LIFE AFTER '80: Environmental Choices We Can Live With

Edited by Kathleen Courrier
with a foreword by Richard Munson

BRICK HOUSE PUBLISHING COMPANY
ANDOVER, MASSACHUSETTS

Production Credits Advisors: Bill Haughey
                              Jack Howell
                              Jim Bright
                    Consultant: Ray Paquin
                    Original Cover Artwork: Curt Witt
                    Final Cover: Jill Weber
                    Cover Typesetting: Wallace Press
                    Copy Editing: Julie Carothers
                    Production Manager: Richard Katzenberg
                    Production Coordination: Deborra Doscher
                    Typesetting: Mary Ellen Wyatt and staff of
                    Country Type
                    Staff: Mary Podevin
                           Diane Russell
                    Printed by Hampshire Press, Inc.

Published by Brick House Publishing Company
3 Main Street
Andover Massachusetts 01810

Library of Congress Cataloging in Publication Data
Life after '80.

   1. Human ecology — Addresses, essays, lectures.
   2. Environmental protection — Addresses, essays, lectures.
   I. Courrier, Kathleen, 1949-
GF49.L53   304.2'8   80-11783
ISBN 0-931790-13-1

The Solar Lobby is a membership organization based in Washington and dedicated to supporting pro-solar and energy-conservation legislation, to putting quality-of-life issues on the national agenda, and to making the emerging solar industry responsive to the public interest.

The Center for Renewable Resources analyzes energy policy, comments on regulation, sponsors networking and educational activities, publishes and disseminates information, and facilitates community energy planning.

Both groups grew out of the first Sun Day—May 3, 1978—and they work together to hasten the transition to the use of renewable resources.

Solar Lobby/CRR
1001 Connecticut Ave. NW
Floor 5
Washington, D.C. 20036

TABLE OF CONTENTS

Foreword

The age of limits began 90 years ago. In 1890 the U.S. Census Bureau declared the American frontier closed. Coming to grips with the end of westward expansion, small groups of Americans formed a conservation movement to utilize our natural resources more efficiently.

But despite these efforts to preserve unique land, concern for the environment was to most Americans of only trifling importance during the first half of the Twentieth Century. Their heads had been turned by unprecedented prosperity and the promise of technological wonders. Around 1970, however, seemingly unrelated events undermined this conventional wisdom. In 1969 an oil spill damaged the ocean and paved the beaches around Santa Barbara with tar. Lake Erie was declared dead, the Cuyahoga River—filled with pollutants—caught fire, and the Club of Rome's computer calculated that our exponential growth in consumption was depleting our resources.

In that same year, domestic oil production in the continental 48 states "peaked out." Oil companies began to turn to frontier areas and foreign lands to fill the gap between a rising demand for oil and falling domestic production. With the emergence of the OPEC cartel, Americans found that their supply of petroleum products was more expensive and vulnerable to interruption.

But the news in 1970 was not all pessimistic. A decade ago a widespread public concern for the quality of the physical environment emerged—a concern whose expression culminated with Earth Day. The public began demanding an end to oil spills. It called on industry to "scrub" the effluents from fossil-fueled power plants. It questioned assurances that the nuclear fuel cycle was "foolproof," and for the first time it saw overpopulation as a social, economic, and environmental problem.

Concern for the planet grew rapidly, combining with social unrest to give rise to geopolitics on the one hand and a return to the outdoors on the other. In the United States, Congress sensed the sentiment and approved the Clean Air Act, the Clean Water Act, the Endangered Species Act, and other landmark bills. New institutions, including the Environmental Protection Agency, and new businesses involved in pollution control and resource management came into being. "Ecology" and "natural" became buzz words first in conversation and then on Madison Avenue. And a political constituency, designated neutrally as "environmentalists" and with less understanding as "eco-freaks," appeared on the scene.

Throughout the decade, though, other constituencies began to take up pro-environment issues. The United Auto Workers' Walter Reuther, a leading organizer of Earth Day 1970, inspired other labor leaders to see the positive impact of a clean environment on employment. The Urban League, Operation PUSH, and other minority groups organized conferences and approved resolutions to improve their health and environmental quality. The National Council of Churches proclaimed stewardship for the land to be a moral issue. The National Farmers Union and other rural organizations began to identify the dangers of some pesticides and declared the need to husband our soil. The Environmental Protection Agency and economists outside the government calculated that environmental regulation was good for the economy. And the Energy Project of the Harvard Business School concluded that our wisest energy investments are those made in conservation and renewable energy.

Still, the growing understanding of environmental issues ·wasn't enough: environmentalists didn't achieve the overnight successes predicted at some of their rallies. Throughout the 70s, oil spills became larger and the air in Los Angeles and other major cities became more polluted. Our thin layer of fertile soil eroded further; forests decreased in size while deserts grew; the pain of cancer increased; and the threat of nuclear destruction lasted out protests and near catastrophes. At the same time, a growing number of industry's leaders expressed louder criticism of "environmental excesses," claiming that the new regulations stifle the economy and upset the status quo. Toward the end of the decade, environmental lobbies lost important battles over the Tellico Dam and synfuels development.

The new decade promises political struggles over conservation and preservation. Billions of dollars, the health of communities, and the survival of ecosystems are at stake. While Congress may approve few sweeping legislative measures during the 80s, local communities will confront chemical companies dumping toxic wastes, utility companies building nuclear reactors, developers expanding urban limits, packagers and retailers promoting the throw-away ethic, and a highway lobby paving neighborhoods. Each gain and adjustment will be part of a larger movement toward the natural stability that permits social dynamism.

This transition to a sustainable society is no one-way passage to utopia. Social and racial tensions have survived every other major transition and are likely to survive this one. But the shift from single-minded preoccupation with physical growth will necessarily involve a shift in power. Instead of the rapid consumption of resources, the economy will favor efficiency. Instead of the centralization of power in ever-larger corporations and government institutions, communities will seek increased self-reliance. In the course of the transition, we have the opportunity to express greater concern for harmony and justice.

This planet's frontier is closed. The opportunities to improve the quality of our lives remain open. ❦

Richard Munson
Coordinator of the Solar Lobby
and the Center for Renewable Resources

Introduction

Ten years ago talk shows, teach-ins, symposia, celebrations, and demonstrations introduced millions of Americans to the biosciences and to their own culpability, as consumers and voters, for the state of the environment. The awakening was exciting, for the promise of renewal contained the promise of social renewal. But it was also alarming. Along with industrial chemicals, nuclear wastes, and automobile exhaust, the catalyst had been let out of the bag. Widescale meddling with the environment (and with our perceptions of the environment) had given rise to serious problems, some of them death-dealing, and some of them permanent. There was to be no going back.

Whether we have gone forward is another question. Consciousness was raised, but was the quality of life? And have economic expectations come down even a notch in response to the gravity of the environmental bind? Those whose thoughts fill these pages are not of one mind on these matters. Some point to the passage of the Clean Air Act and the Endangered Species Act, others to the poisoning of Niagara Falls and the steady loss of topsoil. Even those who spy a new equilibrium in these ups and downs entertain doubts about such a marriage of opposites.

But if we lack answers, at least resource analysis has graduated in the last decade from the "if pigs had wings" school. Few now contend that we can have more and more of everything and still side with the angels on such issues as environmental preservation, social equity, full employment, worker health, and energy conservation. Now all our choices are seen as circumscribed by biological, economic, social, and technological limits. If such choices lack the glamour of the "boom or bust" variety typical of the closing era, they are perhaps ultimately easier to make. And, good news, many of them will be personal decisions made at the household level by people more or less in command of the variables.

Trading in a little dazzle for durability, we also acquired other serviceable bits of wisdom. We discovered the limits of the "us and them" view of environmental problems. We finally thought to ask whether efforts to re-establish man's right relation with nature stand much of a chance of working if they divide people from each other. We were also forced by experience with cumulative environmental threats (such as the build-up of toxic substances) and postponed environmental impacts (such as radiation-induced cancers) to admit that identifying clear-cut thresholds below which degradation or pollution is harmless is difficult at best, and in some cases impossible or pointless. We relearned the inexorable law of causality: muck up or push too hard and somebody somewhere pays the full cost, later if not sooner. And we annexed energy analysis and population issues to the environmental agenda. We learned anew that everything is connected—that nature is quintessentially inter-disciplinary and no respecter of national boundaries or I.O.U.s.

In theory, these lessons could have come from books. Any recent physics text reveals more about the environmental prospect than most of us imagine. Henry Adams' classic interpretation of the future as manifested in the present, "The Virgin and the Dynamo," came out in 1918. Thoreau's meditation on man's place in a closed economy and a closed eco-system has been required reading in American schools for the "better" part of this century. And the Old Testament can be read as an epic history of plagues and floods and famines brought about by humankind's defiance of nature's laws.

On balance, though, books alone can play but a small part in socio-evolutionary history because we want for wisdom more than knowledge, the key distinction being that one cannot be abused and the other can. Equally important, the split between doers and thinkers has been as much a part of environmental politics as it has of most other key issues in American history. As perceptive readers of our national literature have pointed out, while Huck Finn was keeping a diary and screwing up the courage to "strike out for the territory" (the vestiges of the wilds), Paul Bunyan was doing his damnedest to cut the wilderness down to (human) size. In a way, this traditional split explains the beginning of the dichotomy between a healthy environment and a healthy economy— a dichotomy we now know is false, though persistent and confounding.

So why another book on the environment? Will the doers read it? Does a vein of wisdom run through the deposits of data? By way of answering for yourself, consider two or three propositions. One is that the choice between thinking and acting is no longer ours. Those who act now and ask questions later—a breed whose early-century triumphs were reported by Theodore Dreiser and Frank Norris—have lost their welcome in business and government as well as among the advocates of low growth and non-nuclear futures. At the same time, the "all talk and no action" mode amounts to an abuse of the right to freedom·of speech. So it is in this volume that every assessment and hypothesis is coupled either tacitly or explicitly with a social choice.

Proposition two is that in environmental affairs, American history must be kept in mind but mainly as a subset of world history. Environmental problems (and environmental benefits) are increasingly global in nature. Some, such as the Greenhouse Effect and injury to the ozone layer, are obviously so. Others, such as the impact of tropical forest degradation on national economies and international trade, are subtler. Beyond that, world history contains precedents of many of the types of resource problems that have thus far played no part in U.S. history, but might yet. We don't know what it is like to live through a nationwide crop failure like the Irish Potato Famine or a pandemic like the Black Plague. We might do well to dust off our history books and re-read them with a fresh eye. True, the next ecological reaction to human mismanagement will not likely come from the same quarter, but there might be discernible patterns in successful survival responses and in creative efforts to prosper and cope. Maybe nature itself is imitable in this respect. Many of the contributors to this book think it is.

If Americans take this wider view, then America will truly come of age. Already among the longer-lived republics, it may also develop the mettle needed to last as long as the world's great cultures. Its chances are excellent, in part because it is a prime piece of property in a prime location, two of nature's unrescindable gifts. For that reason it is also in a unique position to understand the plight of nations and peoples who, through no fault of their own, have a lesser biological inheritance: poorer soils, less access to fresh water or the sea, fewer ores, no agriculturally attuned rains. Without that understanding, we won't be able to subdue world poverty, a force even more environmentally disruptive than the industrial countries' deployment of roughshod technologies and the worldwide use of chemicals that scorch, spoil, and kill.

The third proposition is that an anthology is a peculiarly fit form for the current phase of the environmental debate. It can stretch farther than can the work of any one mind. It can accommodate contradictory truths without falling to pieces. And, like nature, it can encompass a lot of solid evidence and a number of systems whose operating principles can be examined, but resists the yoke of a strong thesis. We don't know what nature is up to. We only know that, unmolested, it keeps its ducks straight. Better while the planet is still habitable to figure out our own agenda in light of what we know about the biosphere than to try to rewrite natural law. In this book, nature is discussed in terms of givens, and social options as the variables. Unknowns crop up in both categories, sometimes the objects of disagreement.

Less inclined now to mouth purely aesthetic defenses of nature or those reductionist economic arguments that becloud efforts to perceive our place in the grander scheme of things, we might without self-congratulation call ourselves wiser. But wise enough? That we don't know and may never, at least until our analyses become truer to life. At any rate, of rationalizing and autopsy we have had enough. Assessments, interrogations, provocations, and proposals are needed now. The stuff of decisions, they spur individual and collective action, which must be the last word. For whether or not the 70s were the years of environmental activism, the 80s and the 90s will be. 🌱

Kathleen Courrier

Acknowledgements

The contributors to this book deserve more than the customary round of thanks. All gave of their best and did so on short notice. Special thanks also go to the staff members of the Solar Lobby and the Center for Renewable Resources. Each helped the book along, either by taking on new responsibilities or doing without resources temporarily diverted to the project. In particular, Dick Munson and Diane MacEachern proposed some of the topics and contributors, and Valerie Dow helped select articles and handled permissions with characteristic good humor and care. Kim-Dung Nguyen typed most of the manuscripts during precious off-hours, and Karen Hughes and Janet Crooks helped as time permitted. Pat Lark proofread under pressure without relaxing her high standards.

A number of the friends of the Lobby and the Center—especially Jacob Scherr of the Natural Resources Defense Council, board members Rick Katzenberg and Bruce Anderson, and Linda Starke of Worldwatch Institute—offered indispensable assistance. Many more commented on individual essays.

Reserved for Laura Janis are the heartiest thanks of all. As a researcher she proved thorough, tireless, and unflappable. ✤   K.C.

I. THE ELEMENTS

The Commandments
of the Sea

Jacques Cousteau

On Earth is only one body of water, which is constantly traveling from one river to one lake to one ocean. Water frozen today into glaciers and icebergs is tomorrow bathing tropical shores. Unchanged, perennial, the water of the ocean runs along the coastlines of deserts, paradise islands, rocky cliffs, flat marshes, and a hundred varied countries. These hundred nations differ by their people, their degree of development, their religious beliefs, their political regimes, and their administrative structures. But to all, the sea is a bonus, soothing climates, washing beaches, feeding animals and people, and connecting nations.

Pregnant with resources of all kinds, the sea is nevertheless sensitive and vulnerable. The seat of its tragedy is the contrast between the indivisibility of the ocean and the selfish way it is handled by each individual country. The way the moving ocean is exploited and polluted is no longer a matter of "internal affairs," since it may severely affect other nations, now and for generations to come. When the ocean is at stake, the sacrosanct principle of national sovereignty should be irrelevant.

In 1977 I engaged my ship, *Calypso*, in the first completely thorough study of pollution in the Mediterranean, a sea bordered by and polluted by eighteen countries. The crew analyzed the content of water and sediment samples, collected plankton and benthic specimens and visited sites recommended for protection. We also interviewed fishermen from many countries as well as mayors, governors, and heads of state. We collected more than three thousand samples of marine life in 148 locations.

Everywhere we found an increase in pollution associated with the careless coastal development of tourist facilities, industrial plants, and residential areas. We had expected to find pollution from sewage and other wastes; that was no surprise. But what impressed us was the extent of the mechanical destruction of the once colorful and vital sea floor. People were aggressively expanding their land-base at the expense of the sea. Bulldozers pushed acres and acres of ground into the sea for landfills, smothering communities of marine creatures in a solid rain of dirt, making moonscapes of breeding- and feeding-grounds of fish.

We also found fishermen competing with each other to catch as many fish as possible with little regard for the management of fish populations. As a result, Mediterranean fishermen have been able to maintain the level of their catches only by switching to new species after depleting the populations of species important in the past. They fish in spawning areas, catching fish before they have a chance to reproduce. They use shallow trawl nets to scrape along the bottom in ten feet of water, uprooting rocks, stirring up clouds of sediment, damaging the bottom prairies, and destroying any sign of life near the coastline. They also use dynamite to blast schools of fish to the surface where they can easily collect them, in the process devastating pockets along the bottom. And when they have eliminated almost everything, the spear fishermen come and go, seeking out and killing the last fish in their last retreats.

When we finished our study, I reported to the United Nations and to the International Commission for the Scientific Exploration of the Mediterranean. But I also wanted to alert the public to the damage done by mechanical aggression and to the need for international cooperation to halt this disaster. Over the years the public has awakened to the insults of pollution. But mechanical aggressions—landfills, dumping, overfishing, misbegotten diversions of rivers—pose a less known threat that may turn out to be even more harmful than chemical pollution. Governments, spurred by their citizens, must develop policies to halt these practices. They must learn to share responsibility for protecting and managing ocean resources, rather than clamoring to exploit them.

As a guide to governments in forming these policies (and to citizens in urging their governments to form policies), we have drafted a set of principles. The principles are very simple; we call them the Ten Commandments of the Sea. With the help of marine science and policy experts, The Cousteau Society Council of Advisors, headed by Dr. Edward Wenk of the University of Washington, translated these principles into recommendations for a national ocean policy for the United States. We submitted them in 1979 to the President and to Congressmen involved in ocean policy. Similar recommendations should with due haste be made in other countries.

The policy paper is lengthy; but the commandments are short, simple, universally relevant, and adaptable to national objectives.

The first commandment is that _Ocean policy must be global._ The seven seas are a single body of water, the only water supply we have on spaceship Earth. Since both use and abuse of the sea are of consequence to all people, a common set of rules and guidelines is therefore necessary.

The second is that _We must give first priority to our obligation to future generations._ We have the right to take options—to develop resources—for ourselves, but we do not have the right to destroy options for future generations. We must leave them resources so they can make a free choice about how they want to live. They may choose a path that is different from ours, but that choice is theirs.

The third is that _Ocean policies must extend to all freshwater systems and to the atmosphere._ The ocean, freshwater systems, and the atmosphere are so closely related they share an identity: all are phases of the water cycle. Polar ice caps, for example, lock up great quantities of water that govern the level of the ocean. These icecaps are highly sensitive to natural or human-made climatic changes. If we make severe mistakes in the way we handle the atmosphere (burning too much coal and thereby raising the global temperature, for example), we might have 100 to 150 feet of water on the streets of Washington, D.C. The Washington monument might make a good navigational beacon, but boating under such circumstances would be without pleasure.

And CO_2 build-up is not the only atmospheric threat to the oceans. In the United States, over one hundred new chemicals are produced _every year._ Many of these find their way into the atmosphere, into freshwater systems, and eventually into the ocean before they are properly tested for their effects on living organisms. DDT, still commonly used in many countries, has been found in plankton samples around the world and in the tissues of Arctic seals and Antarctic penguins. PCBs have been found in the same places. These chemicals travel from their point of origin along air currents, which effectively distribute them around the world. They rain and snow into the sea and into the marine food web.

The fourth commandment is that _We must develop the resources of the sea without depleting them._ The wisdom of this rule seems so obvious, yet it is not being followed. We must manage our resources like a banker manages money, using only the interest, not eating up the capital. That is sound management, while what we are doing is not. If we want to have fish next year, we must not invade their spawning grounds. Over millions of years the ocean has developed intricate food chains and complex life systems. By blindly upsetting these relationships we are eroding our capital, behaving like irresponsible heirs gambling away the family fortune. Yet we could live quite comfortably off the interest. With proper management and with aquaculture we can produce enough fish. Deep-sea mineral resources can be developed with care. The tremendous and renewable supplies of solar energy in the oceans can be tapped. All these modes of sea harvesting require combining technology with an understanding of the intricacies of the sea and a commitment to reaping the sea's bounty without destroying it.

The fifth commandment is that *Ocean vitality must be preserved.* The diversity and health of ocean species vitally affect all life on the planet. Once we destroy this vitality we have destroyed our capital base. To forestall worldwide biological impoverishment, we must focus our efforts on the three areas most crucial to sea life: the coastal margin, the surface waters, and the bottom waters. Because of the heavy concentration of people along the edges of the ocean, coastal waters are the most threatened.

Few people realize that the ocean is not uniformly abundant in fish and other creatures. The open ocean is by and large a kind of liquid desert. Most of the sea's life is concentrated along the world's coastlines, where plankton-rich currents pass across convenient hiding and attachment surfaces shallow enough to be touched by sunlight. Of the 140 million square miles of ocean surface, a mere 14 million square miles near shore contain the sea's most important habitats. About 90 percent of the world's food fish spawn, mature, and get caught in these coastal areas.

Unfortunately, the land adjacent to these productive waters along the ocean's rim is where human populations also gather, where many industries locate, and where the largest amounts of destructive waste matter are dumped. Of the twenty largest metropolitan areas in the world, sixteen are coastal cities or cities on rivers that empty relatively quickly into the ocean. In the United States, 70 percent of the population lives within a day's drive of the sea. The country's rivers, of course, *all* reach the sea, and a 1977 study found that 95 percent of the country's river basins were polluted.

Some areas of the coast must be kept free from any development and left to wildlife. Industrial pollutants that poison marine creatures, especially in their nurseries (wetlands and estuaries), must be treated at their source, not mixed into a noxious, lethal soup that can never be purified. Dumping barrels of these chemicals on the ocean bottom should be prevented, since the wastes eventually escape their containers and are almost impossible to retrieve.

By far the largest amount of matter entering the sea is sediment from the land. This is a natural process, but human mismanagement of the land has greatly escalated the phenomenon. Now, a thick global wave of muddy water pours into the sea, suffocating life, blanketing reefs, clogging the life-sustaining mechanisms of many ocean species. Scientists estimate that in prehistoric times about five billion metric tons of sediment flowed into the ocean each year. That figure is now 18 billion metric tons per year. In the United States the load of silt reaching streams, rivers, and coastal habitats is about seven hundred times greater than the total sewage discharge of the country. Not only is this unwelcome deposit destructive to marine life, it is also a shameful waste of the precious soil needed to grow crops, forests, and gardens.

The seventh commandment is that _Ocean shipping must be safe._ Today's maritime safety rules constitute a scandal. They are weak to the point of ineffectiveness. Huge oil tankers are built with only one engine, one propeller, one oil system. They completely lack any emergency back-up systems. They are sailed by unqualified crews under flags of convenience. About 94 percent of the American-owned tankers fly Liberian or Panamanian flags of convenience and use low-paid foreign crews. Meanwhile, tens of thousands of American crewmen are on unemployment, costing taxpayers more than the shipowners are saving.

Compared to the strict rules for air traffic control, maritime traffic controls are unspeakably lax—witness the accident record for oil tankers. Today about seven thousand tankers deliver oil to every part of the world. Between 1973 and 1977 these ships were involved in five thousand separate reported incidents—strandings, collisions, rammings, fires, and explosions. The upshot was a loss of ninety ships and one thousand lives. And when a ship like the _Amoco Cadiz,_ the _Argo Merchant,_ or the _Torrey Canyon_ spills its cargo, causing environmental damage, no country, much less company or person, is willing to bear the responsibility. Going to sea has always been a hazardous endeavor, but the hazard in this case can be substantially reduced if shippers are forced to use only safe, sound vessels and to abide by the practices of good seamanship. Satellite monitoring and navigation systems could be used to aid maritime traffic control, and the size of these ships and the damage their spilled cargoes can cause makes strict regulation imperative. But until such regulation comes into force, the amount of oil spilled in the sea will escalate. In the past five years oil spills from tankers have increased 300 percent. In 1974, there were 17 tons of oil spilled per tanker year; in 1978, 63 tons.

The eighth commandment is that _The ocean should be used for peace, not war._ That is our position, though it is not a matter we can do much about. The ocean and the air are highways among warring nations. In peacetime, the ocean becomes the dumping ground for obsolete weaponry. After World War II more than thirty thousand bombs and cannisters containing poisonous gases—along with other unwanted munitions, mostly German—were dumped into the southern Baltic Sea in 295 feet of water. In 1969, these rusting cannisters came back to haunt Baltic shorelines. Leaking mustard gas injured fishermen and upset bathers along the coasts of Sweden and Bornholm. Danish fishermen caught at least sixteen mustard gas bombs in their nets. Similar incidents elsewhere have foretold personal injury and water contamination, yet governments continue to dump their dangerous but unwanted weapons in the sea.

The ninth commandment is that _Nations must take responsibility for their offshore waters._ The 200-mile zone set by the Law of the Sea

Conference is considered by most nations to be an economic zone. Nations were given the right to control the amount of foreign fishing and mining in this area, but most countries see that simply as a way to plunder more resources for themselves. Instead, nations should see this area as a "zone of responsibility" for which they must become care-takers and managers of resources—the minerals, the fish, the water quality—for themselves, for other nations, and for future generations.

The tenth commandment is that *We must create a world ocean authority*. No part of the ocean can be fenced off for the use or abuse of a single country, and the actions of any nation inevitably affect the ocean all of us need and use. Seawater and much of the life within it are in perpetual migration. Whales, for example, may be protected along one shoreline and fair game along the coast of another nation one day's journey away. Therefore, some agreement, some common standard, is necessary to preserve the sea's health. A world ocean authority could define and update rules. It could make sure that the exploitation of the ocean is balanced and equitable and monitor the conservation of marine resources. This authority could also help devel-oping nations strengthen their technical capabilities so they can share both the benefits of the sea and the responsibilities of cultivating those benefits.

People have long looked to the sea for sustenance, but we are only beginning to discover how bountiful it can be if wisely managed. We are on the brink of tapping its food, mineral, and energy resources. These commandments represent the constraints we must work under if we are to realize its true potential for humans. Some of the commandments are nature's own laws: we are merely recognizing and stating the work-ings of the water system. Others are born of common sense and of a sense of responsibility to each other and to our children.

If we approach it with respect, creativity, and ingenuity, the sea can offer us more than we dared imagine. If instead of recklessly depleting natural fish populations we engaged in large-scale ocean fish farming, 25 years from now we could realize fish yields five times higher than today's maximums. Of course, a catch of this size would include more than the luxury species—lobsters, oysters, and trout. Among the new concepts we must test and develop are miniature fish-raising ranches and massive bacteria cultures. We must learn to use treated sewage as a nutrient base for fish farms and to farm algae as a protein supplement for both people and livestock. As long as these waters are vigilantly guarded against contamination, we can also link marine farms with power plants to take advantage of warm water effluents.

Seabed mining has recently captured the interest of several coun-tries and corporations. Manganese nodules lying in some parts of the ocean floor contain nickel and other valuable metals. Mined safely and distributed equitably, they can meet critical resource needs.

Beyond mining, the ocean affords us the unique chance to farm minerals. In numerous locations, the ocean contains *renewable min-*

erals. In deep-sea volcanic zones minerals bubble to the surface of the sea floor at temperatures of 300 degrees. Continued research on these "hot brines" could help us develop methods for capturing these minerals.

Energy from the sea could satisfy most of our energy needs within a few decades. Ocean thermal energy, bioconversion, wind currents, salinity gradients—all are being studied and show great promise as energy sources. While all of the untapped ocean energy sources are safe and unlimited, learning how to plug into them will be expensive, but not impossible. Developing a sensible global policy for the ocean and learning to mine its resources without destroying them will most of all require a huge commitment by governments, industries, and citizens. About $1 trillion will be needed worldwide over the next 30 to 35 years. The U.S. share of this would be about $400 billion—less than the aggregate cost of developing and producing nuclear bombs.

In most countries the public is more aware of the importance of the ocean and the magnitude of its potential than their political leaders, government agencies, and industrial decision-makers are. Throughout the world, pressure is building for a global ocean policy and for rational management of oceanic resources.

The ocean conceals the most formidable potential resources of our planet. But to tackle them—to accept this challenge—we must think big, think unselfishly, think globally, and think far ahead. ❦

Our Inland Waters

David Zwick

Drought and coming shortages. Poisoned drinking water. Skyrocketing sewer and water bills. Mountains of unmanageable sludge. Destruction of rivers and wetlands.

These are familiar headlines from the news of the 1970s. They trace the story of America's most precious, limited natural resource—water.

No human activity—food production, the manufacture of goods or energy, or whatever—can be sustained without water. Where there is not enough clean fresh water, there can be no factories or farms or cities. Water is one of those few basic substances that is a vital link in the fragile ecosystem upon which all life depends.

For this most precious commodity, the 1970s was a decade of discovery. It brought a loss of innocence, the first widespread public recognition that our country's limited supply of water is seriously threatened. Pollution, waste, mismanagement—throughout the decade, these and other threats to water came into clearer public focus.

The techniques to protect water are known and affordable, but too little used. Why? The obstacles are, for the most part, political and institutional. The story of what happened to America's water in the 1970s is the story of a struggle over power, a struggle over who controls the water and has the right to determine its fate.

The Coming Crisis

America is living on borrowed water and borrowed time. While energy shortages dominated public attention during most of the 1970s, a coming water crisis has crept up close behind. Just as the great gas crunch of 1973–74 foretold a future of permanent energy shortages, the droughts of 1975–76 —now nearly forgotten even in some of the places where they were most severe—warned of America's worsening water problems.

Wasting water has become an essential element of the conspicuously consumptive lifestyle. Noting that in Los Angeles leaves are now *blown* off driveways with a spray hose, the *Washington Post* recently designated the leaf rake an endangered species.

Water use trends show part of the picture. If past patterns continue, the country will literally run out of available fresh water by the end of the century. What will happen instead, some experts optimistically predict, is that rapidly rising prices and severe shortages will spur recycling and hold down future increases. The implications of those predictions are important: *at best,* there will be shortages and soaring prices.

A bellweather statistic to watch is the trend in *consumptive* use of water. Water consumed is not available for recycling and reuse, and consumption is expected to keep climbing.

What are the trends? While the 1970s saw some tapering off in industrial water use, the development of a water-gulping synthetic fuels industry in the 1980s could reverse the slowdown. Irrigated agriculture got more greedy during the 1970s, increasing its share of the total take. The General Accounting Office recently reported that at least half of the water used for irrigation in this country is wasted.

Noting what lies ahead, the chairman of a Congressional committee on water resources recently remarked that "if we don't do something," the coming water shortages could make the energy crisis look like "a pink tea party." If our water supply picture seems to be following in the footsteps of the energy mess, that resemblance is not coincidental. Many of the same forces are at work.

1. *Might makes right.* While the concentration of control over water is nowhere as great as concentration of resource ownership in the energy industry, most of the water is used—and wasted—by those economic and political units, businesses, and cities big enough to convert their size (which is subsidized by their water waste) into considerable political muscle. The water laws of many of the states, particularly in the West where large agribusiness operations dominate water use, allow the rich to get richer and the poor to get nowhere. The use of water taken from public waterways, often for free, becomes a property right to the same amount of water. The upshot is that everyone has an incentive *not* to cut back.

2. *Distorted Pricing.* The biggest water wasters have over the years banded together with their boosters in Congress to push for billion-dollar federal subsidies for water projects. The water projects provide irrigation water at a fraction of its real cost. A utility in Utah, as an example, recently had to pay $1750 per acre-foot (the equivalent of

325,000 gallons) of water while in California's nearby San Joaquin Valley, farmers were being piped taxpayer-subsidized water for which they paid less than $10 per acre-foot. And when the price is right, water wasting comes easy.

Predictably, the biggest benefits go to the biggest businesses. The federal law limiting the provision of federally subsidized water to farms of 160 acres or less has gone unenforced, giving huge quantities of artificially cheap water to the largest farm operations, which successfully lobbied against what turned out to be a far too feeble Carter Administration effort to get the law enforced.

Pricing policy plays an important part in urban water waste, too. In 1977, some of the big water-wasting cities, including New York and Chicago, which neither meter nor charge residential and commercial consumers on the basis of the water they use, successfully pushed for repeal of a federal law that would have forced them to start basing their charges on actual use as a condition of getting federal subsidies for city sewage treatment. In the same year, a coalition of industries and municipalities got Congress to stall enforcement of a law that would have required industries using cities' treatment plants to pay back a portion of the cost of constructing their fair share of the sewage facility. Until that moratorium is lifted, industries get a cut-rate deal when they dump into a municipal sewage plant. The more water they use and dump, the bigger capital subsidy they get.

Residential water consumers are being sent the same inverted signals. When they do conserve water, their utility often responds by threatening to raise their rates to make up for lost revenues, as the Washington Suburban Sanitary Commission in the Maryland suburbs near Washington, D.C., did in 1979. Two underused remedies to these problems are water rate structures that reward lower use with lower rates and make up the difference by charging the big users more, and building and sizing water facilities with conservation in mind.

3. *Dependence on "foreign" water.* Artificially cheap subsidized water, artificially cheap energy with which to pump and pipe it, and the aggressiveness of the government agencies that do the transporting—especially the Army Corps of Engineers and the Bureau of Reclamation—have blinded many cities and businesses to the limits on their water supplies. When local supplies run short, they look to get their life-giving liquid from remoter sources.

The result is a pattern of addictive dependence on imported water that is spreading around the country and producing new second-order dependencies in its wake. New York City's needs are too great to be met by its own polluted Hudson River, so it goes next door to the Upper Delaware for more. New York's tapping of the Delaware causes Philadelphia, downstream, to run short, so Philadelphia has its eye on the Susquehanna River. Water from the Colorado River is shipped to quench the insatiable thirst of Los Angeles, ever in search of other faraway rivers to raid. The water-short High Plains states, from Texas to Nebraska, hope for help in the form of a water pipeline from the Mississippi or Arkansas Rivers.

Some water hunters look to even further frontiers. The Ralph Parsons Company of Pasadena, California, has proposed a $120 billion scheme for delivering water to the dry Southwest from the water-rich wilds of British Columbia, the Yukon, and Alaska. For $65 million, inventor Joseph Connell of Torrence, California, says he will take a giant Antarctic iceberg in tow and park it off the California coast. With his patented system, Connell claims, he can deliver the iceburg 120 days from the time the order is placed. His idea has excited interest among Arabian sheiks, who face home-country water prices already greater than the price of oil on a per-barrel basis.

Some of the greediest water-grabbers come from the Sun Belt, where the development of irrigated agriculture in the desert has greatly exceeded water capacity. Arizona's desert farms, built on non-renewable groundwater supplies, have made such great demands that the water table has dropped by more than 400 feet in some areas. To make sure water does not run out, Phoenix growth boosters have been lobbying for the Central Arizona Project, a gigantic federal water project that would use large amounts of energy to pipe in water from the Colorado River.

The possibility of being temporarily bailed out by long distance projects like these, because they encourage development far beyond natural supplies, is promoting today's water waste and engineering tomorrow's droughts and catastrophes—economic and environmental. Increases in the price of energy for pumping portend troubled days ahead even for many areas that buy time with a water importation project. And as expensive transport schemes drive costs to new heights, fights over the distribution of "domestic" and "imported" water and battles over rationing and price controls can be expected.

4. *Public works for private profit.* How do these economically indefensible water-wasting projects come to be? The almost proverbial principle of the three "P"s—Profits, Programs, and Politics—is at work. The bigger profits go to private interests such as developers or large farmers. The bigger programs are for growth-minded agencies like the Army Corps of Engineers. And for the politicians who back these projects, bigger political dividends take the form of friends who stand to make a fortune from a political favor and who owe a favor in return. When the three "P"s come together, a boondoggle water project is born.

Each year Congress debates a long list of pork-barrel water projects as part of an annual package of public works proposals called the Water Projects Appropriations Bill. President Carter was the first president to speak out forcefully against these annual giveaways. In 1978, he vetoed the bill, claiming it contained too many boondoggles and too few projects with real public benefits. Congress dropped the offending projects that year, but in 1979 President Carter signed the bill with that year's crop of objectionable projects intact.

5. *Shortsighted energy policies.* The water crisis and the energy crisis are inextricably intertwined. While artificially cheap energy has fueled false hopes of endless water from afar, expanding energy production has been directly draining away available water supplies, adding to demands for new water sources and energy to tap them. The new Intermountain Power Project, for example, will use 45,000 acre-feet of water and take 15,000 irrigated acres out of production in south-central Utah to generate electricity for consumers in California. The Western States Water Council, a regional group that does planning for an eleven-state area, predicts that new energy projects—including nuclear power plants, coal slurry pipelines, and synthetic fuels developments like coal-gasification plants and oil shale conversion facilities—will take an extra 2.3 million acre-feet of water by 1990, an amount that could irrigate nearly one million acres of agricultural land or maintain streamflows for dwindling fishery resources. Losing agricultural water and lands could, in turn, stunt development of low-cost renewable energy crops, including those needed to make gasohol.

6. *Entrenched interests and bureaucratic inertia.* Wrong-headed local building and plumbing codes and health ordinances, especially those set to suit entrenched interests, frustrate sensible water-conservation practices all over the country. The State of Virginia, for example, has proposed adopting rules that would restrict the wider use of several known water-conservation techniques, calling them "experimental" because they are not widely used in Virginia now. Resistance to change by pollution officials and by a powerful constellation of construction companies, engineering consulting firms, sewer pipe and control equipment manufacturers, and chemical companies that do billions of dollars of business each year in conventional water-wasting sewage systems has made the nation's mammoth federally subsidized sewage-treatment program one of the country's leading water wasters. For example, while water-short California imports irrigation water from several states away, it dumps valuable water—the sewage effluent from its cities—into the ocean, losing many recycling opportunities. Kentucky has irrigation regulations that all but outlaw recycling on the land. New York State subsidizes conventional sewers and systems but not decentralized alternative systems that save water.

The Carter Administration's response to the droughts of the mid-1970s was to promulgate an ambitious and enlightened policy that required federal agencies to build water-conservation requirements into their activities and grants. But the policy has floundered for lack of publicity—the President set up no fireside chats, made no clarion calls for water conservation—and for lack of sufficient follow-through. The water-saving potential of the Presidential directive remains mostly untapped.

7. _Leaks._ Older Eastern cities lose large amounts of water because their pipes—many of them laid in the last century—leak. Stemming this hemorrhaging will be expensive.

The 1970s were in a way to the water crisis what the 1960s and early 1970s were to the energy crisis. They brought an abundance of early warning signals to those who were watching. During the decades ahead the struggle over water will mount. Upcoming developments will make it as difficult—and as necessary—for communities to achieve water self-sufficiency as it will be for our country to become self-sufficient in energy.

As the water crisis worsens, those who control large quantities of water, including many of the biggest water wasters, will profit at the expense of everyone else. The only way to avoid this and other disastrous consequences will be to develop new incentives that reward conservation over consumption, and incentives that force us to live within our means and within the limits of our local ecosystems. Needed is a new ethic that treats water as a resource to be renewed—to be managed, not mined.

Waters Beneath The Earth

Groundwater, our great hidden water resource, cannot be thought of as separate from the network of surface rivers, lakes, and streams that have become so despoiled. Groundwater is an integral part of the circulation of water in the ecosystem.

Increasingly, as clean surface supplies have reached their limits, we have turned to our underground stores. In 1975, groundwater accounted for about 24 percent of the fresh water used in the United States. It made up a disproportionately large share of the water most Americans rely on—more than half of all municipal water, for example, and more than 90 percent of the water for rural homes. From 1970 to 1975, use of underground freshwater supplies increased by nearly 22 percent while use of surface fresh water rose by just over 5 percent.

Groundwater differs from our surface waters in two significant respects. First, it is more vulnerable to permanent harm. Groundwater is slow to return when depleted, and can take centuries to recover when polluted. Second, groundwater enjoys less legal protection than do surface streams. Our underground waters have been nearly as invisible to law-makers and regulators as they have been to the naked eye.

The consequences of this neglect caught up with us in the 1970s. The most frightening stories of chemical contamination of water came from the communities located near the Love Canals and other industrial poison pits. During 1979, EPA listed 103 known hazardous waste-storage sites, and that number will surely grow. There may be more than 50,000 storage spots for hazardous wastes in the U.S., thousands of which may be seeping deadly juices into nearby waters. The late 1970s saw drinking wells closed in Pennsylvania, New Jersey, New York, Maine, Connecticut, Tennessee, Texas, Michigan, and California, among other states. The chemicals being found in well supplies and nearby hazardous dumps are associated with a host of human ailments, including headaches and dizziness, brain and nervous system damage, seizures, loss of hair, paralysis, cancer, and scores of other illnesses.

Serious attempts to protect groundwater have scarcely started. EPA is still gearing up to begin enforcing a new Resource Conservation and Recovery Act to upgrade landfills. In December 1979, the Justice Department sued Hooker Chemical, Love Canal's polluter, for $134 million in clean-up costs. And, as the decade ended, more than four years after the Safe Drinking Water Act's 1975 deadline for setting standards protecting groundwater from improperly operated underground waste injection wells, EPA—under pressure from the oil industry—had still not set the standards.

Legal protection of underground water from over-pumping is also weak. Groundwater tables are dropping dramatically in many parts of the country. For example, experts believe that the great Ogallala aquifer, the underground reservoir underlying some 98,000 square miles of water-fed farm country in Texas, Oklahoma, New Mexico, Kansas, Nebraska, and Colorado, is being depleted to the crisis point.

The lack of legal restrictions leaves the law of the jungle in effect in many places. Pumping by Georgia's Union Camp plant has helped lower Savannah's groundwater level by more than 150 feet. Union Camp's president's comment on the matter betrays an attitude widespread in industry: "I had my lawyers in Virginia research the question, and they told us that we could suck the state of Virginia out through that hole in the ground and there was nothing anyone could do about it." Another example is an advertisement by TRW Company. The suck-it-dry philosophy of too much of the water-pumping world is all to plain: "We're learning the hard way that there is only so much water on our planet. Or in it . . . Men everywhere are pumping water out of the earth's water table faster than it can be replenished. . . . As the world water table goes deeper, so does a TRW pump."

America's Lethal Liquid

The struggle for water will be all the more severe because there is so little "clean" water to fight for. Pollution is creating shortages in places where water—or what used to be water—is plentiful.

In 1972, the President's Council on Environmental Quality reported that over 90 percent of our watersheds were more than "moderately" polluted. Many urban waterways had become so over-burdened with municipal and industrial excretions that they were fit for little else besides navigation and continued pumping.

The 1970s ushered in a burst of activity aimed at correction. The Clean Water Act of 1972 set clean-up deadlines, and the new Environmental Protection Agency set out to make polluters meet them. What did all this achieve? The results are mixed. Disease-causing organisms are down. (Fewer fecal colliform bacteria—a commonly checked-for organism that indicates the presence of other pathogens—are being found in most places than were earlier.) The total volume of oxygen-consuming wastes being dumped into our waters held about even over most of the decade. Eighty-five percent of the nation's industries met the Clean Water Act's 1977 deadline for the first phase of improved treatment, though only 30 percent of the municipalities did.

In contrast to the 1960s, when federal clean-up efforts made no discernible difference in a major body of water, the 1970s produced some visible changes. Fishermen are now hauling small-mouth bass, coho salmon, brown trout, and perch out of the once-dead Detroit River. A number of other formerly fetid streams—including the Arkansas, Tombigbee (Alabama), French Broad (North Carolina), Naugatuck (Connecticut), Mohawk (New York), and Pemigewasset (New Hampshire) Rivers—have made striking comebacks, complete with fish and, in a few cases, swimming. In 1976, EPA identified 50 waterbodies, from Maine's Annabessacook Lake to Hawaii's Pearl Harbor, that are seeing better days.

On the darker side, eutrophication (a rapid pollution-caused aging) of lakes has worsened overall, due to increasing pollution from nutrients such as phosphorus and nitrogen, which feed the growth of slimy green and blue algae. Then too, all reports have us falling far behind in the march to meet the Clean Water Act's original goal of "fishable and swimmable" waters by mid-1983. At the same time, pollution from health-threatening chemicals has become more prevalent and more dangerous.

That last bit of intelligence is perhaps the most telling and certainly the most disturbing. It means that many people are ingesting more dangerous contaminants in 1980 than they were ten years before.

Americans used to be only vaguely aware that many of the same waterbodies that polluters use as private sewers do double duty as the source of many food items, including our most important foodstuff—drinking water. Over the last decade, the water drinkers of America were regaled with one numbing discovery after another about the extent to which many chemical poisons are making their way into the tap. Available evidence has pointed increasingly to water pollution and drinking water contamination as possible contributors to many human ailments, including heart disease, cancer, birth deformation, decreased productive capacity, and genetic damage.

The 1970s news read like a menu of chemical cocktails. Mercury pollution led to restrictions on sport and commercial fishing in twenty-one ·states and Canada. Kepone ran amok in the James River. Polychlorinated biphenyl (PCB) contaminated the Delaware River. Every day brought new revelations.

Logically, we might have expected some years ago that these water-borne intruders might be infiltrating our drinking water distribution systems and homes. Operations of drinking water facilities around the country were using obsolete purification technologies that had been developed to conquer the mass epidemics (the typhoid and cholera out-breaks) of the last century. These technologies were not designed to screen out the alphabet soup of complex new chemicals that industries had been pouring into rivers and lakes for the past forty years. Large-scale chemical contamination of drinking water was not a problem primarily because no one was looking very hard for trouble. When we started looking, we started finding.

Tests of drinking water in 113 cities during 1976–1977 turned up at least traces of suspect chemicals in every single metropolitan area, and high levels of known or suspected carcinogens in many. Analyses of tap water over the past several years have identified 700 distinct organic compounds in drinking water around the country, many of them be-lieved to be harmful. These compounds, the ones that researchers have been able to identify so far, amount to only a small fraction of the much larger mass of organic chemical contaminants being found in drinking water.

Stopping these poisons at the source has proved harder than detect-ing them. The most important immediate objective of the 1972 Clean Water Act was controlling toxic pollutants. It did not work. In a victory of inertia and expedience over intelligence, EPA clamped down first on the more innocuous pollutants, leaving the truly hazardous substances until the last. Control officials began to catch up only after the Natural Resources Defense Council and other environmental groups won a court judgment against EPA. With the late start, most of the results will not show for several years.

With prevention of dangerous pollutants at the source years away, the Safe Drinking Water Act of 1974 was aimed at catching them at the other end, by pulling a complacent drinking water treatment industry into the Twentieth Century. The Safe Drinking Water Act passed in an epidemic of Congressional concern over findings that suggested a corre-lation between cancer death rates in New Orleans and consumption of contaminated water from the pollution-choked Mississippi River. The new law required EPA to set drinking water safety standards and testing requirements. If utilities could not meet the standards, they would have to notify their customers who could then press for improvements. Enforcing the Safe Drinking Water Act was a chance to make some headway toward human and environmental health while taking on the larger task of cleaning up lake and river pollution. But for the first three years after the law passed, EPA failed to propose any standards at all for cancer-causing chemicals in drinking water.

An Environmental Defense Fund (EDF) lawsuit and a 1977 visit from Ralph Nader and EDF's Robert Harris persuaded the EPA to pro-pose in 1978 the first protections against cancer-causing chemicals. One proposal was for a maximum allowable concentration for trihalo-methanes (THMs), compounds produced when organic chemical pollu-tants in water link up with the chlorine used to disinfect it. (Some THMs—including the ubiquitous chloroform—cause cancer in test animals.) The other part of EPA's proposal was to take care of that inevitable mysterious larger batch of difficult-to-identify organic chemicals. For drinking water systems serving over 75,000 people, EPA prescribed filters of granular activated carbon when high concentrations of these pollutants were found. Such filters remove the whole organic mess.

That proposal was the most important of this century in terms of drinking water protection. At last the dormant drinking water industry was roused—not to meet the standards but to fight them. Mobilizing to defend the public's right to consume dangerous pollutants, water utilities joined to form a group with the misnamed "Coalition for Safe Drinking Water." Leading the dirty drinking water lobby were several of the water utilities that are serving up the worst water in the U.S. to their customers, including New Orleans, Louisiana; Passaic, New Jersey; and Louisville, Kentucky. Tests of these utilities' water have turned up some of the highest concentrations of cancer-causing chemicals found in the country. Most of the utility coalition's members have billed their drinking water customers for their campaign against the safeguards, and some of the money they collected has gone to hire high-priced "experts" (many of them defectors from government) to help push their cause.

The utility lobby created confusion by distributing factually inaccurate information about the proposed standards to local water utilities all over the country. Utilities began visiting their Congressmen and finally got introduced a still-pending bill that would repeal EPA'S authority to prescribe treatment for cancer-causing chemicals. Frightened, EPA postponed the carbon filter installation requirement and went back to the drawing boards to draft a new proposal. Consumers did not lose all way round, however. In December of 1979, nearly two years after it was first proposed, a standard for THM in drinking water was officially set by EPA. It will be several years more before the standard, which is not particularly strong, goes into effect. And when it does it will basically do little more than bring THM contamination in the worse half of the country's communities to the current safety level of the better half. But while environmentalists had hoped for more, this measure is an important start.

Putting this outcome in perspective requires understanding that the water utility lobby (a pipsqueak when stacked up against the big Washington powers) has had a field day so far, in large part because their consumers—for whom they typically claim to speak—are seldom on the field at all. Few communities have large numbers of organized citizens demanding safe drinking water at affordable prices. That helps explain why, five years after the legal foundation for drinking water clean-up was first laid at the federal level, Americans have just one weak standard to protect them against the thousands of dangerous chemicals in drinking water.

To go farther and faster in the 1980s, larger numbers of drinking water consumers will have to move the next steps beyond expressing concern. They will have to be better organized and more politically active.

The Forgotten Polluters

Many businesses—agriculture, forestry, mining, and real estate construction, for example—do not send their wastes down to the nearest stream in a pipeline, as cities and industries customarily do. Instead, the pollution from these activities is blown or washed off millions of acres of farm and forest lands, construction sites, and mines into America's rivers and lakes.

"Nonpoint source" polluters like these are, in terms of sheer volume of waste output, the worst polluters in the nation. For example, agricultural lands contribute most of the more than four *billion* tons of sediment produced each year in the United States (compared to between 30 and 40 *million* tons of organic wastes and suspended solids from all industries and municipalities combined). This massive movement of dirt—carrying pesticides and other chemicals and turning our rivers into oxygen-less mudholes—is wasting both our waters and our best farmland topsoil.

Nonpoint polluters have always confounded law-makers and pollution-control officials (many of them sanitary engineers). It is hard to assign blame when you cannot follow up a pipe back from the water's edge. And nonpoint pollution problems are not solved simply by laying a sewer or building a better treatment plant. The response of pollution-control officialdom has been to focus first—and sometimes almost exclusively—on cleaning up the point-source industries and cities.

In 1972, Congress toyed with the idea of requiring nonpoint clean-up with deadlines and federal enforcement and then dropped it, leaving it up to federally funded local planning activities (called Section 208 plans), which depend entirely on local and state enforcement. So far, many of these planning efforts appear unlikely to produce much beyond protracted debate. Where they do, it will be because an active local citizenry demands changes like zoning rules and land-use decisions, sediment control programs, restrictions on chopping down trees and paving over green space, and so on.

Wetlands

Bogs, marshes, swamps, and prairie potholes—each locale has its own type of wetlands, those muddy and often reedy areas where water meets land.

America's tens of millions of acres of wetlands began to come into their own in the 1970s, gaining both new legal protections and long overdue recognition as one of the country's most valuable natural resources. Wetlands are the spawning grounds for fish and a vital link in the aquatic food chain. They are nature's own free systems for flood protection, groundwater recharge, and pollution-filtering.

Wetlands are as vulnerable as they are valuable. When developers and other commercial interests look at wetlands, they often see something else in their place—shopping centers, second-home developments, high-rise apartments, and other potential profit-makers. This country's first two centuries have seen half its original 120 million acres of wetlands disappear to draining or filling. Pressure to turn much of what remains into "quick cash" projects is increasingly intense.

This intense interest in wetlands led to one of the most controversial environmental battles in Congress during the 1970s. It started in 1975, when the U.S. Army Corps of Engineers was ordered by a court to belatedly put into effect the "Section 404" permit program that had been called for by the 1972 Clean Water Act. Section 404 states that anyone wishing to dump, dredge, spoil, or fill material (dirt, trash, or whatever) into the country's waters or wetlands has to meet environmental standards set by EPA and get a permit from the Army Corps. Up to 1975, the Corps—itself the country's largest dredger—had been enforcing the law only where it mattered least, in the large rivers and lakes it had historically regulated to protect navigation. That left unprotected not only the vast numbers of smaller lakes and streams (98 percent of the country's total stream mileage) but also more than 85 percent of the country's wetlands.

The 1975 court decision ordering wetlands protection to expand was a threat to the plans of a host of special interests. A powerful anti-wetlands coalition—including dredgers, land developers, construction operators, timber and mining companies, and many other business groups—began to pick up support. With the U.S. House of Representatives' majority leader Jim Wright and other powerful Democrats championing their cause, they pushed to change the Clean Water Act to cut legal protections back so they applied to only the large navigable channels. Citizens groups rallied to the defense of Section 404, and the battle see-sawed back and forth for two years. Wetlands supporters finally won, keeping federal protection standards for the nation's wetlands in the Clean Water Act of 1977.

With the federal law saved, the decisive battles over wetlands promise to be the ones still to come—the battles to see that controls are actually carried out. That will take, among other things, increased funding to boost EPA's meager wetlands staff. It will also take expanded citizen vigilance and action wherever wetlands are threatened.

Sewage Treatment

At $3.4 to $5 billion a year, the cost to federal government for sewage treatment is just part of an ever-mushrooming national bill for treating our country's wastewater. States and localities spend billions more each year.

A sewage-treatment system is to most communities roughly what a home is to most families: the single most important (and most expensive) purchase they will ever make. Ballooning municipal budgets (and even bankruptcy), skyrocketing sewer and tax bills, suburban sprawl, downtown neighborhood deterioration, critical water shortages, housing and land scarcity, soaring farm fertilizer costs, waste of energy and other resources, massive environmental destruction—all these can be costs of making the wrong decisions.

The national sewage-treatment effort promises to become the biggest domestic public works spending program of all time, bigger even than the interstate highway program. The wisdom with which this national shopping spree is conducted will obviously have enormous consequences for our communities, our waters, and our pocketbooks. Up to now, much of the fast-paced funding has been funneled into conventional technologies and institutional arrangements that are both economically wasteful and environmentally destructive.

The conventional sewage-treatment systems in widespread use typically screen out a portion of the waste and then dump the partially treated effluent in streams and lakes, where it can still cause considerable pollution. The screened-out waste—the left-over "sludge"—is taken somewhere else where it typically causes more pollution. It has been dumped into the ocean, incinerated to cause air pollution, land-filled, and disposed of in any number of ways. Advanced versions of this conventional plan use heavy doses of expensive chemicals and energy to produce a purer effluent, but have many of the same problems, plus astronomical costs.

There are available and widely proven alternatives which are environmentally superior and usually cheaper: treatment systems that use the fertilizer value of sewage in crop irrigation, for example, and sewerless systems for the home or neighborhood that turn waste into compost.

Use of alternatives like these has been stifled by the sewage-treatment industry, with a multi-billion dollar financial stake in the status quo, and by the private and public establishments that have grown up around it. Simply put, converting from conventional treatment means loss of profits for the conventional consulting firms, manufacturing, construction, and chemical companies that Ralph Nader has called a "tightly organized sub-economy" that lacks "the insecurity of competition."

Reversing this misdirected momentum takes patience and power. Environmental groups have for years campaigned to revive the EPA-smothered alternatives to conventional sewage-treatment technologies and methods. Finally, in 1977, an amendment to the Clean Water Act— many of the details of which had been proposed by the Clean Water Action Project and backed by a national coalition of citizens organizations—passed. It meant that communities that adopted alternative sewage-treatment plans, including those for recycling, would be rewarded.

. For sewage treatment, the 1980s look to be a critical and transitional time. EPA's top officials and the federal law favor alternative systems. But the progressive perspectives are taking a long time to percolate down to lower levels of government. Many communities long ago planned new conventional systems that they would someday build, and boosters of such conventional technologies have now mounted campaigns to dust off these old plans and push ahead. At the same time, longstanding but wasteful water-management arrangements remain in force. In particular, EPA has delayed approval for alternative plans while quickly giving conventional models the green light. A final complication is that some communities are trying to bail out failing conventional systems by bringing users from surrounding areas on board to share the misery. For the foreseeable future, the best defense for communities is to organize and to ally themselves with enlightened officials.

Zero Discharge

The decade of the 1970s opened, fittingly, with the enactment of the National Environmental Policy Act (NEPA). Signed into law on January 1, 1970, NEPA was followed by an unprecedented burst of environmental law-making. As if in chain reaction, the major laws protecting water—including the wholesale revision of the Clean Water Act in 1972, the Safe Drinking Water Act of 1974, and the 1977 amendments to the Clean Water Act—came in rapid succession. The years following the enactment of each of the laws were consumed with the writing of volumes of federal regulations to implement them. Never again is there likely to be such a concentrated outpouring of activity aimed at producing environmental laws and regulations. Nor does there need to be. While important gaps (especially in groundwater protection) will need to be filled, the 1980s begin with much of the basic legal foundation for protecting water laid.

Elements of the foundation include national _goals_, and _standards_ that EPA must set to achieve these goals, clean-up _timetables_ and _deadlines, enforcement_, authority that allows the federal government to go to court or issue enforceable clean-up orders when standards are not met (the Clean Water Act makes federal enforcement _mandatory_ in some situations), authority for _citizen suits_—legal actions initiated by citizens or citizens groups—in federal court against either the polluter or the federal government when government enforcement is not doing the job, and legal _protections for workers_ against being fired or otherwise penalized for reporting their employers' pollution violations and against "environmental blackmail" (employers' threats of lay-offs if pollution standards are enforced). All of these elements, now part of federal law, had earlier been demands of the citizens' lobbying campaigns of the 1970s.

The most controversial element of the clean water laws, and the one with the greatest potential for bringing a major reshaping of environmental protections in succeeding decades, has been the "zero discharge" goal of the Clean Water Act, which proclaims an objective of ultimately eliminating all discharges of pollutants into our navigable waters. This concept was completely at odds with the conventional wisdom in pollution control, which always regarded the stream and its "assimilative capacity" as the final (and sometimes the only) stage of waste-treatment. When in 1971 *Water Wasteland* called for a zero discharge goal, pollution-control officialdom denounced the notion as an unrealistic and dangerous heresy. Congress ran into the same kind of resistance in 1972 when it made the zero discharge objective the cornerstone of the new Clean Water Act. As the target date Congress first set for reaching the goal—1985—draws nearer, the likelihood of that original timetable being met by all polluters grows smaller. But the wisdom of the goal grows clearer with the passing years.

The point of the zero discharge goal is simple. It is based on an appreciation of how difficult it is to separate out, let alone even detect, an ever-changing assortment of thousands of pollutants once we allow them in our waters. Its proponents recognize that these pollutants are really resources out of place, needing to be wisely managed and not just "controlled." Throwing away the valuable nitrogen fertilizer in sewage is just as wasteful as damaging the river into which the sewage is released. The zero discharge goal makes it a national objective to find cost-effective ways to recycle and reuse our resources rather than dump them in our drinking water.

Since 1972, this once-radical idea has already become a prevailing practice in a growing number of industries and communities. Our environmental problems in the decades ahead will be solved as we understand and apply this fundamentally different perspective to all those misplaced resources that have been poisoning Americans for so long.

The Challenge of the 1980s

With the legal foundation for protecting water largely laid, a central problem for the 1980s and beyond is fulfilling the law's promise and potential. This will be more difficult; changing the world is harder than changing the law. Probably the most important lesson to be drawn from the experience of the 1970s is that real headway will not come without some hard-fought larger realignments of economic and political power. Water has been damaged because its biggest wasters, polluters, and misusers have more power than the larger number of losers. Altering these relationships will be difficult, in part because it will mean dislodging many of the same entrenched powers that control other essential commodities. It will take more than decrees to alter their activities. Regulators will not enforce a law if they fear their action will result in their own dismissal or the law's repeal. Local politicians will not take the stands needed to protect water unless they are propelled by a citizenry with the political strength to defend the tough decisions and make them stick.

Fortunately, the problems and accomplishments of the 1970s have created the conditions for expanded citizen strength in the 1980s.

Among these conditions are the connections between water problems and other problems. Pollution, water pricing, sewage-treatment choices, water supply projects, preservation of agricultural land, energy conservation and generation, the availability and price of housing, economic development—all these concerns and others are directly related. From now on, strategies that do not recognize and take into account these relationships will fail. The relationship between the problems of energy and water will deserve special attention; the inevitable reconceptualization of energy systems in the 1980s will force a retooling of all our water-management structures as well.

With this growing complexity comes growing opportunity. The next step beyond recognizing the emerging relationships between problems is forging relationships between their victims. The coming water and energy shortages, rising prices and expenditures related to water, and expanding physical disruption of communities as outmoded water-management structures reach their illogical outer limits—all these give more people and groups a bigger shared stake in the solutions. The citizen coalitions of the coming decade can include community and neighborhood groups; consumers, taxpayers, and senior citizens—people who care about housing and the economic health of their communities, be they central city or rural area—workers, small farmers, and enlightened businesses and professionals; fishermen and outdoor sports groups; and others. They can include all those people and groups who feel squeezed now and who believe that all Americans deserve access to sufficient supplies of safe water at affordable prices.

The major victories of the 1980s will not be new laws passed in Washington. Instead, victories will come at the community level with each practical advance and each exercise of citizens' legal rights. They will come with wetlands saved, alternative sewage systems started, rate structures reformed, and boondoggles beaten back. The challenge for the 1980s is building citizen movements and organizations strong enough to return control of the people's resources—their dollars and precious waters—to the people. ❦

Deforesting and Reforesting the Earth

Erik Eckholm

Our dependence on trees is easy to forget in the asphalt and plexi-glass jungle. In the rural Third World the importance of forests—the source of essential cooking fuel and building materials—is obvious enough. But economic advancement does not reduce a society's reli-ance on forest products. As countries develop, wood remains a basic raw material for construction and also takes such useful forms as furni-ture, railroad ties, power poles, cellophane, rayon, and plastics. Trans-formed into paper, it serves as an essential tool for government, commerce, education, and communications. Soon it may also provide liquid fuels and a wide array of petrochemical substitutes.

Forests provide far more than economic products and recreation. They assist in the global cycling of water, oxygen, carbon, and nitro-gen. They lend stability to hydrological systems, reducing the severity of floods and permitting the recharging of springs, streams, and under-ground waters. Trees keep soil from washing off mountainsides and sands from blowing off deserts; they keep sediment out of rivers and reservoirs and, properly placed, help hold topsoil on agricultural fields. Forests house millions of plant and animal species that will disappear if the woodlands are destroyed.

Tree Count

Important as forests are to human well-being, knowledge about their extent or the rate at which they are disappearing is surprisingly incom-plete. Only about half the world's forests have been surveyed in depth, and only a fraction of these have been surveyed more than once so that changes over time could be documented.

At present, the best available global survey is that compiled by Swedish analyst Reidar Persson. In his data, he has usefully distinguished between "closed forests," where tree crowns cover 20 percent or more of the ground when viewed from above, and "open woodlands," where a scattering of trees provide a crown-cover of 5 to 9 percent. According to Persson's calculations, closed forests covered about one-fifth of the earth's land in the mid-seventies. The true proportion is quite likely to be lower since only outdated surveys exist for many regions, and areas recently cleared or severely degraded are almost certainly included in the totals. Open woodlands cover perhaps another 12 percent of the earth's land area.

In terms of the sheer tree-covered area, Latin America and the Soviet Union lead by far among regions, with 680 million hectares* of closed forest in each. From an economic perspective, however, such totals can be misleading. While most of the Soviet Union's trees are conifers, whose soft woods are sought after for construction and papermaking, a good share of them stand in remote, cold areas where harvesting is commercially unfeasible and growth extremely slow. While the Soviet Union does enjoy a wood surplus, the widespread notion that it will become a major supplier of forest products to a wood-short world has no grounds in economic reality.

The total for Latin America is so high largely because of the Amazon Basin, the world's largest tropical moist forest. But forest-product industries have not yet begun to make good use of most of the incredibly numerous species in rain forests. Much tropical timber exploitation to date has been wasteful and of little lasting benefit to nearby residents.

As of the mid-1970s, there were about 0.7 hectares of closed forest for each of the world's four billion people. The disparities among regions, and among countries within regions, in per capita forest area are huge. Two or more hectares of forest stood per person in the USSR, Latin America, North America, and Oceania; only half a hectare or less per person existed in Africa, Europe, and Asia. Again, though, aggregates can mislead. Many Latin Americans, especially in Central America and the Andean countries, live amid barren hills and wood scarcity; the richness of rain forests elsewhere in the continent means little to them. By the same token, Europe's well-managed forests produce far more harvestable timber—year after year—than the numbers suggest.

Nearly all the shrinkage in closed-forest area is occurring in the humid tropics, where, according to one recent estimate, the forested area is declining annually by about 1.2 percent—by 11 million hectares, an area the size of Bulgaria or Cuba. Covering 935 million hectares in the mid-seventies, tropical moist forests have already been reduced from their natural domain by more than 40 percent.

*one hectare = 2.47 acres

In North America and Europe, the forest area is roughly stable; in fact, the modernization of agriculture over the last half-century has allowed a considerable reversion of farm to forest. In these regions, today's challenge is less one of simply preserving forest lands than of balancing competing environmental, recreational, and industrial demands.

Throughout most of Africa, Asia, and Latin America, the forest itself is shrinking and usually not according to any rational land-use plan. Areas that were densely settled long ago—such as the Middle East, parts of North Africa, the Andean region of South America, and most of China and South Asia—lost the bulk of their forests in ages past, so the absolute decline, if any, in closed-forest area today is small. But many developing countries, especially those in the humid tropical belt, are now experiencing rapid and massive destruction of forests.

Worldwide, the extent to which tree planting is offsetting forest losses is impossible to ascertain. Most data on reforestation and plantation programs do not distinguish between the restocking of existing forest lands and the extension of tree plantations to new areas. In 1978, the United Nations Food and Agriculture Organization (FAO) estimated the current world planting program to be "about 4 million hectares a year." China and developed countries undoubtedly account for most of the total.

With governments alarmed about forest losses and firewood scarcity and with a flurry of reforestation programs now being initiated, the planting totals are probably rising fast. Still, the current pace of tree planting looks pitifully slow when compared with the gargantuan demands that will be placed on the world's forests in the decades to come. Real prices for forest products are sure to rise as worldwide consumption of wood for all purposes grows from 2.5 billion cubic meters in 1976 to 4 billion cubic meters in 1994 (FAO estimate). Commercial wood demand is rising particularly fast in less developed countries, most of which combine rapid population growth and relatively high economic growth rates with low current levels of industrial wood consumption. The FAO projects that Third World consumption of wood-panel products and paper will quadruple over the next two decades, and that consumption of sawn wood will rise by 50 percent a decade.

Even as the demand for industrial wood soars, one-third of humanity will continue to rely on firewood for cooking and home heating. Optimistically assuming that wood-conserving stoves and cooking alternatives such as biogas plants and solar cookers will spread, one World Bank analyst estimates that 20 to 25 million hectares of new wood plantations will have to be in place by the year 2000. But at current rates, only about one-tenth of that area will be planted.

Causes, Not Culprits

The spread of agriculture, firewood collection, and short-sighted timber harvesting usually precipitate deforestation. But behind these causes lurk more basic ones: agricultural stagnation, grossly unequal land tenure, rising unemployment, rapid population growth, and the incapacity to regulate private enterprise to protect the public interest. In a way, forest losses are a measure of broader social failures.

The spread of agriculture, today as it has been throughout most of human history, is the principal threat to forests. Most of the farmland in nearly every country was once at least moderately tree-covered. Although its extent is often exaggerated, some potentially arable land yet remains under forest in parts of Africa, Latin America, and Southeast Asia. Given the population increases in store for these regions, converting much of this land to agriculture over the coming decades will be necessary and, in many cases, the wisest feasible land-use choice. But the method of conversion may be anything but wise. The spread of agriculture is often characterized more by chaos and ecological destruction than by rationality, even when it is "planned" by governments. Politicians always find it easier to hand out unoccupied land than to redistribute proven farmland, however unequal the ownership of the latter may be. In the tropical rain forests, where in many cases little is known about soil conditions and potentials, both legal and illegal colonists are trying to carve farms out of the jungle. But much tropical land colonization, as U.N. analysts observed a decade ago, "is indiscriminate . . . an ill-advised use of the land . . . merely a process of trial and error."

In Central and South America, increasing areas of tropical forest have been cleared to create grazing lands, too often a transition of dubious social value. Despairing at last of populating the Amazon Basin with peasant cultivators, the Brazilian Government has granted huge concessions in the region to both domestic operators and foreign corporations to raise cattle. New pastures account for a good share of the million-plus hectares of forest that disappear in Brazil's portion of the Amazon Basin each year. Likewise, large landowners in Venezuela are transforming forest into pasture while, throughout Central America, virgin forest is rapidly giving way to pastures created by cattle ranchers anxious to cash in on the lucrative U.S. export market.

Often blamed for forest destruction are shifting cultivators—those who slash and burn a clearing in the rain forest, grow crops for a few years until the fertility of the thin topsoil dissipates, and then move on to clear a new patch. While itinerant farmers are major agents of deforestation, not all take the same approach and not all the same toll on the forest. Some practices just now being developed and pushed by tropical foresters, such as agro-forestry systems (in which trees and crops are rotated on the same land), are in a sense efforts to build the ecological soundness of traditional shifting cultivation into new forms of continuous land use. Today, many traditional peoples in areas such as the Amazon Basin, Central Africa, and the more remote parts of Southeast Asia are still practicing shifting cultivation (alternating cropping with fallowing to allow the soil to recover its fertility) in harmony with nature. It is when such farmers get hemmed in by logging companies, the spread of plantations, or other modern economic forces that they are portrayed as enemies of the forest.

Many of the "shifting cultivators" wreaking the greatest forest destruction today are not traditional practitioners of this art at all. They are rootless, landless people, many of them squeezed from their homelands by unequal land tenure or population growth, who are struggling to make what living they can amidst unfamiliar ecological conditions. Thirty thousand Venezuelan families, most of them practicing shifting cultivation, are living within national parks, forest reserves, and other supposedly protected areas. Accelerated erosion and siltation caused by an influx of shifting cultivators in the watershed above the Panama Canal are jeopardizing both the Canal's future utility and Panama City's water supply—prompting a major new U.S./ Panamanian program of reforestation, agro-forestry, and improved land management.

Firewood collectors also sap the forest. About half of all the wood cut in the world each year is burned as fuel, mainly by the poorest third of humanity, who still rely on firewood for cooking and heating. At least 1.5 billion people each burn anywhere from one-fifth of a ton to well over a ton of wood a year, putting on the world's vegetation an awesome pressure that is often ignored in official statistics. The outright destruction of living trees to meet fuel needs occurs most commonly around cities and towns, where commercial markets for firewood and charcoal are located.

Worldwide, the operations of the lumber and forest-products industries do not rival the spread of agriculture as a direct cause of deforestation, though the two forces often work in tandem. Still, improperly managed logging is unquestionably helping to deplete the earth's forest resources. Heavy cutting can reduce wood output even from an area that appears to remain covered with trees. Moreover, logging sometimes depletes or destroys resources of great daily value to people living in or around the forest, while the profits and consumer benefits of the operation flow mainly to people in faraway capital cities or foreign lands. In evaluating the economics of timber operations, governments can easily overlook the multitude of products and services that the forest renders to local people; in some cases their combined value may rival or surpass the value of the forest as timber. The trouble is that most of these other benefits do not accrue to those who hold power over the destiny of the forests.

Logging in humid tropical forests—much of which has been done by multinational corporations—usually involves not clear-cutting but the "creaming" of the forest's small proportion of commercially valued species. However, the process of cutting and removing selected trees amid dense foliage and on delicate soils usually wreaks far more destruction of vegetation and wildlife than the bare statistics suggest. One

Indonesian study revealed that logging operations damaged or destroyed about one-third of the trees left behind.

Apart from the responsibility with which it is practiced, logging in many tropical forest areas contributes inadvertently to the permanent loss of forests. Wherever loggers build roads and settlements, other people follow. With or without government approval, cultivators move along new logging roads and into newly logged areas, hoping to put down roots. The widening clearings and tell-tale smoke plumes of slash-and-burn cultivation are normal sights around new roads throughout the humid tropics. When these farms fail, cattle pastures or useless, tenacious grasses sometimes take their place. Even when cultivation doesn't follow, logging can leave the forest permanently bereft of the more valuable species.

The price of the extensive degradation of tropical forests will be paid the world over. More and more of the world's wood and fiber supplies will have to be produced in the tropics, where year-round sunlight and warmth permit much faster growth than is possible in temperate zones. Even as logging depletes the major commercial species of many tropical forests, technologies are being developed that use virtually all species, if not for lumber then for chipping and reconstitution as particle board, fiber board, and paper.

Like many new technologies, "all-species use" is a two-edged sword; because of its uncertainties and dangers, it has been termed a "Faustian bargain." Used carelessly, it can ultimately prove more harmful than traditional logging practices are. Most of the nutrients in rain-forest ecosystems are contained in the vegetation rather than the soil. Remove the biomass, as all-species use does, and future tree growth may be stunted. Replanting is supposed to follow clear-cutting, but the jury is not yet in on the long-term productivity of intensive tree plantations on rain-forest soils. Unless governments regulate more stringently than they have in the past, there is no guarantee that serious reforestation efforts will always follow denudation in any case.

On the other hand, more intensive use of smaller tropical areas offers a means of breaking the current vicious pattern—extensive creaming of prime species followed by reckless cultivation and grazing. Implemented carefully and responsibly, all-species use could simultaneously relieve the pressure on other lands and enable forest-rich developing nations to maximize forest productivity. If forest clearing is combined with sustainable tree planting, the tropics can supply prodigious amounts of wood and fiber; and man-made tropical forests can produce five to ten times the wood temperate-zone forests can.

What Price Inaction?

What are the full consequences of uncontrolled deforestation? Curiously, the substantial literature on forestrial economics includes practically nothing on the economic and social consequences of failing to put forestry on a sustainable footing. A better understanding of the price of inaction is clearly needed.

One outcome of neglect or abuse can be a rising dependence on imported forest products. Already most Third World countries are net importers of forest products, particularly paper. As a whole, they enjoy a slight positive balance in forest-product trade, but four tropical timber exporters—Indonesia, Malaysia, the Philippines, and the Ivory Coast—account for that edge. If these four timber giants are removed, the developing world has a net trade deficit of billions of dollars in forest products.

Trade-deficits aside, some of the most negative social impacts of wood scarcity are felt by low-income people even in timber-*exporting* countries. For one thing, the major forest products used by most poor-country residents never enter the market economy; when berries or firewood become scarce, people either do without or they switch to noncommercial alternatives rather than to imported goods. For another, foreign exchange shortages, import restrictions, and high prices can hold a nation's wood and paper consumption well below their true needs.

With inflation now rampant nearly everywhere, the extent to which forest-product scarcity is one of its driving forces deserves close scrutiny. An inadequate supply of forest products is already an inflationary force worldwide, and appears certain to be even more of one in the coming decades. The deepening timber shortage in Pakistan, to take one example, has driven the price of domestic lumber skyward. In the Rawalpindi market, one popular species that sold for 15 rupees a cubic foot in 1967 sold for 80 rupees in 1976. A simple board costs twice as much in Pakistan as in the United States though the income of the average American is 46 times that of the average Pakistani.

Naturally, timber-price inflation boosts construction costs. The social impacts of such increases are especially pernicious in poor countries. In the booming cities of less-developed Asia, about three to four million housing units are being built each year, but housing starts amount to less than a third of housing needs. Even if governments were to make this challenge their top priority, where would they find adequate wood supplies? Right now, the Indian state of Gujarat's ambitious plan to construct huts for landless laborers is being derailed because raw materials are in short supply. The program requires 25 million wood poles, but only 400,000 of these become available each year.

Soaring firewood prices also drive inflation. Almost everywhere commercial firewood markets exist, prices have multiplied over the last decade—in some cases faster than oil prices. In parts of West Africa and Central America, urban families spend one-fourth of their income on wood or charcoal for cooking; it can cost more to heat the pot than to fill it. Even those who gather wood instead of buying it—typically women and children—pay in time and labor what can be a tremendous price. In central Tanzania, 250 to 300 days of work are required to provide the annual firewood needs of a household. In parts of India, a family member must spend two days gathering a week's worth of wood.

With firewood unavailable, rural people switch not to fossil fuels, which are often unavailable and always expensive, but to crop residues and dried cow dung. The resulting diversion of organic matter and nutrients from field to fireplace carries its own negative economic effects. Each ton of dung burned means a loss of about 50 kilograms of potential grain output.

Rising prices and outright shortages of paper have been yet another forest-related source of inflation and hidden hardships. Recent global surges in paper prices reflect boom-and-bust cycles in the pulp-and-paper industry rather than a shortage of wood for pulping. Still, the paper industry requires huge amounts of wood and production increases in parts of the Third World will be severely constrained by shortages of raw materials.

Seldom expressed in economic terms, the environmental consequences of deforestation can directly influence economic output as well as human welfare in the broader sense. Better analytical techniques for evaluating both the environmental benefits forests provide and the environmental results of continued forest losses would undoubtedly help us cut our losses. Decades of research have proved, for example, that deforesting watersheds can increase the severity of flooding, reduce streamflows during dry seasons, and increase the load of sediment entering waterways and reservoirs. Yet, most efforts to combat such problems have entailed engineering measures—dams, embankments, dredging—that address their symptoms rather than their causes.

Some of the environmental costs of current forest trends are by nature incalculable, but are nonetheless massive. Should the clearing and disruption of tropical rain forests continue at recent rates, thousands and possibly hundreds of thousands of plant and animal species, many of them not yet named, will become extinct. As ecologist Norman Myers points out, it is a statistical certainty that numerous sources of beneficial drugs, foods, and industrial products will be unknowingly wiped out. And who can calculate the full ecological repercussions of such an unprecedented biological massacre? Or the costs?

Scientists studying the rising level of carbon dioxide in the atmosphere, which is likely to lead to global climatic shifts, have voiced yet another reason for concern about the loss of tropical forests. A vast amount of carbon is stored in the extensive forests of the tropics, particularly in the massive older trees of virgin forests. The release of that carbon through deforestation and burning could add significantly to the atmosphere's carbon dioxide. Concern for the economic prospects of deforested and wood-importing countries aside, issues like species extinction and climatic change should make the fate of the world's forests a matter of concern to people everywhere.

At Root

All in all, a host of forestry measures that could slow the pace of forest losses await wider implementation. With agro-forestry systems, shifting cultivators can make a good living as they rebuild rather than destroy forest resources. Intensive plantations in selected areas can supply a large share of needed wood and fiber, freeing other areas from the chainsaw. Community-controlled woodlots around villages, and in and around cities, can provide fuel, poles, and a stable and pleasant environment. More intensive management of North American and Soviet forests could boost their output considerably. Logging practices can be regulated to protect the interests of future generations, while waste in the post-harvest processing of timber can be cut.

But essential as they are, such forestry measures alone will not be enough to solve the deforestation problem, for many of the underlying sources of deforestation originate outside the scope of forestry per se. Halting the destructive spread of cultivation will require providing the destroyers with alternate ways to feed themselves. In particular, crop yields and employment must be boosted on the lands best suited to farming. Sound forestry policies can contribute to these efforts but broader decisions on investment priorities, land tenure, and the choice of farm technologies will be even more critical.

Woodland depletion by firewood gatherers can be greatly mitigated by tree-planting, but broader attention to rural energy needs, appropriate alternative energy sources, and national energy priorities is also essential to revitalizing rural environments. The conservation of forest products—by the poor through the adoption of efficient wood-stoves, by the rich through recycling and wise use of wood—is another partial but long-term solution that requires a broad social commitment. Underlying all the sources of deforestation to varying degrees is, of course, human population growth; more people demand more firewood and farmland in some countries, more veneer furniture and unspoiled wilderness in others. The sooner population growth slows, the brighter will the prospects be for preserving forests ample enough to meet both environmental and economic requirements. Wide-scale tree planting is essential over the coming quarter-century, but getting at the deeper roots of deforestation requires far more. ❦

Soil Erosion
and Cropland Loss

Lester Brown

Ever since agriculture began, people have gone hungry when land is scarce in relation to their numbers. When crops are poorly nourished, so are many of the people they sustain. The Tigris-Euphrates Valley, once described as the Fertile Crescent, may formerly have supported more people than it does today, and the food-deficit lands of North Africa once served as the granary of the Roman Empire. But the scale of cropland loss and soil deterioration, a problem that affects rich and poor countries alike, is unprecedented. Natural soil fertility is now declining on roughly one-fifth of the world's croplands.

Pressures on the world's croplands have escalated since mid-century as our numbers have increased, raising doubts about long-term food security. In 1950 there were 2.5 billion people in the world. In 1975 there were 4.0 billion. By the end of the century, there will be 6.3 billion of us if current projections prove correct.

Soil erosion is direct evidence of the mounting pressures on the global cropland base. So is the spread of deserts and the loss of cropland to nonfarm uses. In the Central Sudan and Northwest India, sand dunes now cover the traces of abandoned villages. In the midwestern United States cornfields have given way to shopping centers. Factories are being build in southern China on land that previously yielded two rice harvests each year.

Indirectly, excessive pressures surface as falling crop yields, growing food deficits, and economic instability in the world food market. During the seventies, the prices of wheat and rice have in times of scarcity more than doubled. After a quarter-century reprieve, famine returned to claim hundreds of thousands of lives in Bangladesh, Ethiopia, and Africa's Sahelian zone. The food shortages that led to these deaths were initially blamed on poor weather, but weather was in many instances only the triggering event that brought into focus a more fundamental problem—the growing pressure on local land resources.

Competing Uses of Land

As world population and economic activity increase, more land is needed for purposes other than food production. Chief among them are urbanization, energy production, and transportation, each of which now claims precious cropland in virtually every country.

Most data show the growth of cities to be the leading contributor to cropland loss. U.S. cities are consuming cropland at a record rate. Land-use surveys by the USDA in 1967 and 1975 indicated that over 2.5 million hectares of prime cropland were converted to urban and "built-up" uses during the eight-year span. A study of urban encroachment on European grasslands and croplands from 1960 to 1970 shows that West Germany was losing 1 percent of its agricultural land every four years. For France and the United Kingdom, the comparable figure was nearly 2 percent for the decade.

No one knows exactly how much cropland cities claimed during the third quarter of this century, much less how much will be converted by century's end. But information on the expected growth in urban numbers provides some gauge of future land needs. U.N. figures show that the urban share of world population, which was 29 percent in 1950 and 39 percent in 1975, will likely reach 50 percent by 2000. This means the urban population would expand from 1.547 billion in 1975 to 3.127 billion just 25 years later. The absolute increase in the number of urban dwellers during the final quarter of this century will nearly double the increase from 1950 to 1975. If it is assumed, perhaps conservatively, that those additional 1.580 billion people will need only .04 hectares per person, then the world's cities would occupy 63 million hectares of additional land by 2000. If it is further assumed that 40 percent of this total is cropland, expanding cities will cover 25 million hectares of cropland between now and the end of the century.

Although this loss would amount to only 2 percent of the world cropland base, the share of world food output involved would be larger, for in most countries cities occupy the most fertile land. Canadians studying their land-use patterns report that "half of the farmland lost to urban expansion is coming from the best one-twentieth of our farmland." Assuming average levels of land productivity, this loss of 25 million hectares represents the food supply of some 84 million people.

In the Third World, too, cropland is lost each year to village growth. Analyzing village spread using data over several decades for his native Bangladesh, Akef Quazi of the University of Wales finds a close relationship between growth in the number of families and growth in the area occupied by the village. Homes are "made of locally available materials, such as bamboo, thatch, and corrugated iron sheets, and, as such, are never strong enough to hold an upper story." In a country that consists largely of rainfed rice fields, almost every new village homestead is being built on cropland. Occasional exceptions aside, Quazi's general point is sound. Sprawl has come to the Bengali countryside.

China, the world's most populous country, is also losing cropland to cities and industry. USDA China specialist Alva Erisman reports that "water control projects, urban growth, and the appropriation of agricultural land for roads, railroads, airfields, industrial plants, and military uses have removed good farmland from cultivation." Dwight Perkins, a scholar of Chinese at Harvard, lays part of the blame to China's 10 percent industrial growth rate. The Chinese commonly site factories on the edges of cities. Perkins believes Chinese planners are taking account of this continuing loss of cropland. But, he says, "there is no way around the fact that good farm land (flat, located near transport, et cetera) often makes an excellent factory site."

Rivaling urbanization as a claimant on cropland is energy consumption. During the final quarter of this century, as during the third, energy consumption is projected to increase even faster than food consumption. Already hydroelectric dams have inundated vast stretches of rich bottomland and many electricity-generating plants each require hundreds of hectares. More often than not, oil refineries and storage tanks are built on prime farmland along rivers and coastal plains, while strip-mining coal and diverting irrigation water to the energy sector both tend to reduce the cultivated area. The energy "crunch" we don't hear much about is that of the bulldozer on cropland.

A particularly voracious consumer of cropland is the automobile-centered transport system. An enormous amount of U.S. cropland has been paved over for the automobile. Just parking for the nation's 143 million licensed motor vehicles requires millions of hectares. But even parking, paving, and dotting the land with service facilities do not account for all land losses. Urban sprawl is an indirect consequence of over-reliance on the automobile, as are the development of commercial strips and ex-urban shopping complexes.

The amount of cropland that will be paved over, flooded by a dam, built on, or strip-mined by the end of this century is unknown. But, if world population does increase by 2.3 billion people, every nonfarm claimant on cropland—urbanization, energy production, and transportation—will increase, further reducing the cropland total.

Biting The Dust

Over much of the earth's surface, the topsoil is only inches deep, usually less than a foot. Any loss from that layer can reduce the soil's innate fertility. Forty years ago, G.V. Jacks and R.O. Whyte graphically described the essential role of topsoil. "Below that thin layer comprising the delicate organism known as the soil," they said, "is a planet as lifeless as the moon."

Soil erosion is natural. It occurs even when land is in grass or forests. But when land is cleared and planted to crops, the process invariably accelerates; and when it exceeds the natural rate of soil formation, the layer of topsoil dwindles, eventually disappearing entirely to expose subsoil or bare rock. Once enough topsoil is lost, the cropland is abandoned. But the gradual loss of topsoil and the slow decline in inherent fertility that precedes abandonment may take years, decades, or even centuries. Throughout this process, the size of the cropland base may remain stable, but its productivity declines.

As population pressures mount, farmers itensify cultivation and bring marginal soils under the plow. Ironically, some of the techniques designed to boost land productivity in the near term lead eventually to excessive soil loss. In the American Midwest, corn is now continuously cropped. Gone are the traditional rotations of corn, grass-legume mixtures, then corn again. The advent of cheap nitrogen fertilizers that replaced nitrogen-fixing legumes has abetted the transition to continuous cropping of corn. These chemical fertilizers can replace nutrients lost through crop removal, but they do nothing to make up for the loss of the topsoil needed to maintain a healthy soil structure.

In 1977, the U.N. Conference on Desertification issued a summary report that indicated that just under one-fifth of the world's cropland is now subject to degradation that cannot be tolerated over the long run. Productivity on this land has been reduced by an estimated average of 25 percent. Interpreted at the national level, this statistic is startling. In the Soviet Union, attempts to regain food self-sufficiency by investing heavily in agriculture are stymied because soils have lost some of their inherent productivity. According to Thane Gustafson of Harvard, that Soviet government's agricultural planners must reckon with "50 years of neglect [that] have left a legacy of badly damaged soils."

Nepal too must pay the piper, as must poor countries the world over. The Nepalese Government estimates that the country's rivers now annually carry 240 million cubic meters of soil to India. With wit born of adversity, His Majesty's Government has called this loss Nepal's "most precious export." In Ethiopia, a drought that culminated in famine in 1974 has brought soil deterioration into focus. A mindful foreign ambassador in Addis Ababa noted in 1975 that Ethiopia was "quite literally going down the river," and more recent U.S. AID mission reports say the same. "There is an environmental nightmare unfolding before our eyes . . . It is the result of the acts of millions of Ethiopians struggling for survival: scratching the surface of eroded land and eroding it further; cutting down the trees for warmth and fuel and leaving the country denuded."

Official observers in Indonesia and Pakistan have witnessed similar environmental degradation. A report from the U.S. Embassy in Jakarta indicates that "soil erosion is creating an ecological emergency in

Java . . . laying waste to land at an alarming rate, much faster than present reclamation programs can restore it." An AID officer in the Punjab in Pakistan reports that several thousand hectares of cropland are abandoned each year because of severe erosion and degradation.

In the Andean countries of Latin America, skewed land-ownership patterns aggravate this problem. Wealthy ranchers use the relatively level valley floors for cattle grazing, forcing small landholders onto steeply sloping fields to produce subsistence crops. This peculiar land-use pattern leads to severe soil erosion on the slopes, impairing the productivity of both the mountainside and the valleys.

Even well-equipped and well-informed U.S. farmers are losing top-soil at an unsustainable rate. The USDA Soil Conservation Service reports that U.S. farmers are not managing highly erodible soils as well today as their forebears did a generation ago. Adopting conservation measures is easy enough when the system has excess capacity. But when grain prices are high and food is scarce, the temptation to forego these essential measures intensifies. A nationwide survey by the Soil Conservation Service indicated that "in 1975, soil losses on cropland amounted to almost three billion tons or an average of about 22 tons per hectare." These losses would have been even more excessive had farmers followed no conservation practices, but "worst case" scenarios offer small comfort. The surveyors concluded that if U.S. crop production was to be sustained, soil loss would have to be reduced to 1.5 billion tons annually—one-half today's level.

With an acute shortage of productive cropland in sight, any loss of topsoil is cause for concern. Even with large quantities of fertilizers and the best tillage practices, creating an inch of new topsoil can take 100 years. Left to nature, the process can require centuries.

Land Productivity Trends

Demand pressures upon the soil are now becoming so great in many parts of the world that the soil's inherent productivity is at stake. In tropical and subtropical regions, where fallowing has evolved as a method of restoring fertility, mounting population pressures are forcing shifting cultivators to abbreviate the rotation cycles. As cycles are shortened, land productivity falls. Students of African agriculture refer increasingly to the continent's "cycle of land degeneration."

In Nigeria, where both the addition of marginal land to the cropland base and a shortening of the fallow cycle are lowering cropland fertility, cereal yields have been falling since the early sixties. "Fallow periods under shifting cultivation," says a World Bank study, "have become too short to restore fertility in some areas." In some locales the original cropping cycle of 10 to 15 years has already shrunk to five years. Since 1950, the harvested area in Nigeria has multiplied two-and-one-half times as marginal land has been put under plow and fallow cycles truncated. Not even the combined contribution of all advances in agricultural technology (including chemical fertilizers, seed varieties, and irrigation) can compensate for the resultant decline in productivity.

Similar pressures on the land are evident in Latin America. A U.N. study of Latin American agriculture ties the falling potato harvests to soil erosion in the Peruvian Andes, the region that gave the world the potato. In Venezuela, FAO researchers have found abundant evidence that "with growing population pressure, the fallow period is becoming increasingly shorter so that soil fertility is not restored before recropping." The upshot is a decline in the soil's organic content and water-holding capacity. Those loses, in turn, contribute to soil compaction. "In other words," say the researchers, "with the population of modern times, formerly stable shifting cultivation systems are now in a state of breakdown."

On the Indian subcontinent, the story is much the same. German geographer Robert Schmid describes a situation in Nepal that is strikingly similar to Peru's: "During the last century man in search of more arable land had greatly extended the terraced fields. . . . Increasingly, the farmers had to be self-sufficient, and therefore marginal land was taken into cultivation." The farming of increasingly marginal land, Schmidt goes on, combines with progressive deforestation, as trees are felled for wood and branches are lopped from remaining trees for use as animal fodder. Soon, the cycle of soil erosion and deterioration is complete.

In dryland farming regions, another influence on the productivity of cropland is shrinkage of the fallowed area. As world wheat prices rose, U.S. summer fallow land dropped from 17 million hectares in 1969 to 13 million hectares in 1974. This decline led Kenneth Grant, head of the USDA Soil Conservation Service, to warn farmers that severe wind erosion and dust bowl conditions could result. Snapping at the lure of record wheat prices and short-term gains, warned Grant, might cost farmers the long-term productivity of their land. In other dryland regions, agricultural history ran a similar course during the late sixties and early seventies. The Soviets consistently fallowed 17 to 18 million hectares in the dryland regions until the massive crop shortfall 1972. They then reduced the fallowed area to between 11 and 12 million hectares, the level at which it has remained.

The continual substitution of marginal land for prime land also jeopardizes the inherent productivity of cropland. In Canada, land being lost to urbanization includes some of the most productive in the country, whereas land being converted to agricultural land is far less productive.

An even sharper fall-off in land quality, commensurate with greater population pressures, is reported in China. Leslie T.C. Kuo, a specialist on Chinese agriculture, reports that "the use of one acre of cultivated land for construction purposes must be offset by the reclamation of several acres of wasteland." In Brazil, the amount of land harvested has more than doubled since 1950, but simultaneous increases in the use of fertilizer and modern agricultural techniques have not increased the crop yield per hectare. Here again, the poor quality of successive additions of land has apparently offset production gains made possible by advances in agricultural technology and the increased use of fertilizer.

Even as the inherent fertility of as much as one-fifth of the world's cropland declines, the backlog of agricultural technology waiting to be applied in the agriculturally advanced countries appears to be dwindling. Consider Neal Jensen's analysis of the long-term historical rise of wheat yields in New York State. Applying his findings to agriculture in general, Jensen predicts that the rate of productivity increase will become slower until it eventually levels off. Plant breeders and agronomists in the more advanced agricultural countries are finding it difficult to come up with new techniques to measurably raise yields.

An historically unique influence on agricultural yields deserves the last word: the fivefold increase in the price of petroleum during the seventies. Price jumps slow the growth of energy use in agriculture directly by curbing the use of fuel in tractors and irrigation pumps and indirectly by slowing the production of chemical fertilizer, an energy-intensive commodity. Coupled with rising energy prices, they make the loss of inherent soil fertility and the outright loss of cropland much more serious than they otherwise would be.

Regional Prospects

In 1950, opportunities for adding to the world's cropland base were still substantial. Then, the potential for expanding the area under irrigation was also impressive, particularly in the developing countries. Today, grounds for optimism have disappeared. In North America, the cropland base has been shrinking for three decades, while opportunities for new land reclamation in Western Europe have been assessed as negligible by the Organization for Economic Cooperation and Development. The countries of Eastern Europe have been hard pressed to maintain their cultivated land area over the last 15 years, while in the Soviet Union cultivation has already been extended into highly marginal rainfall areas.

In densely populated Asia, the prospect does not ignite hope either. China has little new land to bring under the plow, and irrigation development is already so extensive as to limit opportunities for further expanding the area that is multiple-cropped. In India, the region's other leading food producer, the cropland area is expected to increase little, if at all. There, however, room exists to expand the area harvested through multiple-cropping, since much of the irrigation potential, particularly on the Gangetic plain, is still to be developed. The one area in Asia that could sustain an increase in both cropland area and the intensity of cropping is the Mekong Valley and delta, local politics permitting.

Save for that in a few undeveloped pockets, opportunity for greatly adding to Africa's cropland is limited. In the vast northern section, the Sahara is expanding in every direction, claiming land in nearly a score of countries. The one country with potential for markedly increasing the area harvested is the Sudan, since it has developed only part of the share of the Nile water reserved to it by treaty with Egypt. To the south, the principal hope for more farmland lies in opening the tsetse fly belt to cultivation—*if* a way can be found to eradicate the tsetse fly.

In Latin America, the cropland area can be expanded by plowing up some grasslands, as Argentina has been doing during the seventies. But this approach would reduce the scope for grazing livestock. The other major avenue of expansion, opening new lands in the Amazon basin and the rest of the continental interior, is also overrated. The principal constraint here is the limited capacity of fragile tropical soils to sustain cultivation over time.

All available data show a sharp fall-off in the productivity of recent additions to the cropland base. They confirm what some analysts have suspected—that the world's farmers have most of the productive cropland under the plow. Rough projections by John McHale, which incorporate both additions and losses of cropland, show that the former will offset the latter and that the cropland base at the end of the century will be essentially the same size as today's. A USDA model of the world food economy, which assumes a real increase in commodity prices of roughly 50 percent between the 1969–71 base period and the year 2000, shows an increase over the harvested area of cereals in 1975 of only 6 percent.

On balance, it is difficult to see how the world can increase its cropland area by more than 10 percent during the final quarter of this century without a dramatic rise in the price of food. Such an increase would be much smaller than the one that occurred between 1950 and 1975, when for the first time the increase in cultivated area fell far behind that of population and accounted for only one-fourth of the gain in food output. The small increase before us is of a piece with a decline in the rate of increase.

If population grows during the final quarter of this century as projected, cereal land per person will decrease from .184 hectares to .128 hectares even if the 10 percent increase in croplands materializes. In absolute terms, this per capita decline of 0.56 hectares is almost exactly the same as the .057 hectare decline of the third quarter-century. But in relative terms it is much larger. From 1950 to 1975, the area per person shrank by scarcely one-fourth, while the reduction during the current quarter will be closer to one-third.

How then, are we to satisfy the projected growth in world food demand for the final quarter of this century? If U.N. projections are correct, world food demand could double between 1975 and 2000, and if this cropland assessment is correct, total cropland area will expand by 10 percent at most.

Nothing except increasing yields per hectare can make up the difference, and recent trends indicate that the potential for a continuing rapid rise in crop yield per hectare may be much less than we thought. Between 1950 and 1971, the modest expansion in world cropland area and the unprecedented rise in crop yield per hectare raised world grain production per person from 276 kilograms to 360 kilograms. Since 1971, per capita grain production has actually declined, averaging only 354 kilograms over the following six years.

Far from our minds as we eat, drive, use energy, or break ground for new urban developments is the balance between people and cropland. Yet few things are more critical to our welfare and survival. If recent population and cropland trends continue, that balance will almost certainly topple and upset the economy and politics, too. Avoiding such upheaval requires making a mammoth effort to protect cropland from nonfarm uses, to improve soil management, and, most important, to reduce the rate of population growth. Our present lack of well-developed land-use policies harks back to an earlier era when land was relatively abundant. Now, the frontiers are gone. There is no more room to play out high-risk social and agricultural experiments, no more excess agricultural land to waste or exhaust for the sake of expanding industry, urbanization, and energy production. In a world of continuously growing demand for food, land must be viewed as an irreplaceable resource, one that is paved over or otherwise taken out of production only under the most pressing circumstances and after careful, far-reaching consideration.

Historically, land in most countries was allocated to various uses through the marketplace. But the free market is almost blind to purpose and the competition for cropland is fierce. As cropland becomes scarcer, land-use planning becomes more critical, whether at the national level, the local level, or both. The mechanism—be it land-use restrictions, government decrees or tax incentives— is a matter of preference. Each society will need to employ approaches suited to its own circumstances. With acute pressures on its land resources, Japan has faced the issue first and in so doing has developed a model for other countries to follow. According to OECD reports, it is the only country with comprehensive zoning nationwide. In 1968, the entire country was divided into three land-use zones—urban, agricultural, and other. In 1974, the plan was further refined to include specific areas for forests, natural parks, and nature reserves.

In some situations, adjustments are needed in land use within agriculture as well as between agriculture and other sectors of the economy. For example, intelligent land-use policies would reverse the anomalous use in several Latin American countries of valley floors for grazing and mountainsides for farming. In effect, existing social structures in some countries are simply incompatible with the wise management of land resources.

In many countries, preventing erosion and stabilizing soils are such vast undertakings that they will require a strong national political commitment and a detailed plan of action. Such a program has been outlined for the United States by the Soil Conservation Service, which

has called both for changes in cropping practices and for heavy investments in land improvements. All these prescribed changes in farming
practices are monumental in scale, involving half of all U.S. cropland,
and some run counter to the immediate economic interests of farmers
and consumers, since they would lead to a 5 to 8 percent increase in
food production costs. Thus, the U.S. faces the same obstacles many
poor countries do—getting the broad political support needed to fund
and administer plans drawn up by soil scientists. Doing that means
inculcating a broader understanding of the social costs of failing to act.

Balancing food demand and cropland also requires us to assess population policy yet again. No other single factor is so critical to the
balance. Growth in human numbers generates simultaneously a demand
for more cropland and pressures to convert cropland to nonfarm uses.
Acute land hunger, food shortages, soaring food prices, and widespread
social unrest all make it clear that land-use policy and population policy
address different dimensions of the same issue—the equilibrium of
resources and demand. The issue is not whether this equilibrium will
eventually be reestablished. It will. If the deterioration is not arrested
by humankind, then nature will ultimately intervene with its own
checks. The issue is whether a new land ethic and a new reverence for
land will be forced upon us by wisdom or regret.

Man-Made Deserts, Man-Made Sorrows

Erik Eckholm

Early history was made in the deserts. The first civilizations were born in desert soil, and so were three of the world's major religions. Now the deserts themselves make news. In the 1970s, world attention was drawn to arid lands—to some because of the oil beneath their sands, and to some because ecological deterioration had culminated in human disaster.

Although more than a third of the earth's land is arid or semi-arid, less than half this area is by nature too dry and barren to support human life. Year after year, however, additional areas are converted to useless desert by people who are in many cases forced by circumstances beyond their control to compromise their futures. As a result of over-grazing, overcropping, and denudation by firewood gatherers, deserts are creeping outward in Africa, Asia, Australia, and the Americas. Worse, the productive capacity of vast dry regions in both rich and poor countries is falling.

Often called "desertification," the degradation of arid lands was once little known outside narrow scientific circles. Global recognition of this problem came only after catastrophe. In the early 1970s, haunting television images of starving Africans forced the U.S. and the rest of the world to realize that all was not well in the deserts.

Disasters in the desert are nothing new; droughts and crop failures have always plagued arid lands, as Joseph recognized in ancient Egypt when he advised the Pharaoh to set aside grain reserves. But both the scale of suffering when the rains fail and the scale of destructive pressure on delicate ecosystems are reaching unprecedented proportions in many desert regions as population growth outstrips agricultural reforms and progress.

The Geography of Desertification

Land deterioration south of the Sahara has been especially well publicized, with good reason. In the Sudan, for instance, the desert boundary has been pulled southward by 90 kilometers over the last two decades, and crop yields and range productivity have fallen in areas far away from the desert fringe. Along the Sahara's northern edge, the story is the same. In North Africa, some 100,000 hectares of pasture and cropland degenerate into desert each year.

Desertification has a particularly strong foothold in the Middle East, where some areas support fewer people today than they did thousands of years ago when they spawned the earliest civilizations. Desert-like environments are also replacing richer ecosystems in Argentina, Brazil, Chile, Peru, and Mexico.

Apart from intensively irrigated regions like the Nile and Indus Valleys, northwestern India is the world's most densely populated arid zone— a distinction that may turn out to be an epitaph. As farming spreads into marginal areas, grazing lands shrink commensurately. Yet, the number of grazing animals continues to rise. The two trends represent a sure-fire formula for overgrazing, wind erosion, and soil deterioration. Crop yields have declined there already and most pastures are only 10 to 15 percent as productive as they once were.

In the U.S., desertification is less virulent than it is in the less developed countries, but no more welcome. Recent surveys of federally controlled rangeland in the United States revealed more than 20 million hectares to be in "poor" or "bad" condition because of overgrazing.

One of the most dramatic and, in human terms, costliest examples of desertification in the United States is that of the huge Navajo Indian Reservation in northern Arizona and New Mexico. Encouraged by the U.S. government to become sheep farmers after their nineteenth-century subjugation, the Navajos proved to be adept shepherds. But, as the flocks multiplied in the absence of proper range-management techniques, the land—and ultimately the people living off it—paid an enormous price. Locations described by mid-nineteenth century travelers as lush meadows are today vistas composed of scattered sod remnants amid shifting sands and deep gulleys. Only a small fraction of the potential economic benefit is being harvested from these dusty, sagebrush-dotted lands that were once largely carpeted with grass.

In one zone that range specialists recently calculated could safely support 16,000 sheep at most, 11,500 Navajo people with 140,000 sheep were trying to wrest an existence. Before a new stock-reduction program took effect in the mid-1970s, their lot was growing increasingly difficult. In essence, individual families have been caught in an economic bind in which short-term self-interest dictates behavior that undermines the tribal patrimony. Yet, if herd reductions, careful grazing management, and reseeding can restore this zone to peak conditions, its carrying capacity will eventually rise above the current level by a factor of ten.

While desertification clearly plagues rich as well as poor countries, the same processes of deterioration can have quite different effects on human life in different social contexts. Wealthier countries with diversified economies and public welfare programs can generally absorb localized declines in productivity without human catastrophe. In the U.S., for example, many of those whose cattle are degrading public rangelands are well-off ranchers or investors, and even those Americans who can ill afford financial losses from desertification can sometimes migrate to better prospects or, if nothing else, collect welfare funds that at the least keep starvation at bay.

In contrast, tens of millions of Africans, Asians, and Latin Americans have nowhere to turn for aid as the basis of their livelihood erodes. Left in the wake of the global development process, they face chronic destitution and, when the rains fail, possible famine. But agricultural output is not the only gauge of desertification. For some people, a decline in the quality of the land means a decline in the quality of the diet, chronic ill health, and an increased vulnerability to famine when the rains fail. By reducing a region's opportunities for productive employment, desertification can create "ecological refugees" who must leave the land in search of a livelihood—and who swell the ranks of migrants gathering in the cities of the developing world.

Learning from Nomads

Manifested as an ecological phenomenon, desertification is at base a human problem. Any scheme for enhancing the productivity of desert lands will fall short of the mark if it isn't grounded in an understanding of the cultures and economic predicaments of desert dwellers—and in the recognition that people undermine their own futures only when they see no alternative. In the existing institutional context, what is essential to the short-term survival of the individual who lives on arid lands can fly in the face of what the long-term survival of society dictates. Nomadic families or clans, for example, need many animals each just to meet their basic needs for milk and milk products—generally their principal foods. To these people, surplus livestock represent both an investment and insurance against drought losses. Nor does the individual farmer, who has little choice but to plow up high-risk marginal fields, count his contribution to desertification as anti-social behavior. To him, it is a matter of survival. And anyway, yields on the better farmlands may be inadequate to feed the local populace, or even falling as population pressures or the extension of cash cropping undermine traditional fallowing customs. Small wonder, then, that individual parents in desert lands place a premium on having large families. To them, the children are needed to tend herds, gather wood, and carry water—they are not seen as part of a global population problem but as vital members of the household economy.

Hope and help for the people of the arid lands, thus, depend upon forsaking a system in which personal aspirations lead to social suicide for one in which hard-working people can promote their own and society's welfare at the same time. How can this be done? For one thing, livestock will have to be valued for its quality rather than its abundance, and farmers will have to have the knowledge and equipment they need to grow enough food for all on the best-suited lands without running down these lands' long-term fertility. Besides that, the advantages of small families will have to be apparent to all couples.

In the desert, as elsewhere, planners have much to learn from the plants, animals, and cultures that have withstood centuries of environmental adversity. If the ecological balance historically maintained by most nomadic groups was wretched, predicated as it was on high human death rates, these people used the life-defying desert remarkably resourcefully. The popular notion that nomads wander aimlessly has little basis in fact: nomadic movements nearly always harmonize with the seasonal rhythm of climate and plant life.

Returning to an earlier historical age is no more desirable than likely. The harsh natural selection that underlay nomadic life in the past runs against the grain today. In any case, rudimentary modern medicine has trickled into the arid zones well ahead of advanced agricultural technology, helping to push down death rates, so the law of the desert is no longer the "law of the jungle." At the same time, national boundaries now divide natural ecological zones artificially and restrict the traditional movements of nomadic groups, while the spread of farming into grazing areas further squeezes the nomads. Clearly, there is no going back.

But while many traditional nomadic practices no longer work, adopting some modernized version of the nomadic way of life may be the only way that those in the desert's arid fringes can safely tap these areas' protein-producing potential. Huge regional management schemes, in which clan leaders regulate grazing and migratory movements according to natural conditions and the advice of range specialists, are one possibility. Ruled thus, nomads could retain their flexibility while preventing overgrazing and making use of modern methods to improve livestock quality.

Improving farming in areas where the cultivators stay put is as crucial to arresting desertification as controlling grazing is. Agricultural progress means food, employment, and income, but it also means preserving pasturelands by halting the spread of cultivation onto them. In past decades, cash crops such as cotton and peanuts for export have been the object of research and investment, as have large-scale irrigation schemes intended to bring desert regions under intensive production of food or fiber. Simple subsistence farmers, growing millet or sorghum for family consumption and trade with nomads or urbanites, have frequently been neglected—with sorry consequences for the land.

Export crops, a principal source of foreign exchange for many arid countries, can bolster economic progress. But if their expanded cultivation is not accompanied by careful land-use planning and if a major share of the income produced is not earmarked for rural development, the lot of the rural poor may deteriorate and environmental stresses intensify. All too often, the foreign exchange and taxes collected from export crops wind up mainly supporting bloated government bureaucracies and the pampered urban elite.

In many dryland farming areas, population growth has made impossible a return to the ecologically sustainable systems once used with success. The only alternative is to adopt new cropping systems that minimize erosion and that employ crop rotations, water-conserving techniques, animal manures, green manures, and in some cases chemical fertilizers. Sustainable dryland farming methods have been developed and proved effective in Israel, Australia, the Soviet Union, and the United States. Indeed, their use could be enhanced if agricultural technologies and experiences were exchanged among developing countries—a generally neglected form of technology transfer. Ecologically sound methods of continuous cropping that involve the heavy application of human and animal wastes to the fields have evolved in Northern Nigeria, for example, and these practices could well prove workable in other areas.

The quest to modernize agriculture should lead governments and aid agencies to shape land-tenure patterns to insure that social development goals are not undercut by the concentration of landholdings and production benefits in the hands of a few. Land in many arid regions is still allocated by traditional tribal criteria; but as land becomes more scarce or when its value suddenly jumps after it is irrigated, traditional tenure patterns begin to break down. If "progress" entails the emergence of huge mechanized, irrigated farms owned by wealthy individuals or corporations—as it now does in arid northern Mexico—then the welfare of large numbers of people may actually be worsened, and the meaning of "progress" had best be reassessed.

Alongside improved agricultural methods, tree-planting programs are urgently needed nearly everywhere that dryland agriculture is practiced. In the U.S. Great Plains, the thousands of windbreaks planted during and after the 1930s helped stabilize a system that once threatened to become a permanent dust bowl. Besides reducing wind erosion around fields and, in some circumstances, stabilizing sand dunes, tree-planting programs can also help relieve the critical firewood shortage (for cooking) that now plagues every arid region in the developing world.

A problem as awesome as desertification has not gone totally unnoticed. For decades scientists have warned that trouble was brewing in the deserts, but their warnings fell on deaf ears. Individuals who have witnessed environmental deterioration and have felt its impoverishing impact have had no choice but to do all in their power to survive, even if their actions (such as building large herds or plowing up pasturelands) posed a long-term social threat. Virtually every national government in the desert areas has sponsored programs to combat one or another aspect of desertification. But most have been too scattered or too weak to reverse widespread degradation.

Some striking successes do exist. Much of Israel's Negev Desert, which has suffered thousands of years of overgrazing and deforestation, is now productive and prosperous as a result of innovative irrigation practices, improved dryland farming, and controlled grazing. China, too, has halted deterioration and boosted productivity in many of its huge desert areas. Arresting the march of the "sand dragon" by, among other things, planting trees has been one of the Chinese government's priorities. The American Great Plains, once parched and dusty, are now productive and prosperous.

That massive efforts to protect and enhance the productivity of the world's arid lands make good economic sense has been well established. By U.N. estimates, degradation of rangelands and farmlands in dry regions has reduced their combined annual productivity by more than $16 billion below the potential. Fortunately, however, few of the degraded areas have yet passed the point of no return.

Political Timeframe

The technologies needed for reversing desertification are for the most part on hand. Missing is a political commitment commensurate with the size of the challenge. Faced with immediate crises—famines, strikes, and political intrigues—governments find it difficult to devote substantial resources to combatting a seemingly long-term and nearly invisible problem such as ecological deterioration. Their reluctance is particularly great when shifting national priorities and investment patterns go against the short-term personal interests of powerful elites. A political fact of life is that those in power often prefer to channel development funds to lucrative export crops and through large land-owners rather than to subsistence food production and through nomads or small farmers.

Eventually the cows come home, though. Governments that procrastinate too long may one day find their deteriorating agricultural landscapes mirrored in deteriorating social and economic conditions. Undernutrition and famine, unemployment and migration, deepening poverty and human desperation—none of these consequences of desertification is far afield. ❦

Climatic Limits to Growth: How Soon? How Serious?

Stephen Schneider

If present energy consumption and production growth trends continue, the earth may undergo potentially major and possible irreversible global climatic changes. State-of-the-art climatic models suggest that the changes could by the year 2000 rival any since the end of the last ice age.

The earth's surface temperature has varied by only about 5° centigrade between glacial and interglacial extremes, so a degree or two is a matter of some magnitude. And until very recently, all climatic changes have reflected natural events such as volcanic eruption or changes in the earth's orbit. Ours is the first generation with the potential to create significant inadvertent global climate modification through energy use, and we have every reason to expect this anthropogenic influence on the climate to grow along with net energy consumption.

If climatologists' current understanding is correct, the largest single influence on future climatic conditions is expected to be caused by a steady increase in atmospheric carbon dioxide (CO_2) concentration—a result of the extended burning of fossil fuels such as oil and coal. An infrared radiation absorber, CO_2 tends to re-radiate to earth some of the heat our planet normally radiates out into space. This is the so-called "Greenhouse Effect" that many climate models suggest could raise the global mean surface temperature about 1°C by the turn of this century and 2° to 3°C by the middle of the next. These seemingly insignificant changes are sufficient to upset the earthly heat and water balance (if not those policy-makers concerned with our environmental future).

Other trace gases with strong infrared absorptions in the atmosphere could also increase in concentration, thus affecting climate. Notable among these is nitrous oxide (N_2O), a by-product of chemical reactions in the soil and oceans. N_2O might be increasing as a result of the rapidly increased use of nitrogen fertilizers—essential ingredients needed to step up food production for the world's growing population.

Relatively little is known about the overall global climatic implications of the nitrogen cycle, but some evidence indicates that an increased amount of N_2O in the atmosphere could contribute to an alteration of the ozone layer—our stratospheric protection against harmful ultraviolet rays of the sun. Enhanced dosages of UV radiation could lead to more cases of human skin cancer and biological damage to plants and animals.

These are still highly controversial issues, owing to large uncertainties about both photochemical and climatic factors concerning ozone. Less controversial is the possibility that N_2O could also contribute to the Greenhouse Effect. Although human activities—most notably the increasing use of nitrogen fertilizers—interfere significantly in this geochemical cycle, the combustion of fossil fuels for energy is likely to bear much graver consequences for global climatic change. The future temperature impact of N_2O on climate will probably not exceed about 1°C by the middle of the next century. In contrast, current estimates of CO_2 effects signal a temperature difference of several more degrees.

The Critical CO_2 Factor

CO_2 is a relatively stable gas chemically, and estimates are that somewhat less than one-half of the added CO_2 goes into solution in the oceans or is taken up by some of the world's forests. Yet, tropical forests may be shrinking at the hands of loggers, farmers, and developers, so the biosphere may not be absorbing as much CO_2 as it normally would. If that is so, then deforestation could contribute to the CO_2 increase.

Observations show that the CO_2 content of the atmosphere has increased from its pre-Industrial Revolution level, which is estimated to have been between 265 parts of CO_2 per million parts of air and about 290 ppm, to a present value of 335 ppm (about 0.33 percent of the atmosphere). Assuming a continued increase of 3 to 4 percent annually in fossil fuel use, of which roughly one-half continues to remain airborne, the level will approach 400 ppm by the year 2000 and may double its present value by the middle of the next century. This amount of CO_2 could raise global surface temperatures by several degrees C.

Oceanographers have concluded that, even though the entire ocean volume has an enormous capacity for the added CO_2, surface water and deep water mix so slowly that the oceans would need centuries to absorb most of the excess airborne CO_2. Thus, much of the CO_2 we are adding will probably remain in the atmosphere long enough to commit our descendants to endure the consequences for generations.

Dust in the Air and the Physics of Clouds

Burning fossil fuels or vegetation also adds particulate matter (aerosols) to the atmosphere. Current mathematical model experiments with atmospheric anthropogenic aerosols are more ambiguous than the CO_2 experiments, so we don't know whether aerosols might heat or cool the earth's surface. (This is because white dust cools the climate by reflecting light, while black dust heats it by absorbing light, and actual dust is a variable mixture of both kinds.) Nor do we have a clear understanding of how they might influence the physics of clouds. They could act as cloud condensation nuclei or as ice nuclei, in which case they could alter rainfall patterns. The results of most climate models do not indicate whether aerosols help cool or heat the climate, let alone gauge an overall magnitude of effect. Of course, this does not mean that aerosols therefore pose no serious global climatic problem. On the contrary, there is evidence that aerosols, locally and regionally, may contribute to precipitation anomalies around urban areas. Particularly serious is the contribution to the acidity of rainfall in or downwind from industrial areas. This aerosol case exemplifies a risk whose outcome is largely unknown.

Local and Regional Effects

Urban-industrial activities cause local changes in temperature and probably also in rainfall, thunderstorms, and related climatic elements. Most likely this is so because a significant quantity of heat is released locally and much of the area is paved over, so the cooling effects of evaporation are mitigated. Also, burning fossil fuels adds particulate matter to the atmosphere. Preliminary evidence suggesting that anthropogenic aerosols act as cloud condensation nuclei or ice nuclei indicates that anomalous precipitation occurs around urban areas where more particulates are produced. This subject too is poorly understood, though it is widely believed that extremely large concentrations of surface heat could trigger some atmospheric convective instabilities that might lead to severe convective storms. And who might be liable for damages from such storms? That is a legal question that has not been sufficiently considered.

At any rate, a larger problem than this local-scale modification may arise in the future if present increases in energy use continue. Such growth has the potential for creating regional "heat islands." As urban sprawl advances and the number of energy-generating power parks increases, cast-off heat could force changes in atmospheric patterns that affect the climate of more than a particular region. One capital city could grow dryer or wetter as another's population or industry grows in size.

What Would Life be Like in A Greenhouse?

Should CO_2 prove the dominant human influence on climate, what changes can we expect as the earth warms? First, the agricultural belts would shift. Some models suggest that land areas in the subtropics may become more productive as a result of a more favorable rainfall, that the growing season will be longer at high and mid-latitudes, and that rainfall will be lighter in some places that are now the worlds' "bread-baskets," the midwestern United States for one. The southern Rocky Mountains or the sierra watershed regions could also be seriously affected.

Energy-induced climatic changes also affect human health, eco-systems, and sociopolitical systems. Human health is often strongly influenced by local climates, and animal species (including humans) or an ecosystem (such as food crops) in a marginal environment may not be capable of a stable existence under prolonged climatic stress.

Lowered crop yields that in some places would result from in-advertent climate modifications would most likely place severe stress on human societies, causing hunger and competition for scarce resources. Some areas could, of course, benefit from climate changes—the proverbial silver lining of the cloud—but so far atmospheric scientists don't know enough to say where these beneficial changes would occur. The most significant problem of all is perhaps the least quantifiable—the long-term impact of climatic changes on the political fabric.

The Values of Facts

It still remains to refine present knowledge of the climatic system and to improve substantially state-of-the-art estimates of inadvertent climatic effects of human activities. Tackling these subjects not only requires further research, but also some social definition of "acceptable risk."

Most likely, scientists will not be able to predict reliably the magnitude, timing, and consequences of potential climate modifications before the atmosphere "performs the experiment" in question itself. Certain proof of the CO_2 greenhouse theory will come only after roughly a generation, since if the present models are more or less correct, climatic change attributable to CO_2 increases will be unambiguously detected by the end of this century. At that point, the warming predicted will, to use the terms of communications theory, be a large enough "signal" (about $1°C$) to exceed the "noise" (about $0.5°C$) of the natural climatic fluctuations.

Do we want to chance adopting a "wait-and-see attitude" until present estimates can be verified? If we have underestimated the effects of CO_2, then we could already be moving toward significant climatic change for which additional years of study only commit posterity to an even larger dose of CO_2. Good sense and good science say no.

Since it takes at least a generation to significantly alter energy-production technologies or economic dependence on energy use, public policy-makers must begin to consider the predictions of climatic theory today. That's a problem, since few scientists themselves are satisfied with the state-of-the-art of climatic theory and modeling. But it's a problem that will have to be endured rather than dismissed. The need to carry on the debate in scientific circles should not be allowed to obscure its wider urgency. No scientist has sufficiently expert credentials to tell society what level of climatic risk is "acceptable" or how those risks should be weighed against the benefits of fossil fuel energy. Scientists are experts only in estimating the potential range of risks and benefits, the confidence with which present estimates can be viewed, and roughly the time it will be before research can narrow the range of uncertainties relative to the occurrence of those risks and benefits.

Some scientific issues, including some aspects of the CO_2 problem, are cloaked in uncertainties that appear to be easily reduced by research well before the worst consequences are expected. In such cases, the correct public policy is simply to encourage more of the right kind of research. But with respect to a number of climatic issues, we need to consider taking action now, while we study more, for the seeds of significant consequences are already being sown.

The Genesis Strategy

But what can be done to hedge against the chance that we are committing future generations to potentially irreversible climatic changes? No action (including inaction) in the face of such uncertainties is without risks, and choosing these involves making value choices. Nevertheless, several steps can be taken to minimize society's vulnerability to such changes.

The idea of minimizing that vulnerability by maintaining flexibility and reserve capacities—of food or water, for instance—might be thought of as a "Genesis Strategy," named after the Biblical account of the seven-year "feast-famine" cycle. This strategy involves four steps. First is *learning the range of possibilities so that fact and value can be more easily disentangled.* Personal value judgments of how to react to the risks of CO_2 in the face of technical uncertainty need to be considered now. We can hope present mathematical models have overestimated the problem and continue adding CO_2 to the atmosphere, or we can play it safer and behave as though the models are underestimating the potential adverse effects and act now to reduce CO_2 input to minimize our vulnerability to climatic changes. At a minimum, we could focus on mechanisms (such as water-sharing agreements or conservation techniques) that would help us adapt to an altered climate should it occur earlier than predicted.

Second is *focussing the current energy debate on growth-rate issues, particularly for Third World countries.* We must recognize now the urgency and immediacy of the energy-growth debate and assess what sort of financial support and political muscle it will take to constrain the amounts of CO_2 released into the atmosphere. Many countries are striving to improve their standards of living through the use of more energy, and they are not likely to agree voluntarily to halt such "progress." Should the heavy energy consumers in developed countries compensate by cutting back per capita energy use in exchange for a lowered birth rate in developing countries? How feasible is such a "Global Survival Compromise"?

Third is *conserving energy and developing viable solar and other renewable resources.* Striving to become more energy end-use efficient, curbing wastefulness, and conserving energy are in the ultimate sense protection against climate modification in addition to being economy measures. At the same time, accelerating development of more economical solar, wind, and geothermal power would help us reduce the global pollution impacts associated with energy production.

Fourth is *beginning now to minimize our economic dependence on energy growth.* Decoupling our economic system and its growth rate from heavy dependence on energy growth means minimizing the economic consequences of slowed energy growth. Taking this step as soon as possible would reduce risks associated with growth of all sources of energy, not just fossil fuels.

These suggestions are the barest outline of the kinds of steps we need to consider in response to the energy-climate problem. We do not have ten years' leisure in which to toy with the problem only at the research level. Risks are increasing cumulatively with abuses, and ten years of delay will put us ten years closer to potentially irreversible changes. To decide to accept that risk is to make a value judgment, not to give an expert opinion.

Most of the tough decisions before us are value judgments. They involve weighing risks and benefits in the face of large uncertainties. In many cases, scientists cannot definitively assess the risk/benefit issues and thereby simplify the politicians' decision-making. In such instances, their obligation is instead to narrow these uncertainties as quickly as possible—which means focussing inter-disciplinary research more precisely. In the case of CO_2, waiting for research alone to narrow our uncertainty is an ill-affordable luxury. Needed today are political decisions—assessments of risks versus hedges against those risks. As part of the politics of survival, these assessments are long overdue.

Atmospheric Conditioning: Fine Particulates on the Rise

Frederica Perera,
A. Karim Ahmed,
and Helene Kendler

Scientists and government officials have for years acknowledged that the toxicity of many common air pollutants is enhanced because they take the form of particles too small to be screened out of the lung by the body's natural defense mechanisms. Existing National Air Quality Standards for total suspended particulates, sulfur oxides, and nitrogen dioxide have pressured industry to deploy air pollution control devices that curtail emissions of fine particulates and their chemical precursors to some extent. But we have no regulatory program aimed specifically at controlling fine particulates, despite mounting scientific evidence that implicates them as particularly toxic to human beings, dangerous to the natural world, and destructive of visibility and materials.

The concentration of these atmospheric pollutants is nevertheless on the increase. If no new regulatory action is taken, it will rise rapidly in the coming decades. Should we burn more coal without adequate controls, this trend will be exacerbated, for most coal contains more sulfur and nitrogen than oil and natural gas do, and produces vastly more particulate matter when burned. Should we widely employ the diesel engines to which automobile manufacturers are turning in their quest for better mileage, highly toxic fine particulate matter may be created at accelerated rates. The switch to a diesel fleet could increase human disease, add to acid rainfull, reduce visibility, and sap the productivity of fields and forests.

Some Distinctions

Research studies over the past few years have shown that atmospheric particles are generally distributed into two broad modes—"fine" and "coarse." The fine particulates contain most of the man-made carbon, lead, sulfur, and nitrogen-containing compounds. In contrast, larger coarse particulate matter is composed mainly of natural materials of the earth's crust and originates primarily from natural or mechanical processes such as erosion, rock-grinding, and stone-crushing. Naturally, the ratio of fine to coarse particulates varies widely from cities to rural areas. In general, urban areas directly affected by transportation, combustion, and industrial processes show higher ratios of fine to coarse particulates than rural areas do. Two extremes are Point Arguello on the California coast, where the mass of fine particles has been measured at 2 percent of total particulate mass, and urban St. Louis, where the comparable measurement is 76 percent.

A fine particulate is categorized as either "primary" or "secondary," depending upon how it comes into being. Primary particulates are created by physical or chemical processes that directly inject the matter into the atmosphere. Each year more than five million tons of man-made primary fine particles such as soot, fly ash, condensed metals, and vapors are unloaded into the atmosphere. But most airborne particles in urban areas—about 60 to 80 percent—are "secondary"; that is, they are formed from gaseous precursors in the atmosphere.

The human respiratory system is admirably equipped to filter and remove large natural dust particles, but not man-made fine particles. Particles smaller than one to two micrometers are drawn deep into the respiratory system when a substantial percentage is deposited in the lung's air sacs. There, if insoluble, they can remain for weeks or even years. Furthermore, fine particulates do not confine their damage to the respiratory system alone. A significant fraction of particles may be transported by the lymph or circulatory system to other organs, and once particles are deposited, soluble toxic materials concentrated on their surface can be washed out into the surrounding tissue.

Fine particulates are a complex mixture of pollutants whose combined effects on human health are greater than those of any one pollutant in the mix. They contain a disproportionate amount of inherently toxic substances such as sulfuric acid, arsenic, beryllium, and nickel. And even so called "inert" fine particles can impair lung function and increase susceptibility to vapor pollutants, resulting in greater harm to health than gases or vapors alone can inflict. Clearly, there is no such thing as a "harmless" respirable particle.

In fact, a growing body of knowledge attests to the adverse effects of all respirable-sized particles, particularly the smallest of them. Numerous studies have shown that certain particulates generally found in the form of fine particulates—sulfates and nitrates—are associated with respiratory disease, chronic bronchitis, aggravation of asthma, and cardiopulmonary disease. Death rates from chronic respiratory disease have been rising steadily in the U.S. and are considerably higher for people living in urban areas than for the rural population. Fine particulates, which reach their highest concentrations in urban areas, are undoubtedly an important factor in this observed increase.

Human cancer may be the most serious health effect of fine particulate pollutants. A number of carcinogens—including polycyclic organic matter and certain metallic substances and fibers found in the workplace—are known to be present in airborne fine particles. In addition, carcinogenic organic alkylating agents such as nitrosamines may be associated with atmospheric fine particles. Most disturbing in this respect are studies showing that the increase of lung cancer among non-smoking Americans living in urban polluted areas is about double that for residents of rural areas—a difference often referred to as "the urban factor."

Organic Substances

Organic substances, which comprise 30 to 40 percent of all fine particles, are both directly emitted and secondarily formed by chemical reactions in the atmosphere. Particulate polycyclic organic matter (PPOM) is a major class of organic compounds that includes 19 known animal carcinogens. The most prominent of these is benzo(a)pyrene, whose presence is used as an indicator of the potential carcinogenicity of pollutants found in the air. Most PPOM formation is ascribed to the burning of fossil fuels (especially coal and solid waste) and to the gaseous discharges of industrial processes such as iron- and steel-making.

Of special concern are the large amounts of fine particulate polycyclic compounds found in diesel exhaust. Possibly carcinogenic, diesel fuel emissions recently failed another test. Epidemiologists who studied a mountain town in Switzerland, where 30 percent of all passenger vehicles are diesels, found a strong correlation between increased deaths from cancer among the residents and the proximity of their dwellings to the highway. Cancer mortality was nine times more common in residents whose homes were near the highway than in residents of sections more remote from heavy traffic.

Sulfates

Sulfates account for up to two-thirds of all fine particles in the eastern United States. Fossil fuel-burning power plants and oil refineries disgorge sulfur dioxide, which forms sulfates in the atmosphere. (Hydrocarbons, nitrogen oxides, carbon, metallic oxides—all found in abundance in polluted air—dramatically speed up this reaction.) Sulfuric acid particles, created when sulfur dioxide combines with oxygen, help create acid rain.

Air pollution, it is often said, respects no boundaries. Sulfates may be the perfect example. Today Easterners are exposed to sulfates not only from the power plants in their midst, but also from those operating far away in the midwest. The sulfur dioxide emitted by power plants in Illinois, Indiana, Michigan, Wisconsin, and Ohio travels to the east coast on prevailing westerly winds. Changing into sulfates along the way, it accounts for up to 21,000 premature deaths each year east of the Mississippi alone.

Sulfates are thought to aggravate respiratory diseases, including asthma, chronic bronchitis, and emphysema, and to cause shortness of breath and irritation of the eyes. Some of these ill effects have been observed at sulfate concentrations that are common in Boston, Chicago, Detroit, Los Angeles, New York, Philadelphia, Pittsburgh, and San Francisco.

Nitrates

Nitrates, which are predominantly formed by secondary reactions involving nitrogen oxides in the atmosphere, constitute roughly 7 to 16 percent of the fine particulates in the entire United States. They too have been linked with respiratory illness and cardiovascular disease. Recent EPA studies have shown an association between increased asthma attacks and elevated levels of suspended nitrates in six out of seven communities studied. In another study, families and school-children exposed to a suspended nitrate level typical of that found in many U.S. cities experienced increased acute respiratory disease and increased bronchitis.

Metallic Substances and Fibers

Metallic substances in fine particulates are also a potential threat to health. Trace metals are widely introduced into the environment from fuel combustion, incineration, and industrial emission sources. Metal vapors either condense to form fine particulates or are absorbed on the surface of fine particulates.

Lead, cadmium, nickel, beryllium, mercury, arsenic, vanadium, chromium, and asbestos are all found in the form of airborne fine particulates or fibers. And all can affect health seriously and adversely. It is well known that exposure to lead in high concentrations harms the central nervous system irreparably, but less widely appreciated that even low-level chronic exposure may cause subtle brain damage and behavioral problems in children. Inhaled asbestos fibers have been shown to cause cancer of the lungs and of the pleural cavity. Epidemiological studies have linked nickel, arsenic, and chromium with human cancer too.

Damage to the Environment

Besides the damage that airborne fine particulates can inflict on human health, what of the injuries that they inflict upon the environment? Serious in themselves, all are exacerbated by the natural phenomenon known as long-range transport. Since fine particulates are the most persistent and long-lived of all particles in our air, they are carried by prevailing air currents far from their point of origin. Particles smaller than two micrometers are regularly transported hundreds of kilometers and, in rare cases, as far as 2,500 kilometers from their source. Photo-chemical air pollution created in the New York City area finds its way nearly two hundred miles northeast to Connecticut and Massachusetts. In general, long-range transport of fine particles poses a major air pollu-tion problem that often transcends national boundaries.

Rainfall whose acidity may have been increased as much as ten to one hundred times by sulfates and nitrates holds particularly serious consequences for ecosystems. Besides slowing the growth of trees, acid rain causes leaf damage, dissolves nutrients out of the soil, alters protective responses to disease-producing organisms, and thwarts the germination and establishment of seedlings. Decreases in growth and productivity of a New Hampshire hardwood forest have already been reported. By some estimates, Sweden may suffer a reduction of up to 15 percent of its forest growth by the year 2000 from acid precipita-tion, and so may the northeastern U.S. and Canada.

Acid rainfall can injure non-forest vegetation as well, inhibiting the growth of commercial crops such as cotton, oats, rye, barley, and tomatoes. And, of course, the threat does not confine itself to what lives and grows in soil. The aquatic life in lakes and streams has deter-iorated alarmingly. The number of lakes without trout in Norway has increased along with fossil fuel combustion in industrial and urban regions of Europe. Just as in the human population children are most vulnerable to the health effects of pollution, so it is among fish—the newly hatched more readily fall prey to the destruction of acidic water. Nearly half of the mountain lakes in New York's Adirondack Region contain no fish today; while between 1929 and 1937, less than 4 percent had no fish.

Less visible, though no less significant, are the effects of fresh water acidification on other aquatic forms of life. As the number of acid-sensitive bacterial decomposers declines, organic debris can accumu-late and block the recycling of nutrients from the sediment. In Swedish lakes, algae mosses and fungi have increased while plankton growth has been retarded. Fish food organisms such as plankton are highly sensitive to changes in acidity, and the impact of their dislocation reverberates up through the food chain.

Even Art and Visibility Suffer

One consequence of acid rain and other fine particulate activity that does not directly involve health and survival, but that nevertheless impinges upon the quality of life, is the erosion of coatings, painted surfaces, textiles, and masonry. Particulates contribute to a deplorable decay of works of art, statues, and historic buildings the world over. The incalculable aesthetic loss incurred when, say, the stones of the Parthenon decay as a result of Athens' recent industrialization argues from yet another vantage for more effective control of fine particulates.

The annual loss due to damage of materials and property from particulate air pollution in the U.S. has been pegged at $3 billion. No doubt much of this damage can be attributed to fine particulate pollution.

Of all the environmental damage created by airborne fine particulates, none is more obvious than the effect on visibility. Particles of 0.1–1.0 micrometer in diameter are close in size to the wavelength of visible light, which they therefore absorb and scatter. Since fine particulates reach very high concentrations in urban and polluted air (90 to 99 percent of the number of particles in these settings), they are considered responsible for the marked reduction of visibility in urban areas. In Los Angeles, for example, visibility is frequently reduced to two or three miles. This stands in sharp contrast with very clean areas, where visibility reaches 120 miles.

Perhaps it is true that "on a clear day you can see forever," but such days are now rare. If you stand at the top of a mountain amid the peace and magnificence of the Hudson Highlands, your line of sight will bring you to the New York City skyline 50 miles away; but gaze as hard as you might out of one of the windows located within the city, and the visual favor will not be returned. As emissions of fine particles and their gaseous precursors have increased, this haze has blanketed larger and larger areas. Indeed, particles from the eastern United States now cloud eastern Canadian provinces. As fine particulate concentrations increase, greater visibility loss is inevitable.

Climate Change

A final cause for concern about fine particulates is that man-made airborne fine particulates can significantly alter weather and climate — so much so that the term "urban climate" has been coined to describe the phenomenon. Temperature and humidity are generally higher in the city than in the surrounding area, and urbanites commonly get more cloud cover, precipitation, and fog.

Patterns of cloud formation and weather change as fine particulates act as nuclei upon which water vapor condenses. Emissions from automobiles provide these condensation nuclei, while certain steel mills have been identified as sources of particles called "ice nuclei," which can alter precipitation below 32°F. A five-year field investigation of urban air pollution in the vicinity of St. Louis revealed that rain, thunderstorms, and hail are maximized within the urban area.

Long-lived fine particulates can also absorb energy and re-radiate light, thereby acting as a lid (like the glass of a greenhouse) to prevent the outflow of heat to the atmosphere. This "insulation" cuts down daytime sunlight but retards the night-time loss of radiant energy from heated city air. Increased cloudiness also cuts down on the reflectivity of the earth. Thus, the city tends to be encased in a closed atmospheric system. The net global effect of these two contradictory forces has been a subject of heated scientific debate. Whatever the outcome, small changes in atmospheric conditions look increasingly capable of causing long-term trouble. And if a net heating does occur, fine particulates will exacerbate the serious global problems associated with CO_2 build-up.

What to Do

Singularly able to elude the body's defense mechanisms, fine particulates pose a distinct risk to public health and welfare. What is needed is a comprehensive new program aimed at developing regulations to reduce the concentration of fine suspended particulates in our ambient air. We must make sure that EPA's program for maintaining and improving visibility focusses on the role fine particulates play in reducing visibility. We must design the stationary source performance standards so that stringent controls are exerted over the emission of fine particulates and the gases that form them. We must establish a national air quality monitoring system for fine particulates, and determine—_now_ before our national auto fleet is converted to diesel—how much the increased use of diesel engines will add to fine particulate pollution.

The National Academy of Sciences has stated that in recent years there has been a revolution in knowledge about the effects of fine particulates. To date, however, the government's regulatory program has failed to keep pace with this new knowledge. This failure must be regarded as grounds for one of the most important and far-reaching struggles for healthful air in the coming years.   ❦

II. INHABITANTS

The Population Bomb Revisited

Anne and Paul Ehrlich

The human population has grown by some 20 percent in the past decade, now exceeds 4.2 billion, and continues to grow at approximately 1.7 or 1.8 percent per year. This, however, reflects a slight but significant decline in the rate of population increase since 1970. The slight slowdown in population growth is very good news, particularly if it heralds a continuing reduction of birth rates. But if there is no further change in the growth rate, the global population will double in slightly less than 40 years—allowing only slightly more time to accommodate an additional 4 billion people than did the 36-year doubling time that prevailed until recently.

The growth-rate decline is a cause for celebration for other reasons besides the demographic consequences. Consider, for example, the rather dazzling social change implied by the sudden and unexpected drop in the birth rate in the United States, where the demographic structure of the population indicated a rise in the birth rate was due in the 1970s. The change in reproductive behavior in the U.S. and other developed countries has put those nations on a path that may lead to an end in their population growth within a few decades. A few have already stopped growing, and the two Germanies and Luxembourg have begun to decline. The quickness of the change offers some hope that other social changes required for civilization to survive and make the transition to a "sustainable society" might be made with similar swiftness.

Because of the built-in momentum of population growth and the apparent resistance of people in traditional societies to ideas of birth control, ending growth in Lesser Developed Countries is still a gargantuan task. But the examples of China, Taiwan, South Korea, Hong Kong, Singapore, Costa Rica, Trinidad and Tobago, Barbados and others show that it may not be an impossible one.

Nevertheless, even with signs of a slowdown, momentum will almost certainly carry the total population past six billion by the turn of the century, and the peak population is now expected to reach at least nine billion (assuming birth rates continue to drop and there is no significant rise in death rates) before an actual decline in population size can begin 100 years or more from now. A more moderate, and still optimistic, projection would have population growth peaking at 12 billion.

The reason that such a prospect is alarming, and that we express concern about death rates, is that such a huge population—9 to 12 billion—very clearly cannot be sustained by Earth's life-support systems, certainly not for any great length of time or at a comfortable standard of living for the vast majority. Indeed, signs of strain were abundantly apparent in 1968 and were described in *The Population Bomb*. The appearance of additional deleterious effects of overpopulation was more or less accurately predicted there. Since then, symptoms of population pressure have become increasingly obvious to those who can read them.

Consider some of the non-political subjects of the past decade's news reports: major droughts in areas as diverse as India, the Sahel and California; food shortages, rising food prices, famine; an energy "crisis," quadrupling oil prices, and supply shortages; environmental battles over long-distance oil and gas pipelines, dams and various other projects; battles over nuclear power; inflation, unemployment, recession, balance-of-payment problems and import quotas. All these are related one way or another to growing population pressure on Earth's finite resources, exacerbated by growth in material consumption per person.

The Environment

A great deal has happened on the environmental front in the past 10 years. Public awareness of environmental deterioration has grown enormously, especially in overdeveloped countries where pollution from automobiles and industry are most obvious. Increasingly stringent regulation to control pollution of air and water have been enacted, while in the United States (and a few other countries that have passed similar laws), virtually any development project of any consequence is subject to environmental review. Unfortunately, however, such review does not ensure that badly conceived, highly damaging projects cannot go forward. Litigation by environmental groups is still necessary to stop such projects or to force their builders to use less destructive designs.

Much has been accomplished, but the overall trend of environmental degradation and destruction, though perhaps slightly slowed, is still proceeding.

Indeed, the aspect of environmental deterioration that presents the greatest threat to humanity's future is generally the least understood and appreciated: the accelerating destruction of ecological systems worldwide. Natural ecosystems provide many essential services for human society that society can neither do without nor adequately replace. Among these free services are maintenance of the quality of the atmosphere, control of the climate, production and preservation of soils, cycling of nutrients (including those essential for agricultural productivity), watershed protection (which results in more stable weather and control of flood and drought), control of the vast majority of potential crop pests and vectors of diseases, disposal of human wastes, provision of fishes from fresh waters, and the operation of a vast genetic "library" of potentially useful plants and animals.

The systems that provide these vital environmental services are being assaulted and undermined at an even faster rate in every nation, even though opposition from environmental groups is rising. In the United States recently, several large development projects have been stopped in their tracks because their completion threatened some obscure endangered species of animal or plant. Outraged developers have protested that the threatened species are of "no value" to humanity while their threatened projects represent millions of dollars lost to the economy. Taking each species individually, they may be right (assuming also that the project is really of value). The point is that populations of organisms and entire species are heedlessly being exterminated around the world at an increasing rate, one already far in excess of the rate at which evolutionary processes could replace them with new ones. This is done with no regard whatever for their potential value to humanity (for instance, as an actual or potential source of food, fiber, drug, or any of a myriad other useful substances such as spices, oils, industrial chemicals, hides and so on). And it is done with no regard for their roles within ecological systems. Whether or not a given species is essential to the functioning of an ecosystem is difficult, perhaps impossible, to determine except by removing it. Its importance, in fact, may depend on how much damage has previously been inflicted on the system—for instance, whether other species that could take over its functions have been removed.

The consequences of randomly removing species from ecosystems can be compared to those of removing rivets from an airplane's wings. If you were a passenger about to board a 747 and you saw someone removing rivets at random from the wing of your plane, you might feel compelled to make him stop. You wouldn't know how many or which particular rivets are essential to keep the plane flying, but presumably you would rather not risk your life to find out. Similarly, ecologists cannot say which species or how many of them are essential to the operation of a particular ecosystem. But continued random removal in either case would sooner or later lead to a crash.

This is why ecologists and environmentalists are so concerned about the need for preserving endangered species, wilderness, and natural areas. It is not just that wildlife and wilderness appeal to our aesthetic senses and seem to have the power to soothe and restore one's soul; healthy natural ecosystems are indispensable to the support of human society. Without them there could be no successful agriculture, and we would soon be smothered, choked, and poisoned by our own wastes.

Resources

It is often claimed that clever technology can compensate for lost natural services and allow humanity to support a much larger and denser population than today's. There is truth in this, but only up to a point. Where technological solutions can be applied to problems caused by ecological damage (floods and droughts, for instance), they are rarely as effective as the natural services and are never free. As for supporting larger populations, resource constraints are already making themselves felt in both rich and poor countries. The easily accessible sources of energy and minerals have mostly been exploited already; and though others exist, they will be increasingly difficult and costly to find and exploit. The unavoidable consequences of obtaining, processing, and using ever greater amounts of energy and materials will include still more pollution and ecological destruction.

Some of this destruction might be avoided or mitigated, of course, if civilization switched to solar, wind, and other renewable energy sources. The impact of switching to dependence on nuclear power instead would be borne more heavily by humanity than by the environment, particularly when the risks of accidents or nuclear war are taken into account. Other high-technology "hard" sources, such as oil, shales, tar sands, etc., have severe environmental effects. Even a steadily increased mobilization of energy from relatively benign sources will lead to eco-catastrophe. The level of energy use is the best measure of the impact society makes on the public-service functions of ecosystems.

While the idea that there are limits to growth seems to have been accepted with regard to population (although many still seem to think the limits are set by population density or food production at some preposterously high level), applying the concept to growth in material consumption or economic development seems to elicit consternation bordering on panic in many quarters. Part of the difficulty is that the real limits are not determined by the lack of a single, indispensable, and irreplaceable resource such as living space or fossil fuels. Rather, the limits grow out of the complex web of interactions and interdependencies we have been describing. They are real, but they are hard to perceive and even harder to define with precision.

Consider food production, for example. At first glance it seems reasonably feasible to double world food production in 35 to 40 years.

(This, of course, just keeps production even with population growth, and assuming no change in the present distribution pattern, would mean that one-quarter of the people would still be overfed, one-quarter grossly underfed, and the rest just getting along.) But it is clear that achieving this feat will require the application of huge amounts of capital, energy, and materials, to say nothing of human ingenuity and hard work. And the environmental consequences of doubling agricultural production would almost certainly make it a Pyrrhic victory. The accompanying deterioration of Earth's life-support systems might rapidly reduce its carrying capacity far below that of today, resulting in a catastrophic rise in death rates.

The further complexities of the predicament become clear when one realizes that vast amounts of capital, energy, materials, and human resources in those 40 years also will be required to meet each one of a fairly long list of other human needs and goals:

- Developing and installing new energy technologies to supplement and eventually replace conventional ones, as well as continuing to supply growing needs throughout the 40-year period. Regardless of the choice of technologies made, enormous amounts of capital, energy and materials will be needed for their development.
- Maintaining, expanding, improving, and making more efficient systems of transportation and communications.
- Maintaining, expanding, and improving facilities for processing and manufacturing consumer goods, as well as increasing their output.
- Building and replacing housing and commercial and institutional facilities to accommodate expanding populations.

All these objectives are generally considered essential—even taken for granted by nearly everyone in rich countries and by growing numbers in poor ones. The unexamined goal seems to be to provide something resembling the present-day standard of living of Americans and Western Europeans to everyone in the world within a generation or two (while Americans and Western Europeans go on to double or triple their per capita consumption of materials and energy). But no one seems to have counted up the total cost or attempted to analyze in detail the overall environmental consequences of paying the price.

It is highly questionable whether the goal of reaching an American standard of living could be achieved in 40 years for today's 4 billion human beings without destroying Earth's environmental support systems in the process. But humanity is committed to a population of about 6 billion in only 20 years, and eight billion perhaps 20 years later. Those who think the population bomb has "fizzled" had better think again. 🌱

Garden of Eden to Weed Patch: the Earth's Vanishing Genetic Heritage

*Norman Myers
with Marc Reisner*

Earth is home to five to ten million species. They represent the culmination of at least three and a half billion years of evolution and six hundred million years of diversification among most modern forms of life. Besides adding immeasurably to the richness and comfort of human life, these species constitute a vast genetic reservoir out of which planetary life will continue to evolve. The web they form is at once subtly and incredibly complex and only superficially understood. Yet, if the next fifty years are of a piece with the last, that web will be torn brutally and irreparably asunder.

Widespread disruption of habitats is now the main reason species are disappearing. Indeed, within 20 years we could lose tens, even hundreds of thousands of species, a biological improverishment on the scale of all the mass extinctions of the geologic past combined.

The planet currently suffers from many forms of environmental degradation, but no other is so irreversible, so hopelessly final. When lakes and rivers are fouled and the atmosphere is treated as a garbage can, we can usually clean up the pollution. Species extinction is forever, a legacy visited upon generations to come.

The pragmatic purposes served by the Earth's diversity of species are many and growing. Given the needs of the future—and our own—this diversity can be reckoned among society's most valuable resources. If we lose it, we may be undone.

Abundance & Diversity

Until the mid-1960s, the number of species on earth was estimated at around three million. Of this total, just over half had been given a scientific name and described. The planet was until then believed to support about 4,100 known species of mammals, 8,700 birds, 6,300 reptiles, 3,000 amphibians, 23,000 fishes, roughly 800,000 green plants and fungi, plus many thousands of micro-organisms. The other one and one-half million species were merely presumed alive, sight unseen.

Since the mid-60s, the estimates have risen. Using refined methods of taxonomy and greater knowledge of the earth's environments, scientists have extrapolated their statistical curves for species abundance until they have arrived at an order-of-magnitude conjecture of 10 million species.

The largest of the ten million is a giant sequoia, standing nearly 300 feet tall and weighing about 6,167 tons—as much as a small ocean-going freighter. The oldest is probably a bristlecone pine or a Japanese cedar, specimens of which apparently sprouted from the earth over 7,000 years ago. That with the shortest lifespan is probably the colon bacterium escherichia coli, which divides under favorable conditions after twenty minutes, throwing off billions of progeny each day. The smallest is small indeed. If an average-sized virus enlarged 5000-fold equaled the size of the period at the end of this sentence, a German shepherd dog magnified by the same factor would be about four miles long and two high.

What exactly is a species? Put simply, it is a natural cluster of organisms that share a common pool of genes. All members of the group can interbreed and, generally, they cannot breed with other species. (This definition applies only to bisexual organisms, of course, but it suffices here since it speaks to the point: safeguarding species means maintaining an adequate gene pool.)

A similar system of classification applies to other levels of the taxonomic hierarchy. The lion belongs, together with the tiger, leopard, and other large cats, to the genus Panthera. The genus belongs, with cats small and large, to the family Felidae. The cat family belongs to the order Carnivora, which in turn comes under the class of Mammals, and this belongs to the phylum of Chordates (creatures with a notochord along the back, often protected by vertebrae) within the kingdom of Animals.

Some of these parellel categories have many more members than others. The phylum of arthropods ("jointed feet")—comprised of insects, arachnids such as spiders and ticks, millipedes and centipedes, mites, and their marine counterparts—accounts for four out of five of all known animal species. Some 90 percent of the arthropods are insects, and the number of known insect species is 20 times that of all the classes of higher animals. By one estimate, the planet's bugs weigh twelve times as much as the planet's human population.

Speciation and Extinction

The evolutionary process that spawns new species—speciation—began when life first appeared. As a species encounters fresh environments, brought about by climatic change and other factors, it adapts in different ways in different parts of its range. Eventually, new forms become differentiated enough to rank as new species. The parent form, unable to fit in with changed circumstances, disappears, while the genetic material persists—diversified and enriched. Those species which are less capable of adapting and differentiating, especially those that have become so specialized in their life-styles that they cannot cope with transformed environments, fade away, their distinctive genetic material lost forever.

For much of his last 50,000 years as a hunter-gatherer, primitive man proved himself capable of eliminating species by overhunting them with weapons (some of them rudimentary), and by modifying their habitats with fire. In the main, the process was gradual. But by about the year 1600 A.D., man aided by advanced technology could disrupt environments overnight and overhunt animals to extinction in just a few years.

From this recent watershed stage on, man's impact can no longer be considered on a par with "natural processes" that lead to extinction. Through man's interference, species of mammals and birds alone are now thought to be going extinct at a rate of at least one per year, perhaps many more, as compared to an estimated rate of one per 1,000 years during the "great dying" of the dinosaurs. Sometimes niches open up for new species as established species die out. But accelerated extinction will not lead to accelerated speciation: many old are now making way for a few new.

How Now Brown Cow?

How many species may have existed at each stage of evolutionary history is difficult to say. The fossil record is a pitifully limited reflection of past life. But it now appears likely that after a gas cloud solidified into the planet Earth roughly six billion years ago, it remained starkly barren and lifeless for another 2.4 billion years. Not until about 1.4 billion years ago did the first few nuclear-celled organisms appear, and not until about 700 million years ago did most modern phyla become recognizable. The array of species diversified only gradually for the best part of 400 million years, until it crashed spectacularly with the extinction of many marine organisms toward the end of the Permian period. Thereafter, the abundance and variety of species steadily increased, until another mass extinction some 70 million years ago put an end to about one-quarter of all families, including the dinosaurs and their kind. Ever since, the trend has been towards diversification.

Special Problems

If rarity is defined in terms of absolute numbers, then most species are rare. In an ecological zone with, say, 100 species, a dozen or less might be common and widespread. The rest will be represented by small numbers. In general, the larger the community of species, the longer the list of uncommon species.

Although the fragile status of rarity makes a species susceptible to a sudden decline in range and other problems, a rare species can occupy a narrow and localized niche quite successfully. The idea that a rare species is somehow a "loser" may derive from the fact that many such species are relics, left over after geo-ecological change has eliminated their relatives. Generally, they survive in a few patches of habitat, surrounded by some physiogeographic feature (a sea, for instance) that safeguards them from outside threats. If this protective barrier is breached, however, their decline is usually rapid. Most rare species are either highly localized or highly specialized or both.

Island species are especially localized, specialized, "rare," and thus vulnerable. They tend to evolve with specializations that suit them for survival in a confined world with few competitors and, usually, no predators. This evolutionary equipment leaves them sadly unable to cope with sudden incursions by goats, pigs, rats, cats and other intruders, parasites, and diseases imported by human beings. What were formerly enclaves of security can with the "help" of these outsiders become "killing grounds" without exits. Moreover, many island species have lost the capacity or the inclination to flee. The dodo had no need to fly until the sailor with gun or club in hand arrived in peaceful Mauritius.

In contrast to the dodo and its like, however, are the animal species referred to as "K-selected" species, which are exceptionally sensitive to man-caused disruptions of natural environments. Whales, whooping cranes, and other members of this group can make efficient use of resources once the group becomes firmly established. But they depend on long-term stability in their habitats, and their success at persisting means that they are little inclined to colonize new areas when old ones become unsuitable. Accustomed to stability, they direct less energy to producing many offspring, and more to caring for their young. They are long-lived and reproduce at long intervals. In effect, they trade off a high rate of increase and an ability to exploit transient good times for a capacity to maintain stable populations with low rates of increase and mortality.

This is a fine survival strategy for those species in stable environments, but a high-risk one for those in a man-disturbed world. And, indeed, while K-selected species fared well during prehistoric times, the precise factors that have led to their persistence lead to their undoing when modern man appears on the scene. Worse still, if their numbers fall, they are often unable to regenerate to earlier levels no matter what protection is provided for them. Thus, steps must be taken to safeguard K-selected species while their numbers are still well above what would be acceptable levels in other species.

By contrast, "r-selected" species are usually short-lived, have brief generation intervals, and enjoy high rates of increase. This enables them both to disperse quickly into new environments and to make excellent use of boom times. Opportunistic and prolific, r-selected species are so successful in a man-disrupted world that they often become pests. Two infamous examples are the cockroach and the Norway rat.

Carnivores, K-selected or r-selected deserve special mention here. Not only are they rarer than herbivores in the best of times, but they are also more susceptible to disruption, related to their position toward the end of food chains. Especially disadvantaged are large predators that must roam widely to find their prey: the mountain lion, timber wolf, and golden eagle, among others.

From the standpoint of conservation, certain non-carnivores should likewise be accorded special attention because they need food available only across broad areas of land. A prime example is the ivory-billed woodpecker, with its need for wood-boring insects in recently dead limbs of mature forest trees. This giant, colorful woodpecker once dwelled in about fifteen states from Illinois to Florida, but as logging eliminated the bird's main food sources, it declined in range until it now survives, if at all, only in Louisiana. The amphibians' problems are of another sort altogether. The young must live exclusively in water, and adults cannot be separated from moisture for long. This means that amphibians are unable to move beyond a limited range of habitat, which in turn means they are less able to cope with human interference than are birds, insects, and many other groups. Moreover, frogs, toads, salamanders, and others do not like to spawn in rivers or large lakes, but in ponds, marshes, and similar slack waters—exactly the areas man most readily disturbs. Drainage projects, water impoundments, and other manipulations of hydrological systems can spell ruin to such species.

Another vulnerable category comprises tropical forest birds. Having evolved within relatively stable environments, birds of tropical forests are highly sensitive to disturbances of any kind. Near-victims of their fairly tranquil evolutionary past, they have become unusually specialized in their use of habitat, and they tend to have low reproduction rates. These two factors, together with low populations, make it difficult for tropical forest birds to recover from disturbances, unlike temperate forest birds, which can "bounce back" from severe population crashes within a few seasons. Many of these birds cannot disperse easily from one area to another, which means they cannot escape disturbances in their habitats nor colonize more hospitable areas.

Principal Threats

Man has exterminated many species and threatens many more. He kills animals for food, hide, fur, feathers and trophies, for talismans and superstitious rituals, for the live animal trade, and simply for the sake of killing them.

The toll taken by over-exploitation is already immense. Giant tortoises on the Galapagos and Seychelles Islands, the buffalo of North America, and countless other species have been substantially decimated. Some species of whales have been hunted to extinction and several others survive only precariously. Across all classes of vertebrates, over-kill is believed to have been responsible for the elimination of 33 percent of all mammals and 42 percent of all birds lost since 1960, and for the present plight of 24 percent of mammals, 68 percent of reptiles, and 12 percent of fishes.

But an even more pervasive and destructive form of habitat disruption is the mega-scale technology developed in the 20th century. In the abysmal benthos, where many new species have lately been discovered, mining operations for mineral-rich manganese nodules could cause whole communities of species to be depleted or eliminated. When the Great Lakes were joined by the Erie and Welland Canals, for example, the sea lamprey entered, decimating the lake trout and other fish.

The trend toward disruption of natural environments on every side is significant in still another sense. Economic development occurs as a result of demand by consumers. In the tropics, increasing the amount of available food through extra fertilizer or expanded cultivation would doubtless increase the overall level of nutrition, and the influx of more industrial products would ease the struggle for existence in many ways. But for most citizens of the advanced world, additional food and material goods do not necessarily raise living standards and may even promote physical deterioration and social decline. Yet the demand for products of every kind on the part of the one billion citizens of affluent nations—the most profligate consumers the world has ever known—contributes a great deal to the exploitation of natural environments in every part of the world, since four-fifths of all raw materials traded internationally go to developed-world economies.

What are Species Good For?

Every species adds to the diversity, color, and texture of life on Earth. However, not even the keenest conservationist sheds many tears because he will never see the extinct dodo bird, just as few Greek scholars feel cheated out of the Sophoclean plays that didn't survive. Some loss of species is tolerable to most of us—especially if such loss is a trade-off for, let us say, new cropland that could mean life to starving people. Thus, the _aesthetic argument_ for species preservation, though weighty, is subject to the vicissitudes of human inclination and the exigencies of societal need.

Others argue that the more numerous a community's species and the more complex their inter-relationships, the greater is the system's stability. While they have a point, the matter is considerably more complex than that.

Some natural monocultures—bracken, for example, and the grassy marshlands along the east coast of the United States—are highly stable. When man's agricultural monocultures, notably crops, become destabilized, the fault may lie not so much in their simplicity as in the degree to which they are synthesized—their lack of an evolutionary pedigree. Conversely, the most complex ecosystems, while stable under natural conditions, show surprisingly little resilience when normality is disrupted. Thus, the *diversity and stability argument* is important but it cannot be viewed simply as a question of numbers. They suggest that the paramount consideration should be safeguarding those species that play a critical role in the functioning of a complete and self-sustaining ecosystem.

Another common defense of species conservation is that it preserves the stock of genetic material on earth. Without an adequate gene pool, diversity is ruled out. However, this argument loses some force when one considers the genetic diversity that is hypothetically in the cards. For example, if there are only 1,000 kinds of genes in the world, each existing in 10 different variants, then 10^{1000} different gene combinations are theoretically possible—as compared to the total number of subatomic particles in the universe, estimated at 10^{78}.

This *genetic reservoir argument* too is simplistic. It doesn't take into account that each species—each genetic combination—is a painstakingly evolved, marvelously adapted, and discrete organism with a unique role in life's scheme. Here again, our chief concern should not be preserving genetic stock *per se* but protecting genetic configurations (species) that are important for ecological, practical, aesthetic, sentimental, and other reasons.

Since none of the above arguments, however worthy, is likely to stand up to the overwhelming pressures to manipulate and disrupt natural environments, the goal of species conservation must derive considerable support from the pragmatic purposes served by genetic resources. There is ample basis on which to argue that preserving species brings enormous utilitarian benefits.

One such benefit is to agriculture. New forms of crops have to grow quickly and strongly if they are to be highly productive. They must be able to incorporate protein and two critical amino acids, lysine and methionine. They also need to adapt to disease, climate, and other environmental factors. Thus, plant geneticists must be in a position to utilize a broad stock of germ plasm from the wild. In fact, without sufficient stocks of wild strains of wheat, corn, rice, and other staple foods, we won't be able to maintain—let alone expand—recent advances in agriculture.

The loss of genetic diversity in agriculture has already become one of the world's least recognized major problems. In part, the problem lies with sheer attrition of natural environments through increases in human numbers (and aspirations). In part, too, a major threat is the trend for subsistence farming to give way to commercial agriculture, whereupon food plants that have been selected over centuries for their suitability in local ecological conditions are supplanted by a small range of highly productive and readily marketable varieties, often of external origin.

Any monoculture is vulnerable to new strains of pests and diseases and to climate changes. Yet nearly all cultivated crops in the U.S. now have an extremely narrow genetic base. Around 40 percent of our hard red winter wheat derives from two basic varieties, and all domestic sorghum contains a common plasmic sterilitic component. In this light, consider that some meteorologists say we have just had the wettest 30-year period in the last 1,000 years.

Preserving wild food species is important for another reason: it opens up a whole new range of agricultural possibilities. The planet is believed to contain 80,000 edible plants, of which people have at one time or another used at least 3,000 for food. Yet only about 50 have ever been cultivated on a large scale, and a sum total of 12 now produce 90 percent of the world's food. Most stock species were domesticated by Stone Age people thousands of years ago. While Moderns have not shown much enterprise in looking around for other foodcrops, the possibilities abound.

Like those of plants, the gene pools of domesticated animal species are much reduced and declining rapidly. In France, where the livestock industry appears to be heading for serious trouble, only seven breeds of sheep form over half the national flock. Less drastically, the same applies to cattle, pigs, horses and poultry.

In the United States, for example, diversity among cattle breeds has declined so much that we pay up to $40,000 per head for calves from Britain's Anjou herd. Here, too, preservation and use of wild species may have beneficial results. A U.S. bison bred with domestic cattle has produced a "beefalo" that reputedly produces meat costing 25 to 40 percent less than beef because of the creature's capacity to thrive (on grass) without the $500 worth of feed the conventional steer consumes before slaughter. In addition, the beefalo can reach a weight of 1,000 pounds in half the time a steer usually takes.

Still another use for species is in pharmaceutical and medical research. Sophisticated as modern medicine has become, many advances would not have been possible without plants and animals from the wild. Animal physiology, for example, affords clues to the origins and nature of a variety of human ailments. The stormy petrel, the albatross, and other long-flying birds have contributed to a better understanding of cardiomyopathy, a failing caused by over-development of the heart muscle, which obstructs blood outflow. The near-extinct desert pupfish of the United States could also serve medicine. Its remarkable tolerance to extremes of temperature and salinity, an evolved attribute, might assist research into human kidney diseases. Closely related to humans, primates too are especially valuable for medical research.

Their contributions in the development and testing of new drugs and vaccines, in psychological experiments, and in a variety of other uses, including the space program are well-known. But 95 percent of the 90,000 primates used each year in medical research alone are accounted for by only 13 species, so pressure on many wild populations is unsustainable. How many know that?

All in all, animals and plants have contributed a wide range of medicines and pharmaceuticals, including analgesics, antibiotics, cardioactive drugs, enzymes, hormones, anti-coagulants, narcotics, vitamins, and anti-leukemic agents. Higher plants are especially helpful; for example, some extremely important drugs, the alkaloids, which are largely derived from tropical plants, are used to treat cardiac problems, hypertension, and leukemia, and they show promise in the treatment of several forms of cancer. As many as one-half of all prescriptions written in the United States each year contain a drug of natural origin as sole active ingredient or as one of two or more main ingredients. Yet a mere 5 percent of all plant species have been screened for pharmacologically active constituents thus far.

Industrial processes also depend upon a great variety of plant and animal species. Again, the examples abound. A range of industrial items—gum, latex, camphor, resins, and sources of etherical oil—are obtained from forests of Southeast Asia alone. Following the cyclamate and now the saccharin controversy, there is greater need than ever for a suitable non-nutritive sweetening agent, and Africa and Southeast Asia have several plants whose fruits are extraordinarily sweet. Other plant pigments may serve us well as food coloring, substituting for riskier artificial coloring agents.

Industry's and science's need for new products is constantly expanding. In fact, the list of ways in which wild plants and animals serve man goes on and on. Lichens, for instance, offer warnings against heavy-metals and sulphur dioxide in the atmosphere. Yet, it is precisely these pollutants that are causing lichens to disappear from industrialized countries.

In short, despite the many pragmatic purposes already served by a number of species, we still know very little about the biological, chemical, and physical properties of most species identified by science, let alone about those species awaiting discovery. But in view of what has so far been revealed, it seems certain that the planetary endowment of species materials is of immense practical value to society.

What Now?

The problem of disappearing species may be the great "sleeper" issue of the 20th century. Even many scientists have not begun to fathom the urgency of the situation. Plant breeders create ever more exotic (and vulnerable) hybrids as the wild forebears of the new breeds disappear off the face of the earth; medical researchers press for more laboratory primates as if these species could replenish themselves indefinitely; foresters, agriculturalists, and "planners" continue to chop down and develop the rainforests as if they would never disappear. Lately, more cries of concern have been heard about some endangered species, especially glamorous ones such as whales and dolphins, but by and large species elimination is rapidly gathering momentum, unheard and unseen by the vast majority of the world's people and their governments.

Yet a number of politically realistic measures hold the potential to slow down the pace of extinction. Some are simple and direct; others require fundamental changes in economic and social principles—particularly in the way we calculate costs and benefits. Because of the complexity and the international scope of the problem, remedies must be proposed and carried out largely by governments. Citizen action can certainly help, and a number of conservation organizations are doing what they can, but the dimensions of the issue remain awesome, and the leverage available to conservationists, depressingly small.

First, *we should vastly increase the size and number of protected areas* by establishing parks and reserves. About 1.1 percent of the world's 55 million square miles of land have been set aside as parks and reserves that merit inclusion in the United Nations' list of protected areas. But this network is far from representative of the earth's terrestrial ecosystems. Forty of the world's 120 biotic provinces are represented in no parks and reserves, another 40 in few.

Second, *we should exert pressure against multinational corporations that endanger species.* Multinational corporations are exploiting forests and forestlands in all three main tropical regions. Some of their activities benefit both their own stockholders and the forested countries. But others invite close scrutiny, especially since those corporations represent a vehicle by which the affluent countries intervene in the development process in poorer regions. Emissaries of consumer demands, they can also express worldwide concern for conservation of resources, major unique ecosystems, species, and genetic reservoirs. The principal responsibility for conservation of national natural resources lies with the countries that possess them. But by applying pressure to multinationals whose home bases are located in the U.S., Americans can contribute to survival prospects for species.

Third, *we should require environmental impact assessments for all foreign aid development projects.* All national and international development-assistance agencies should follow the lead of the U.S. Agency for International Development in requiring of their development projects environmental reviews similar to the environmental impact statements federal agencies operating within the U.S. must now submit. These development-assistance agencies sometimes have a considerable impact on local biota. For example, the Jonglei Canal Project in southern Sudan, a joint venture of several international agencies, is designed to channel water away from well over 1,000 square miles of Sudd swampland, an exceptionally rich biotic community.

Fourth, *we should require environmental impact assessments by private corporations, and reward environmental concern.* Corporations should be required by law to take into account the environmental consequences of their. overseas activities. This would allow both the host nations and the U.S. to foresee the likely consequences of their activities. To complete a potentially effective carrot-and-stick approach, conservation measures taken by multinationals operating abroad could be encouraged through taxation systems in their home countries. For example, were a forestry enterprise to leave part of its concession abroad in an undisturbed state, the company could be granted a tax rebate.

Fifth, *we should establish a governmental compensation system.* Rich nations should demonstrate their concern for species preservation and human welfare by inaugurating a system of compensatory payments similar to the U.S. Soil Bank program. Under such a scheme, the U.S. might, say, compensate Brazil for foregoing exploitation of areas exceptionally rich in species.

A garden will invariably become a weed patch if left untended for long. By the same token, our planet, unless properly cared for, will steadily turn into a weed patch, too. If we continue to plunder and disrupt its ecosystems—heedlessly, irresponsibly, thinking only of our immediate material gain—we will create a habitat ideal for weeds and pests but intolerable for most species. As population pressure, technology, and sheer waste and greed combine to cause the greatest evolutionary wipe-out ever recorded, we will lose countless species before we even understand their roles in functioning ecosystems or appreciate the benefits they could bring to humankind.

A decade ago in "The Tragedy of the Commons," ecologist Garrett Hardin described the demise of the common grazing lands in 18th Century England. Since they belonged to no one, yet were used by everyone, nobody felt responsible for protecting them. As a result they were overgrazed, and soon they were useful to no one at all. We are now seeing this tragedy re-enacted, but on a grand scale, with the entire planet as our commons. It remains to be seen whether we can avoid the fate of the English sheepherders by upholding new standards of planetary stewardship. But see we shall. ✤

Requiem for the Snail Darter/Lament for a Smaller Planet

Thomas Lovejoy

The closing of the floodgates of the Tellico Dam brought to an end a very important battle, not just in the history of conservation, but also history in general. For most, it probably seemed little more than a silly battle to save an insignificant minnow, the snail darter, at large cost to society. Few Americans are aware of the trivial justifications for the Tellico Dam itself, or that it will yield a tiny amount of energy while valuable farmland will be destroyed at a time when there are already too many ill-nourished people in the world.

The significance is far greater than the particular issues involved, for while societies have undertaken campaigns against disease and pest species, this does represent the first time that legislative and executive branches of any nation have deliberately and consciously acted to allow a species to go extinct. In one sense, it is refreshing in that the decision was made publicly and consciously; myriad species have gone and are going with little or no attention.

In another sense, it is deeply discouraging. Pressed to face the undesirable reality that even the United States, one of the most advanced nations, would not be able to protect all species within its domain, Congress had provided a means for measured and thoughtful decision when seemingly irreconcilable conflicts arise between the future of a species and a social enterprise. It is a less-than-inspiring commentary that the decision from this thoughtful and established process was ignored. What should have been essentially a scientific and technical decision became solely a political one.

The larger meaning of all this is that we have reached a point where either we can try to decide thoughtfully which species we try to keep and how many, or we can let the axe fall as it may and find out later, but only in part, what the consequences will have been. It in fact seems absurd that there be any question as to which route we might take. After all, if, as we believe, ours is one of the highest forms of intelligence ever evolved, how can anyone not be concerned about the planet's basic biology of which we are a part?

There is little question that the biology of the earth is being assaulted to a degree never before experienced in our history. Yet endangered species are all too easily seen as isolated phenomena, instead of being recognized as signs of ecosystems under stress, and, collectively, as indications of the deterioration of the planet's ecological systems. It is harder yet for most people to realize that the loss of species in far distant and tropical lands may forever crimp the future of medicine or agriculture. Hardly any city-dweller knows how many species he or she draws on daily—either directly in food, medicine or clothing, or indirectly in terms of their effect on the chemistry of air and water. It is terrifying that the loss of tropical forests may result in the net loss of 10 percent or more of all species, not to mention the biological potential for the support of human populations. It is even more frightening that such a loss would be so great as to possibly disrupt the fundamental planetary cycles of carbon, and alter atmospheric composition and world climate. Those who scoff at such a possibility are generally unaware that the present atmospheric composition is a product of past biological activity. Our lives are indeed linked with those of other species, however distant and however abstruse the link.

Part of the quandary is that endangered species tend to get treated as problems on a one-by-one basis; thus, the effects of human intervention in nature are often perceived only when the problems are far advanced and hard to reverse. The built-in surge in population and development is hard to check once ecological problems begin to be recognized, so much so that it is fair to say that a nation beginning to lose its wildlife and other natural resources has already overreached itself biologically.

Only 120 years ago Darwin's publication of the *Origin of Species* provided people with a greater perspective of our place in nature, and an understanding of how evolutionary change works, how diversity is created, and indeed how we came into being. It is interesting that our current predicament involves questions of just this sort.

We certainly are affecting the course of evolution, and hence future diversity, in a massive way by snuffing out evolutionary lines prematurely and fragmenting populations and wildlands. Had the Mexican valley in Jalisco (where wild perennial corn was discovered very recently) been converted to agriculture, the evolutionary line concerned and the possibility of a perennial corn agriculture with all its attendant benefits for society would have been forever lost. Fragmentation may lead to additional biological loss: small populations such as bighorn sheep will suffer and perhaps disappear due to inbreeding problems. Fragmentation also leaves patches of habitat unable to support some species; some of our migratory warblers may be affected by such problems both in North America and on their wintering grounds. Fragmentation also generates problems by removing barriers. Breaking up the continuous forests of the southeast has brought the red wolf into contact with the coyote, and now in the course of interbreeding, red wolf genes are being swamped by those of the more abundant coyote.

We are at a point where we will choose what our place in nature is to be. One choice is to remain relatively passive and unconscious of our effect on our biological support base, to allow biological impoverishment to proceed, and by default to leave future generations with a legacy of an impoverished existence. The other is to fulfill a destiny as conscious, intelligent, and prescient creatures, to take charge of evolution (including our own) in a wise fashion, realizing that benevolence toward our fellow species is indeed benevolence toward ourselves. If the snail darter's departure leads us one increment toward making such a choice, we will, unwittingly, have done ourselves a favor. 🌱

III. LEGACIES

III. LEGACIES

Love Canals U.S.A. — Toxic Chemicals at Large

Michael Brown

In the years since Rachel Carson's *Silent Spring,* a great national concern has arisen over air and water pollution. It now appears that pollution seeping into the earth itself has gone largely unnoticed, and in some cases may be far more dangerous as a direct cause of cancer and other severe human illnesses. "Toxic chemical waste," says John E. Moss, who was chairman of the House Subcommittee on Oversight and Investigations before his retirement [in 1979], "may be the sleeping giant of the decade." Not until the nightmare of the Love Canal unfolded in Niagara County, N.Y., did Americans become aware of the vast dangers of ground pollution. But the problem since then seems only to be worsening.

Each year, several hundred new chemical compounds are added to the 70,000 that already exist in America, and the wastes from their production—nearly 92 billion pounds a year—are often placed in make-shift underground storage sites. Federal officials now suspect that more than 800 such sites have the potential to become as dangerous as those at the Love Canal, and some are probably already severely hazardous to unsuspecting neighbors. The problem is how to find them and how to pay the enormous costs of cleaning them up before more tragedy results. So far, federal, state and local governments have been, for the most part, reluctant to face the issue.

School for Scandal

Sometime in the 1940s—no one knows or wants to remember just when—the Hooker Chemical Company, which is now a subsidiary of Occidental Petroleum, found an abandoned canal near Niagara Falls, and began dumping countless hundreds of 55-gallon drums there. In 1953, the canal was filled in and sold to the city for an elementary school and playground (the purchase price was a token $1), and modest single-family dwellings were built nearby. There were signs of trouble now and then—occasional collapses of earth where drums had rotted through, and skin rashes in children or dogs that romped on the field— but they were given little thought until the spring of 1978. By then, many of the homes were deteriorating rapidly and were found to be infiltrated by highly toxic chemicals that had percolated into the basements. The New York State Health Department investigated and discovered startling health problems: birth defects, miscarriages, epilepsy, liver abnormalities, sores, rectal bleeding, headaches—not to mention undiscovered but possible latent illnesses. In August, President Carter declared a federal emergency. With that, the state began evacuating residents from the neighborhood along the Love Canal, as it is named after the unsuccessful entrepreneur, William Love, who built it in 1894. Two hundred homes were boarded up, the school was closed and the nation got a glimpse of what Senator Daniel Patrick Moynihan called "a peculiarly primitive poisoning of the atmosphere by a firm."

But it was clearly not so peculiar. Since then, new dumping grounds have been reported in several precarious places. Under a ball field near another elementary school in Niagara Falls health officials have found a landfill containing many of the same compounds. It was discovered because the ball field swelled and contracted like a bowl of gelatin when heavy equipment moved across it. Officials have discovered, too, that Hooker disposed of nearly four times the amount of chemicals present in the Love Canal several hundred feet west of the city's municipal water-treatment facility, and residues have been tracked inside water-intake pipelines. Across town, near Niagara University, a 16-acre Hooker landfill containing such killers as Mirex C-56 and lindane— essentially chemicals that were used in the manufacture of pest killers and plastics—has been found to be fouling a neighboring stream, Bloody Run Creek, which flows past drinking-water wells. About 80,000 tons of toxic waste are said to have been dumped there over the years.

Still worse, as the company recently acknowledged, Hooker buried up to 3,700 tons of trichlorophenol waste which contains one of the world's most deadly chemicals, dioxin, at various sites in Niagara County between 1947 and 1972. Investigators immediately sought to determine whether dioxin had seeped out and, indeed, the substance was identified in small quantities within leachate taken from the periphery of the Love Canal, an indication that it may have begun to migrate. There are now believed to be an estimated 141 pounds of dioxin in the canal site—and as much as 2,000 pounds buried elsewhere in the county. The Love Canal is above the city's public water-supply intake on the Niagara River but a quarter of a mile away; the other sites are closer—in one case within 300 feet—but down-stream of the intake. However, the Niagara flows into Lake Ontario, which Syracuse, Rochester, Toronto and several other communities make use of for water supply. Although health officials regard the dioxin discovery as alarming, they do not yet consider it a direct health threat because it is not known to have come into contact with humans or to have leached into water supplies. Academic chemists point out, however, that as little as _three ounces_ of dixoin are enough to kill more than a million people. It was dioxin, 2 to 11 pounds of it, which was dispersed in Seveso, Italy, after an explosion at a trichlorphenol plant: dead animals littered the streets, hundreds of people were treated for severe skin lesions and 1,000 acres had to be evacuated.

In early 1980, New York State health officials began to examine and conduct studies of residents and workers in the Niagara University area because of the dioxin concentrations. One local physician there expresses concern over an apparently high rate of respiratory ailments, and union officials say that workers in industries alongside the landfill are suffering from emphysema, cancer and skin rashes. Cats have lost fur and teeth after playing near Bloody Run; some young goats have died after grazing on its banks, and the creek is devoid of all aquatic life.

So far, there are at least 15 dumps in Niagara County alone that have been discovered to contain toxic chemicals. But no one in the county, or anywhere else in the country, is sure exactly where underground dumpsites are. Of the thousands of covered pits suspected of containing toxic wastes in the United States, the U.S. Environmental Protection Agency says it is a fair estimate that as many as 838 are, or could become, serious health hazards. But the machinery to carry out the kind of monitoring and inspecting now being done in Niagara County does not generally exist elsewhere. And the E.P.A., internal memorandums reveal, has not been eager to set it up because of the extraordinary expense and political problems that would inevitably present themselves. In fact, one regional official was reprimanded for trying to get the type of action that must be taken to guard against another Love Canal.

In at least one known case there are symptoms disturbingly similar. Just 400 feet from a residential area in Elkton, Md., is a disposal area that, according to E.P.A. files, was used both by the Galaxy Chemical Company and by a suspected, unidentified midnight hauler. Residents have complained of sore throats, respiratory problems and headaches, all reminiscent of the early days of trouble at the Love Canal. One local doctor contends that the cancer death rate in the area is 30 times greater than elsewhere in the county, though his report is the subject of much controversy. So far, no evidence of direct human contact with leachate is known to have occurred there, as it did at Niagara Falls; nor have residents demanded evacuation.

In Rehoboth, Mass., 1,000 cubic yards of resins left over from a solvent redistilling process were recently ordered removed from a dumpsite that the owner had placed within 10 feet of his own house. In Lowell, Mass., some 15,000 drums and 43 tanks of assorted toxic wastes are at present being removed from a site within 200 yards of homes, and chemicals leaking from the drums are appearing in sewers and a nearby river.

Authorities in Michigan claim that the beleaguered Hooker Company has dumped C-56 into sandy soil, contaminating public wells (which have been closed off) and polluting White Lake, near Montague; the state is trying to force the company into a $200 million cleanup. Hooker has also been involved in lawsuits filed by maimed workers in Hopewell, Va., who became sterile and lost their memories after exposure to Kepone, a pesticide that Allied Chemical and Hooker jointly made and packaged.

The U.S. Comptroller General, at the request of Congress, has mapped out stretches through much of the East, Texas and Louisiana and parts of Oregon, Washington and California as regions with the greatest potential for trouble. "Texans are only now becoming concerned about solid-waste disposal," says Doris Ebner, environmental manager for the Houston-Galveston Area Council. "What will happen is that there will be some disaster to make a flash." But serious ground investigations are still not given a top priority.

Know Nothing, Do Nothing

The tendency not to connect health problems with ground pollution has certainly been widespread. Before last summer, ground pollution was never a major concern in Niagara Falls, either. Because that city is relatively small and has a cheap source of hydroelectricity for chemical firms, most of its people have lived their whole lives on top of or near the hidden strains and goo of industrial pollution. Children near the chemical dumpsites often played with phosphorescent rocks which would explode brilliantly when they were thrown against concrete. Dirt on the old canal had turned white, yellow, red, blue and black; rocks were orangish; and cesspools of caustic sludge gushed from several locations. These manifestations were viewed more as a matter of esthetics than as a health problem.

But indiscriminate dumping—dumping whatever wherever—has been a national way of life. Though American manufacturers of plastics, pesticides, herbicides and other products that produce huge amounts of toxic wastes are beginning to deposit them in centralized landfill sites—which may insure a closer inspection—the common practice has been to dispose of residues and forget about them. This has been true of private individuals as well, from independent haulers to local farmers.

Farmlands, because they make for nicely isolated dumping grounds, have posed special problems. In 1974, a 100-square-mile pastureland around Darrow and Geismar, La., was found to be contaminated with hexachlorobenzene (HCB), which was produced by the volatilization of wastes dumped into pits. HCB, a byproduct of the manufacture of carbon tetrachloride and perchloroethylene, causes liver deterioration, convulsions and death. During a routine sampling of beef fat by the U.S. Department of Agriculture as part of the Meat and Poultry Inspection Program, 1.5 parts per million of HCB was tracked in the meat of a steer belonging to W.I. Duplessis of Darrow. Further samplings showed that cattle were carrying the same toxin. Soil and vegetation were likewise tainted. The dumps were covered with plastic and dirt, and 30,000 cattle were ordered destroyed. The cattle were fed special diets instead of being slaughtered, however, and moved away from the area; their levels receded to an "acceptable" point, and only 27 were deemed unmarketable and killed. No one can be sure how many cattle, grazing near dumpsites elsewhere, have made it to the dinner table undetected.

Several years ago in Perham, Minn., 11 persons suffered arsenic poisoning from leaching grasshopper bait. Those struck with contamination worked for a building contractor who drilled a well 20 feet from where bait had been buried by a farmer 30 years before. Severe neuropathy cost one of the employees the use of his legs for six months.

Much of past dumping has been plainly illegal. New Jersey, one of the most industrialized states and one whose cancer rate has been found to be substantially higher than the national average, has been a favorite spot for midnight haulers, or "scavengers," paid to cart off wastes and unload them in swamps, sewers, pits or abandoned wells to avoid paying for disposal at approved sites. In Conventry, R.I., officials found an illegal and highly toxic dump on a pig farm owned by a convicted gambler. It contained one suspected cancer-causing agent, carbon tetrachloride, and another compound that will ignite at 80 degrees Fahrenheit.

More blatant violators have been known simply to loosen tank-truck valves and get rid of contaminants along roadways in the dark of night. The owner of a New York company that reprocesses electrical transformers is currently on trial on charges of deliberately spilling out polychlorinated biphenyls (PCBs) from his truck onto 270 miles of a highway in North Carolina. 700 residents of the Warrenton, N.C., area recently protested a state plan to create a new dump there for some 40,000 cubic yards of the tainted soil.

In other instances, dangerous conditions have been brought about more innocently. In Missouri, dioxin was discharged into waste oil, which was later sprayed on three race tracks and a farm road to control dust. Some 63 appaloosa and quarter horses, 6 dogs, 12 cats and a large number of birds died as a result. A child who frequently played on the dirt road was rushed to the hospital with severe bladder pains and urinary bleeding.

Drumming Up Trouble

Ground pollution's greatest threat is to the national drinking supply. More than 100 million Americans depend upon ground water as the major source of life's most vital fluid. Springs and wells, as opposed to rivers and lakes fed by running streams, are the main drinking reservoirs in 32 states. Florida's population, for example, is 91 percent dependent on ground water. Pouring tons of chemicals into the earth can be comparable, in an indirect way, to disposing of poisonous wastes upstream from a municipal river intake.

Chemical landfills never lie dormant. When water penetrates buried wastes, it removes soluble components, producing a grossly polluted liquid leachate that extends out from the dump. Therein resides the danger. Leaching can continue, at any given site, for more than 100 years, picking up dangerous, stable materials and spreading them around a surprisingly large area. E.P.A.'s Office of Solid Waste has guessed that the average landfill site, about 17 acres in size, produces 4.6 million gallons of leachate a year if there is 10 inches of rainfall. Last spring the Comptroller General reported that a *billion* gallons of ground water had been polluted near an Islip, L.I., landfill. A contaminated aquifer that was a mile long and 1,300 feet wide spoiled some drinking-water wells, which had to be sealed off and the homes connected to another source. In humid regions, where rainfall exceeds evaporation, the problem is more acute: the more water in the ground, the more leaching occurs.

Several years ago the Union Carbide Corporation contracted with an independent hauler to remove an unknown number of drums from its Bound Brook, N.J., facility. Inside were wash solvents and residues from organic chemical and plastics manufacture. Instead of going to the Dover Township landfill, much of the waste was dumped on a former chicken farm in the Pleasant Plains section of Dover. Mr. and Mrs. Samuel Reich had leased the land to Nicholas Fernicola on the assumption, according to case files, that he was in the drum-salvaging business. When the Reichs smelled pungent odors emanating from the property, they investigated the land and found thousands of containers, both buried and strewn about the surface. Additional drums were discovered in a wooded area near the Winding River, four miles away. The drums were hauled away under court order, but the damage had been done. Sufficient quantities of chemicals had already entered the environment, and early in 1974 residents of the area began tasting and smelling strange things in their water. Dover's Board of Health, in emergency action, passed an ordinance forbidding the use of 148 wells and ordering that they be permanently sealed. Although there were no documented cases of illness as a result, it is difficult to determine how many residents had consumed potentially harmful substances before the odors were noted. Equally difficult is determining where and how far the leachate traveled.

The Government itself has been the cause of serious ground-water contamination. Sloppy storage at the Rocky Mountain Arsenal, formerly an Army production center for chemical-warfare agents, led to the contamination of 30 square miles of shallow aquifer near Denver and, in turn, to the abandonment of 64 wells used for drinking water and irrigation. Waterfowl in the area died, and poisoned soil turned sugar beets and pasture grasses a sickly yellow. An estimated $78 million will be needed to complete the proposed cleanup, but there is no way of recovering the chemicals that have already escaped. One irrigation well that shows traces of contamination is only a mile south of the city of Brighton's public well field. The arsenal dug an injection well 12,045 feet deep for immediate disposal, but such facilities do little to insure against long-range migration; as it turned out, the well caused earth tremors and had to be closed.

Loss of Innocents

Much of the randomness with which chemical companies have chosen their dumping grounds over the years will no doubt continue until the Resource Conservation and Recovery Act is implemented. Even then the problem will not go away. There is simply no such thing as a totally secure, self-contained landfill, a fact even those in the business admit. "There is no proof a landfill 100 years from now won't leach," says Paul Chenard, president of SCA Chemical Waste Services, Inc. He says disposal methods have been improved. Pits can be lined with a special plastic. Waste-disposal firms can excavate on clay-based soil, compact the ground, install standpipes to pump out leachate, and slope the final cover to minimize rain infiltration. But the state of the art is new and no one issues guarantees. Many environmentalists feel that only when there is "cradle-to-death" legislation demanding that wastes be rendered innocuous before disposal will the problem be under control, and there are no signs of that happening in the near future.

The Brunt

An E.P.A. memorandum has listed more than 32,254 storage, treatment, and disposal sites, both on and off industrial premises, as existing in the nation. In an earlier breakdown, California ranked first with 2,985. Pennsylvania, New York, Ohio and Texas were not far behind. Those statistics, officials emphasize, refer only to _known_ sites. And even at the known sites the quality of the treatment is questionable. One estimate is that less than 7 percent of the 92 billion pounds of chemical waste generated each year receives proper disposal. After working in Niagara Falls for several months, Dr. David Axelrod, New York State Health Commissioner, says the overall problems of improper disposal and treatment "are incredibly immense." The Hooker Company—which contends that it did not know the possible dangers and was simply disposing of wastes as everyone else did—is already faced with claim against it in excess of $2 billion, and citizens' demands upon the state are only just beginning. New discoveries of dioxin are prompting new demonstrations, new arrests of demonstrators and new requests for evacuation and relocation. Patricia Pino, whose home in Niagara Falls is now unmarketable, was one of those arrested. "We request a reprieve from death row," she telegraphed Gov. Hugh Carey. "We are innocent of any crime." Her two children have liver abnormalities, and she has learned that she herself has cancer. 🌳

The Immortal Tiger of Atomic Waste

Anne and Paul Ehrlich

The possibility of catastrophic nuclear power-plant "accidents" isn't the only reason why we—and many other scientists—are apprehensive about the spread of nuclear power. Perhaps an even greater danger exists in the radioactive wastes produced within the power generators themselves. Until a means of safely disposing of these materials is found, the production of "no risk" nuclear-generated electricity will be impossible.

Remember that most reactors split uranium 235 (U-235) nuclei to produce heat energy. That heat provides steam, which in turn spins generator turbines. However, when the uranium atoms split they create fragments (called "fission products"), and the waste problem begins. The fragments, for example, contaminate the reactor's fuel rods so badly that the rods must be replaced about once a year. (This replacement is necessary because the fission products "poison" the chain reaction by absorbing neutrons without fissioning. The trapped neutrons are then unable to sustain the "atomic" reactions.)

Furthermore, because many of these fragments remain highly radioactive after they are formed, the fuel rods (in which most of the fragments become embedded) are also radioactively "hot" by the time they're removed from the reactors. These used rods, in fact, are so radioactive that they are normally stored at the power plants for a period of several months, until some of their most dangerous contaminants have decayed into somewhat less harmful materials.

The spontaneous changes in nuclei that result in the emission of radioactivity always transform an atom into something else. If its chemical properties are altered, the atom becomes another element. On the other hand, if an atom's nucleus is changed but its chemical properties remain the same, a different isotope of the same element is formed. Uranium 235, for example, decays in a long series of steps that include the radioactive isotopes radium 226, radon 22, and polonium 218. The end result, finally, is the chemically stable, non-"hot" lead 206.

The process of this breakdown is statistically predictable, even though the instant at which a single nucleus will be spontaneously transformed isn't. For this reason, atomic decay is measured in "half-lives," which indicate the time needed for one-half of the billions of atoms in a small quantity of material to undergo this transformation. For example, one of the major short-lived isotopes used in nuclear fuel elements, iodine 131, has a half-life of 8.1 days. This means that when 8.1 days have passed from any given time, half of the iodine 131 will be gone. After 16.2 days, only a quarter of the original quantity of isotope will be left . . . only one-eighth after 24.3 days . . . and so on. A period of 20 half-lives (which is less than six months in the case of iodine 131) will reduce the original radioactive isotope to one millionth of its initial mass. Thus, if all fission products had half-lives of about a week, the storage of these wastes wouldn't present much of a problem. They could simply be held at power-plant sites for a year or so and could then be disposed of in any way suitable to their chemical characteristics. Residual radioactivity would be—by that time—practically nonexistent.

Unfortunately, however, many of the fission products regularly produced in nuclear reactors have extremely long half-lives. Those of strontium 90 and cesium 137 are 28 and 30 years, respectively. This means that these isotopes would have to be stored for 1,000 years before their radioactivity could be safely ignored. And plutonium 239, which is formed in reactors by the non-fission absorption of neutrons into uranium 238, has a half-life of 24,400 years. This material, in short, should be kept out of the environment for at least one-half million years, which is something on the order of 100 times longer than recorded history.

The magnitude of our radioactive waste problem was made clear in a 1974 study by the now-defunct Atomic Energy Commission. The AEC calculated the amount of hot waste it would expected to accumulate in the United States by the year 2000. Then the commission figured out how much air would be needed to dilute these materials to the so-called "maximum permissible concentration" or MPC. (At the MPC an individual who breathed the waste-polluted air would receive no more than four times the average exposure caused by natural radiation sources.) What the AEC discovered was that by 2000 A.D. the amount of air required to safely dilute the United States' inventory of atomic wastes would be 7,300,000,000,000 cubic kilometers (approximately 1,750,000,000,000 cubic miles). This number represents a block of air 12,000 miles on a side, a mass large enough to cover the entire planet to a depth of 4,000 miles. Even one hundred years after that, 456,000,000,000 cubic miles would still be necessary. Add one thousand years, and the figure is still 36,000,000,000 cubic miles. And even a million years later (1,002,000 A.D.), approximately a billion cubic miles of air would still be necessary to reach the MPC. Remember, too, that these incredible volumes of atmosphere would only serve to dilute the radiation that still remained in wastes that the AEC expected to have accumulated by the year 2000. The figures don't take into consideration any wastes that might be produced after that cut-off date.

The staggering size of these numbers helps to drive home the magnitude of our nation's nuclear waste disposal problem. Still, there are those in the government-industry-nuclear establishment who would prefer that the public didn't understand how overwhelming this problem actually is. General Electric, for example, states reassuringly that the annual wastes produced by a nuclear power plant are equivalent in size to about one aspirin tablet for every person served by the installation. But this statement is a two-dimensional lie. In the first place, University of California physicist John P. Holdren has calculated (using AEC data) that "high level" wastes—in their most concentrated form—actually amount to a mass the size of about ten aspirins for every person served. And those high-level wastes are only the most radioactive residues of the fuel. There is an additional five tablets' worth of waste per person in the form of the intensely radioactive remains of the alloy tubes that held the fuel. Furthermore, intermediate-level and low-level wastes—which contain some very dangerous and long-lived isotopes—amount to well over 3,000 of those aspirin-tablet-sized portions of deadly material per person each and every year.

Remarkably enough, this "understatement" of the volume of radioactive wastes (by a factor of more than 3,000) is actually the less dangerous side of General Electric's lie. The company committed an even more serious deception when it placed emphasis on the amount of the radioactive materials, rather than on the extremely high toxicity of these wastes. As Professor Holdren put it, "If a tablet were to be an apt comparison it would have to be a cyanide tablet . . . and even that would not do justice to the actual toxicity of the fission products." (As a matter of fact, one-year-old radioactive waste is at least 100 times more toxic by volume than cyanide.) Had the nuclear industry been wholly honest it would have announced that "The wastes produced annually by a nuclear power plant are equivalent in size to only several hundred cyanide tablets per person served." But even that unlikely candor would be misleading, because cyanide can be easily detoxified.

Radioactive isotopes, on the other hand, can't be decontaminated either easily or rapidly. In many cases the only practical thing to do with these dangerous poisons is to wait until their own slow decay can render them harmless, which can take generations or centuries or epochs. What can be done with the remaining long-lived wastes that will continue to be deadly for 1,000 to 500,000 years? *In theory*, these reactor by-products can be shipped to a "reprocessing plant." If the wastes have been held at the power plant for 150 days, they will only contain about three percent of the radioactivity that they had when they were removed from the reactor. But, though this figure may sound small, these elements are still emitting an abundance of lethal radiation. Furthermore, the heat generated by continuing radioactive decay is so intense that the used fuel rods would melt if they weren't constantly cooled during shipment. Therefore, any shipment must take place in heavily shielded, cooled casks which can weigh from 35 to 100 metric tons, depending upon whether they're to be shipped by road or rail.

Needless to say, one of the first problems of nuclear waste management has been to design these containers so that they can stand up to possible accidents in transit. What if, for example, a speeding train hit a cask-bearing truck at a grade crossing? Considerable engineering effort has no doubt gone into these containers. We are, at any rate, constantly assured by the nuclear industry that an accident involving cask rupture is virtually impossible. (And, if the industry has its way, we'll get to test the reliability of these containers because by the end of the century thousands of cask trips will be made very year.)

But let's assume the journey from power plant to reprocessing plant is safely completed. What happens then? The fuel rods are chopped up by automated equipment and dissolved in acid so that the various elements can be separated chemically. At this point, reprocessing-plant design allows some gaseous radioactive isotopes to be routinely released from the plants into the atmosphere. In fact, it is here that the largest routine releases designed into the nuclear fuel cycle occur, and these add a small fraction of natural radiation to the burden of ionizing radiation that humanity must already bear. But all is not pure waste. Plutonium 239 and uranium 235—both fissile and thus usable as reactor fuel—can be recovered at the reprocessing plant and shipped back to be recycled through the power plant. The rest of the high-level wastes become concentrated into a highly radioactive liquid (about 10,000 gallons of it per power reactor per year).

While this reprocessing could *in theory* occur, there are at present *no* reprocessing plants in service in the United States. One such installation (a small-capacity plant owned by Nuclear Fuel Services, Inc.) did operate from 1966 until 1971, when it was shut down for repairs and expansion. While in operation this plant's routine emissions were sometimes very close to the AEC's permissible limits. Today, however, that installation couldn't even come close to meeting our newer, more stringent emissions limitations. The plant was scheduled to go back into operation in 1979 at three times its previous capacity, but it was recently announced that the reopening would not take place because of the huge expenditures necessary to enable the installation to comply with current safety standards. So, this highly radioactive structure—with the wastes that it still contains—is currently a ward of the New York State

Energy and Research Development Administration, a monument to the "power of the peaceful atom." Another reprocessing plant was built near Morris, Illinois, by General Electric at a cost of some $65 million. Unfortunately, it didn't work, and was abandoned without ever reprocessing any fuel at all. And yet another plant, scheduled go into service near Barnwell, hasn't done so yet.

In many ways, this so-called "back end" of the nuclear fuel cycle is actually the soft underbelly of the whole atomic power establishment. The shipment and, especially, the reprocessing of spent fuel are hazardous and technically difficult enterprises. They must be accomplished almost entirely by automation, and the barriers between the radioactive materials and the environment tend to be much thinner during these processes than at the power plants themselves. Obviously—as dramatized by General Electric's $65 million fiasco—less is known about how to operate a reprocessing plant than about how to run a power reactor. At this point, in fact, we don't even know if reprocessing plants can be designed with adequate safeguards against catastrophic accidents, tornadoes, earthquakes, and sabotage. In the meantime, spent fuel elements accumulate at power plant sites while we wait for someone to solve the problems.

But let's suppose that this "back end" of the nuclear cycle does become successfully hooked up and large amounts of spent fuel are reprocessed. What then would become of the millions of gallons of highly radioactive, long-lived liquid wastes that would be generated annually? This particular question has vexed the nuclear establishment from the start. The original solution for storage problems posed by high-level wastes from the American nuclear weapons program was simply to store them in tanks above ground. Such a naive solution has been envisioned for reactor wastes, too. Indeed, one AEC official actually testified that this agency would guard the wastes for the required 500,000 years (that is, for half a million years after the last nuclear power plant closes down). One would have to look a long way to find a better example of bureaucratic _chutzpah!_ Imagine a government agency (or a government, for that matter) lasting for 100 times the length of recorded history, let alone carrying out an assigned task for that period. Consider also that during the 500,000 years that the AEC would be "on guard," several ice ages could come and go.

The fact of the matter is, we don't need a crystal ball to evaluate the AEC's performance when it comes to containing radioactive wastes. At the AEC's Hanford Facility in Washington state, for example, wastes have leaked out for years. (Some 150,000 gallons escaped into the soil in 1973 alone.) We can only hope that those radioactive liquids don't migrate through ground-water channels into the Columbia River . . . with unhappy consequences for Portlanders downstream. And we're sorry to say that the record of the AEC (now known as the Nuclear Regulatory Commission—NRC) at its Savannah River, Georgia, site (and elsewhere) is hardly more encouraging.

It's abundantly clear to anyone who has seriously considered the problem that surface storage facilities—no matter how cleverly engineered—are, at best, temporary expedients for the treatment of high-level wastes. This, of course, has led to an extraordinary diversity of suggestions for the permanent disposal of these deadly materials. One solution suggested in the 1950s by Joseph H. Camin of the University of Kansas was to dump the wastes in active volcanoes so that they could then be lofted into the atmosphere and come down as fall-out. (In those days, the AEC sponsored a massive propaganda campaign designed to persuade Americans that fall-out was actually good for them!) Camin's tongue-in-cheek solution, however, has been almost matched by some seriously proposed ones. It's been suggested, for instance, that radioactive wastes be loaded on rockets and blasted off the earth to pollute the solar system. Of course, the record of the technological boondogglers of the National Aeronautics and Space Administration makes it perfectly clear that we wouldn't have to wait very long for a rocket to blow up on the pad or in the atmosphere and create a large-scale radiation catastrophe.

Like space disposal, another alternative—ocean disposal—presents known hazards because a great deal of low-level radioactive waste—encapsulated in steel drums—has already been dumped into the oceans close to our shores. The result? Many of the containers are now leaking, and the degree to which radioactivity will be concentrated in oceanic food chains (thereby threatening humanity) is not yet known.

A suggestion that we bury the wastes in deep trenches dug in the ocean floor is also plagued with uncertainty. The notion that these materials be placed beneath the seas (where the great tectonic plates of earth collide) so that the deadly materials will be drawn into our planet's molten core seems unlikely at best since the ocean floor's rate of subduction (drawing in) is only an inch or so a year, and the probable fate of containers deposited in these geologically active areas is completely unknown.

Actually, the most sensible plan seems to be to solidify the wastes, and then inter them in impermeable geological formations such as deep salt beds. Early in the 1970s, the Atomic Energy Commission actually announced that salt beds were the solution and selected a salt mine near Lyons, Kansas, as it first repository. Here again, the AEC demonstrated the broad-gauge incompetence for which it and its successor, the NRC, are world famous. The experts managed to pick a mine that was as full of holes as a Swiss cheese (the result of early drilling for oil and gas). After the Kansas Geological Survey pointed out this little oversight to them, the AEC was forced to abandon its plans for a "national repository."

Since then, the NRC has looked at other sites, notably salt beds in the Finger Lakes region of New York and near Carlsbad, New Mexico. But it has met stiff public resistance. People sense that our knowledge of geology makes it difficult to guarantee the integrity of burial sites for the requisite hundreds of thousands of years, and they are rightly nervous about the possibility of accidents that may occur in the process of transport and burial. After all, New Yorkers have the spectacle of the Nuclear Fuel Services' failed plant as a constant reminder of the capabilities of the nuclear establishment.

Does all this mean that the nuclear waste problem is insoluble? Our guess is that it can be solved, but only with great difficulty. Burial of solidified wastes in appropriate geological formations may well be the answer, but much more research is required before we know for sure. In the meantime, something must be done to tighten up the much too cavalier treatment of low-level wastes, which—even in the late 1960s—the National Academy of Sciences declared was "barely tolerable . . . on the present scale of operations" and "would become intolerable with much increase in the use of nuclear power."

Finally, techniques must be devised to dispose of the highly radioactive remains of nuclear power plants when their 20- to 40-year service lives are over, to say nothing of the carcasses of failed reprocessing plants. This research should go on. While nuclear fission technology is immature and incompetent today, it is not yet clear that it has no role to play in humanity's future energy plan.

What is clear is that there will be no future for nuclear power unless the NRC (and the rest of the nuclear establishment) changes its ways and restores a credible image, for no sane person today can accept the standard fallback position—that wastes be stored in concrete bunkers on the surface until a suitable permanent solution can be found. After all, who in his right mind would grab an immortal tiger by the tail . . . especially on the word of an incompetent liar who says that someday a way will be found to let go safely?   ✿

The Epidemic of Environmental Cancer

Joseph Highland,
Marcia Fine,
and Robert Boyle

Cancer, a disease that has reached epidemic proportions in the United States, is not caused by some inexplicable miasma, although it may seem that way to the uninformed. In fact, the overwhelming majority of cancers, most scientists now agree, are environmentally caused. As such, they are largely preventable. But failure by the public, industry, and government to recognize this fact and act on it is why we have a cancer epidemic today, and why that epidemic may worsen in the years ahead.

Consider the scope of the epidemic. Of the 216 million Americans alive now, 54 million—one of four in the population—will eventually suffer from cancer. Two out of three persons who contract the disease will die from it. In 1977 more than 380,000 Americans died from cancer, and the fatalities far exceed the number of combat deaths the U.S. suffered in World War II.

About one-half of all cancer deaths in the U.S. occur in people under 65. Cancer is the leading killer of women between 30 and 40 years of age, and after accidents it is the chief killer of all Americans under 35. Among children between the ages of 1 and 10, cancer is the leading cause of death.

Besides the suffering it inflicts on the victim, cancer can also leave the surviving family emotionally and economically destitute. Overall, the cost of cancer is estimated to range from $15 billion to 25 billion a year in the U.S., excluding the costs associated with pain and suffering. It is a mark of the times that an American Family Corporation subsidiary specializing in cancer insurance recently took a full-page ad in *Time* magazine to announce that "we are growing at a faster rate than any other life insurance company in America."

Despite the high toll cancer takes, it would be folly to consider the disease inevitable. Not "everything" causes cancer. The reason we periodically get wind of a new cancer threat, such as vinyl chloride or Tris, is in large part that we market, use, or dispose of products that have not been adequately tested for long-term toxic effects before they are introduced into the marketplace. Also, advances have been made in developing and refining the analytical techniques needed to identify carcinogens (cancer-causing agents) and to detect their presence. It is no longer beyond our ability to deal with the causes of cancer.

What Are the Facts?

The principal fact is that cancer is largely an environmental disease. For years physicians commonly assumed that cancer came inevitably with old age, but in 1964 the World Health Organization reported that 60 to 80 percent of all cancer cases were caused by natural and man-made carcinogens in the polluted air we breathe, the contaminated water we drink, or the food we eat. Cancer may also be caused by exposure to chemicals, cigarette smoke, sunlight, or X-rays. Thus, the incidence of cancer can be reduced by diminishing or eliminating human exposure to carcinogens. Prevention, not "cure," is the key. Not even cancer researchers expect to find a miracle cure.

There are two other important facts to bear in mind about cancer. First, exposure to any carcinogen presents some risk. As the Ad Hoc Committee on the Evaluation of Low Levels of Environmental Carcinogens reported to the Surgeon General in 1970, "no level of exposure to a chemical carcinogen should be considered toxicologically insignificant for man." Second, cancers have a latency period (or lag time). From five to forty years pass between the time of initial exposure to a carcinogen and the time the disease makes itself noticeable. Like a ticking bomb, cancer takes time to explode. Consequently, most cancer cases now emerging originated between the end of World War II and the mid-1950s.

Actually, cancer is not one disease but the collective name for more than one hundred diseases that can affect various parts of the body in different ways. All cancers, however, have one factor in common: the diseased cells multiply in uncontrolled fashion. Most forms of plant and animal life are vulnerable to cancer, but there is no evidence that it is communicable. The ancient Egyptians, Greeks, and Romans were acquainted with the disease. Several mummies show signs of cancer of the bone or the nasopharynx, and Hippocrates, the father of medicine, was familiar with cancer of the mouth, uterus, stomach, breast, and skin. In all likelihood, many cancers in ancient times were caused by carcinogens found in the natural environment. For centuries Egyptian farmers working in the Nile have been infested by a parasitic fluke that may produce chronic changes that can cause cancer. Other carcinogenic agents found in the natural environment are aflatoxin, the metabolic products of a mold that can grow on food staples—for example, peanuts, corn, and lentils—stored in hot, humid places.

Although John Hill, a London physician, reported on six cases of "polypusses" in his *Caution Against the Immoderate Use of Snuff* in 1691, Percival Pott, a surgeon at St. Bartholomew's Hospital in London, is generally acknowledged as the first to recognize that an environmental agent could cause cancer in human beings. Pott studied the high incidence of cancer of the scrotum in chimney sweeps, and in 1775 he attributed the disease to the accumulation of soot in scrotal folds, which usually were not washed.

Other research was long in coming. In 1875 a German researcher, Richard Von Volkmann, linked scrotal cancer in workers to the production of paraffin by the distillation of coal tar, and in 1918 two Japanese scientists demonstrated that the continuous application of coal tar preparations to the ears of rabbits over several months would cause skin cancer. In London during the 1920s and 30s, Sir Ernest Kennaway isolated and identified as carcinogens polycyclic hydrocarbons in coal tar. In the 1940s Dr. Isaac Berenblum of Israel showed that a dose of a carcinogen too low to produce a significant effect in a small group of animals could cause cells to become pre-malignant and stay that way, only to turn cancerous when promoted by another agent perhaps years later. Berenblum was the first to demonstrate that otherwise safe chemicals could interact with carcinogens to enhance their effect.

In the 1940s the carcinogen benzo(a)pyrene was found in cigarette smoke. In 1950 Dr. Ernst L. Wynder of Washington University in St. Louis began to investigate smoking and produced evidence that its increase correlated with that of lung cancer cases. Two skeptics, Dr. Daniel Horn and Dr. E. Cuyler Hammond of the American Cancer Society, both cigarette smokers themselves, began their own study of 187,766 middle-aged male smokers. By the time they were halfway through analyzing the results, both had stopped smoking. Published in 1954, their study demonstrated that lung cancer and heart disease went hand in hand with cigarette consumption.

Much of what we know about cancer comes from studies of the workplace. To mark the two-hundredth anniversary of Pott's discovery of occupational cancer, the New York Academy of Sciences held a symposium in 1975 on occupational carcinogensis. The keynote speaker, Dr. Jospeh K. Wagoner, reported that thousands of coke-oven workers in the steel industry are inhaling substances of the same class that caused scrotal cancer in Pott's chimney sweeps and, "as a result, are dying of lung cancer at a rate 10 times that of other steel workers." Thousands of uranium miners were still working, as of 1971, in environments where radiation dangers were "of such magnitude as to triple their prospects of dying from lung cancer." Eighty years after German surgeon Ludwig Rehn discovered that German dye workers were getting bladder cancer from aromatic amines "thousands of American workers were still literally sloshing in them. . . . Indeed as recently as 1973, 50 percent of the former employees at one benzidine plant in the United States were reported to have developed bladder cancer." And in 1975, "130 years after the observation of scrotal cancer in copper smelters exposed to inorganic arsenic, fully 1.5 million U.S. workers are inhaling the very same substance, and many occupational groups exposed to inorganic arsenic are known to be dying of lung and lumphatic cancers at two to eight times the national average." Wagoner noted that "children living near copper smelters have unusually elevated levels of arsenic in their urine and hair"—which means that carcinogens can spread from the workplace to the general populace.

There is no clearer example than than of asbestos. In the 1960s, Dr. Irving J. Selikoff of the Mount Sinai School of Medicine in New York found that exposure to asbestos caused the disastrous cancer rate later experienced by employees, during the 1940s and early 1950s, who worked for the Union Asbestos and Rubber Company plant in Paterson, New Jersey. Additional studies linked asbestos fibers to cancers diagnosed in persons living near asbestos factories and in members of the workers' families who were exposed to fibers in the clothes worn home. According to Wagoner, "virtually 100 percent of all urban dwellers coming to autopsy show the presence of asbestos in lung tissue."

Studies of migrants have also helped scientists document cancer's environmental origins. In 1968 William Haenszel of the National Cancer Institute reported that within two generations after migrating to the United States, Japanese immigrants suffered a fourfold increase in cancer of the rectum, a rare cancer in Japan, and women acquired a breast cancer rate almost as high as that of American women. At the same time, the normally high incidence of stomach cancer found among native Japanese declined to levels comparable to those of white Americans. The evidence implicates the environment (in this case diet): genetic change is simply not rapid enough to account for these reversals in cancer patterns.

No Relief Map

U.S. cancer mortality rates vary not only by the victim's occupation and ethnic background but by geography as well. Some regions have much higher cancer rates for specific body sites than do others, a fact made compellingly evident in 1975 when the National Cancer Institute (NCI) published the _Atlas of Cancer Mortality for U.S. Counties: 1950-1960_, which depicted geographical variation in cancer death rates among whites throughout the country.

As Dr. Robert Hoover, an author of the _Atlas_, has written, "For various cancers, the maps reveal a surprising number of clusters or hot spots." In the Northeast, cancers of the colon and rectum—believed to be related to diet and other environmental factors—were present at above-average rates in both men and women. The same held true for men and women in the Great Lakes region. By comparison, cancers of the colon and rectum were low in the southern and central U.S. The incidence of breast cancer followed similar geographical patterns, suggesting that whatever causes breast cancer may also cause cancer of the colon and rectum. Men in the Northeast had high rates for cancers of the bladder, esophagus, larynx, mouth, and throat, indicating the influence of occupational factors. Thirteen Louisiana counties were in the top 1 percent nationally for male lung cancer deaths. So were seven other counties along the Gulf Coast and Atlantic Coast from northern Florida to Charleston, South Carolina.

Other patterns revealed scattered high rates for leukemia in men in the central part of the country from Texas to Minnesota. The clustering for women was similar. Eastern New England had elevated rates of Hodgkin's disease for both sexes. Among women, Hodgkin's disease caused excessive mortalities in Minnesota and the Dakotas, whereas among men mortality was high in parts of Kansas, Nebraska, and South Dakota. Female bone cancer showed "a prominent pattern of excess mortality" stretching from Oklahoma eastward through the South into Appalachia. The bone cancer pattern for men was less pronounced, but scattered high rates occurred in Pennsylvania, West Virginia, Virginia, Kentucky, Louisiana, and Kansas.

Drs. Robert Hoover and Joseph F. Fraumeni, Jr., two of the authors of the *Atlas*, carried geographical analysis of cancer mortality a step further by studying 139 counties where the chemical industry is most highly concentrated. They found excess rates for bladder, lung, liver, and certain other cancers among males in those counties. "Of particular note," they said "are the elevated rates of (1) bladder cancer in counties manufacturing cosmetics, industrial gases, and soaps and detergents; (2) lung cancer in counties producing pharmaceutical preparations, soaps and detergents, paints, inorganic pigments, and synthetic rubber; and (3) liver cancer in counties manufacturing cosmetics, soaps and detergents, and printing inks."

Epicemiological studies such as these deal with mortalities from cancers initiated years ago. But what about the future? Since World War II, the chemical industry has undergone a tremendous boom led by petrochemical production, which has increased by more than 2,000 percent since 1945. Within the last decade, U.S. production of synthetic organic chemicals alone has increased 255 percent. More than two million chemicals are known, nearly thirty thousand are in use, and about five hundred new chemicals are put into use each year in this country. Next to nothing is known about the hazards these chemicals might pose because little testing has been done. Most of them may be harmless, but some may be carcinogenic, mutagenic (capable of causing genetic change), teratogenic (capable of causing birth defects), or acutely poisonous.

Paying Later

By polluting the environment, we may have locked ourselves into a cancer growth curve that could in five, ten, or twenty years make us look back upon the present as the good old days. Many of the chemicals found in commodities brought into production since 1940 (and their by-products) are carcinogenic. Although production does not reflect human exposure, it is a good indicator in light of our almost complete failure to regulate the use, discharge, and disposal of these chemicals in the environment. Exposure to these carcinogens may well cause an increase in the national cancer rate in the near future in much the same way that cigarette smoking did in the 1950s and 1960s. As Dr. Bruce Ames of the President's National Cancer Advisory Board recently said: "We haven't seen the effects in terms of carcinogenicity of the modern chemical world. That is going to hit us in the 1980s because of the 20- to 25-year lag period. We'll pay something for it. But whether that's relatively small or relatively large, no one now knows."

Many chemical manufacturers and vendors naturally take issue with not only Dr. Ames' contention that we will "pay later" for our past use of chemicals but also with the notion that cancer incidence rates are increasing. Some argue that if lung cancer incidence rates are subtracted from total cancer incidence rates, then overall cancer rates are in fact declining. Such an argument is both misleading and demonstrably incorrect. The rationale for discounting lung cancer rates is that lung cancer incidence reflects the impact of smoking, not exposure to synthetic chemicals. Although smoking clearly is a causative agent in many cases of lung cancer, it is by no means the sole factor: air pollution and various other factors are also believed to play a significant role. In any case, National Cancer Institute studies show that overall cancer incidence rates for this period—*including or excluding* lung cancer rates—have increased.

Signs of trouble can easily be detected in fish and wildlife, which can serve to sound environmental alarms. Alarm bells have been ringing since 1962, when Rachel Carson roused the public to the menace of pesticides with the publication of *Silent Spring*. Still, in some ways environmental conditions are even worse than Rachel Carson would have supposed. According to the Smithsonian Institution, tumors have become more prevalent in fish as waters have become more polluted. Even fish that look normal can be contaminated with chemicals. In September 1976, after New York State prohibited anglers from possessing coho salmon, Chinook salmon, smallmouth bass, and four other species of fish from Lake Ontario because these fish were contaminated by an insecticide called mirex, the National Water Quality Laboratory prepared a list of chlorinated organic chemicals detected in a single fish, a herring identified as "Lake Ontario alewife sample number NWQL-72416." Besides mirex (a carcinogen), the herring contained detectable quantities of trichlorobenzene, heptachlorostyrene, octachlorostyrene, pentachloroaniline, tetrachloronaphthalene, and eleven homologues of polychlorinated biphenyls (PCBs). Several of these chemicals are carcinogenic, and had the herring also been tested for polynuclear aromatic hydrocarbons, the list of compounds—and carcinogens—found might have doubled.

Although the number of synthetic chemicals in the herring seems overwhelming, the bodies of American people are not much less chemically contaminated. More than a dozen toxic or carcinogenic chemicals have thus far been detected in the fatty tissues of Americans.

Who Cares?

Why should this be? Has government failed to protect both the environment and citizens from a flood of hazardous substances, including carcinogens? Even federal legislation designed to protect citizen health and the environment has not been implemented swiftly or thoroughly enough by federal agencies. Too often promulgation and enforcement of all-important regulations come late, and only in reaction to public pressure. Programs have foundered because they lack direction, and because federal agencies too often yield to pressure from those companies most directly affected by proposed regulations. Moreover, the current governmental structure fragments responsibility among agencies and divisions so that action on one front to protect the public health may or may not be supported by commensurate action on another. There is, in sum, no unified federal approach to the control of carcinogens.

At least a half-dozen federal agencies specifically deal with cancer. First and foremost of these is the National Cancer Institute (NCI). Founded in 1937, the NCI is one of the components of the National Institutes of Health. In 1971, with the passage of the National Cancer Act, the NCI became a major research entity unto itself, with the director reporting directly to the White House. The NCI also began to receive massive infusions of money. But even as spending increased, so did the annual age-adjusted cancer death rate.

Like the NCI the National Institute for Occupational Safety and Health (NIOSH) is a research institute in the National Institutes of Health within the Department of Health, Education, and Welfare (HEW). Established by Congress in 1970, NIOSH develops standards to safeguard the health and safety of workers. So far, NIOSH has done some excellent work, though it has been underbudgeted and understaffed.

NIOSH forwards its recommendations to the Occupational Safety and Health Administration (OSHA), a regulatory agency in the Department of Labor. Responsible for the health and safety of some 60 million workers, OSHA came into existence along with NIOSH in 1970. The legislation that created it sailed through Congress with the support of both labor and the White House, but OSHA has not lived up to its original promise. Preoccupied with such trivial issues as the shape of toilet seats and the space between rungs on ladders, it has been slow to respond to major hazards.

Help may be on the way, though. At present, OSHA is under forceful leadership aimed at altering OSHA's policies. The agency has proposed a sweeping change in the regulation of carcinogens in the workplace, and in 1978 it eliminated some 1,100 trivial regulations for workplace safety.

The Food and Drug Administration (FDA) within HEW is supposed to protect the public against unsafe and impure foods, drugs, cosmetics, and medical devices. In 1958 Congress passed the Food Additives Amendment to the Food, Drug and Cosmetic Act; it includes the so-called Delaney Clause, which prohibits the intentional addition of a carcinogen to human food. The clause also states that no food additive shall be deemed safe "if it is found to induce cancer when ingested by man or animal" or, if the FDA deems appropriate, when taken into the system by means other than ingestion. In 1960 Congress inserted a similar clause into the Color Additives Amendments. But only on rare occasions has the FDA invoked the Delaney Clause to ban an additive in food. The FDA can also set "tolerance levels" for hazardous substances inadvertently added to human food and shipped in interstate commerce, and it can seize foods that exceed the tolerance level. But only rarely has it invoked its power to ban a food additive.

The Environmental Protection Agency (EPA) was established as an independent regulatory agency in 1970 to "serve as the public advocate for a liveable environment." The EPA administers a number of important laws, among them the Clean Air Act of 1970 and the Toxic Substances Control Act of 1976, but its record in carrying out these laws has been deficient at best, partly because the agency is so disorganized. Evaluating the agency in 1976, the National Research Council of the National Academy of Sciences contended that EPA needed more scientists with experience in environmental problems, better coordination of efforts to monitor water and air pollution, and more autonomy from the industries it regulates.

The Consumer Product Safety Commission (CPSC), established as an independent federal regulatory agency in 1972, has the authority to set safety standards to reduce unreasonable risk of injury to consumers from products. In fact, CPSC can ban products it finds hazardous. So far, however, it has an appalling record. It has drawn fire from consumer groups and government alike.

No single example is sufficient to create a true understanding of the ineffectiveness of past governmental action to protect citizens from environmental carcinogens. But preventing cancer involves more than changes in governmental policies. It involves changes in attitudes and, even more immediately, changes in individual lifestyles—none of which will happen until the public fully understands that cancer is an environmental problem, not a fumble of fate, and can be prevented if treated as if it were preventable. ❀

At War with Nature: Military Activities and the Environment

Arthur Westing

The era of bounty and growth is giving way to an era of overextension and reckoning. Humanity is utilizing all of the world's major renewable natural resources—agricultural soils, forest trees, range grasses, and ocean fishes—at rates exceeding their natural abilities to renew themselves. It is consuming fossil fuels and other minerals at ever increasing rates, bringing these non-renewable resources ever nearer to exhaustion. It is introducing pollutants into the environment at levels increasingly beyond the point at which they can dissipate and decompose to insignificance, among them radioactive isotopes from weapon-testing and carbon dioxide from the burning of fossil fuels. It is being forced by fossil fuel shortages to rely (while safe alternatives are developed) ever more heavily upon nuclear fuels that are inexorably coupled with a proliferation of nuclear weapons and other intractable problems. It is becoming poorer by the day (that is to say, despite continued advances in science and technology, the worldwide average standard of living countinues to decline). And its ability to cope with overpopulation and other root causes of this multifaceted dilemma is not improving.

In this light, continuing to devote a substantial fraction of the annual global product to military preparations and to war is tragically *self*-defeating. War not only diverts our energies from civil pursuits and consumes precious raw materials, but it disrupts the ecology of the theaters of operation as well. Even apart from nuclear bombs and other weapons of mass destruction, nominally conventional means of attack can devastate the local ecology. That is one of the lessons of Viet Nam.

The ecological disruptions of war take a variety of repulsive shapes. To begin, warfare disrupts the environment if it exerts a substantial impact on the civil populace. Thus, if a significant fraction of the beleaguered people are killed, displaced, denied their source of food for extended periods, or deprived of homes or means of livelihood, these losses must be considered forms of environmental damage. Second a war disrupts the eco-system directly and physically through its impacts on the land, the vegetation, the water, and the wildlife. Such disruption can be obvious or it can have only a subtle, delayed, or marginal effect on human society.

One measure of the extent of environmental disruption that has been brought about by human society is the increased rate of plant and animal extinctions. The extinction of existing species and the evolution of new species of biota are, of course, natural phenomena. They have always and will continue to occur. For example, the natural turnover rate for avian species—of which approximately 8,600 exist—appears to be on the order of one every 230 years, and that for mammalian species —of which approximately 4,200 exist—appears to be on the order of one every 140 years. On the other hand, between 1600 and the mid-1960s an estimated 94 species of birds and 36 species of mammals have suffered extinction, most at the hand of man. Moreover, the rate is accelerating, and today an estimated 200 or so species of birds and 100 or so of mammals are known to be threatened with extinction.

Some species have been hunted to extinction, others eliminated because they were considered pests. Still others have disappeared because predator or competing species have been introduced by man, either advertently or inadvertently. A few extinctions can be traced to environmental pollutants. But in the great majority of instances, competition between man and the other species for space—the space humanity needs to live and to grow food and industrial crops—is at cause. It is nothing less than tragic that warfare exacerabates this strain on space.

Of particular concern is the disruption of agricultural and wildlands by war, and thus of the ecosystems (and micro-climates) of these regions. The weapons and other means of war available to today's armed forces are increasingly capable of disrupting these natural and semi-natural habitats. Indeed, consider the impact on nature of the "progression" from arrow and sword to firebomb and defoliant.

Chief among the factors that contribute to the increasing military violence against nature are the growing technical and logistical abilities of armed forces to devastate large areas on a sustained basis. Also against nature is a simple lack of restraint. Today armies can devastate the ecology of large areas with nuclear weapons, as well as with chemical agents or biological organisms. Soon, moreover, it may be possible to accomplish the same with so-called geophysical weapons. But one need not turn to unconventional or fanciful weapons for such a purpose.

Of immediate importance, the conventional high-explosive firepower of armed forces has also continued to increase dramatically over the years. By way of example, the reported weight of the salvo that one of the Soviet Union's army divisions can deliver against an enemy increased exponentially between 1923 and 1968.

It is also instructive in this regard to compare U.S. actions during its three most recent wars: World War II, the Korean War, and the Viet Nam War. U.S. battle intensity as measured in terms of the monthly number of U.S. combat fatalities dropped progressively from each of these wars to the next, in the ratio of 15:2:1, respectively. Combat fatalities among the forces opposed to the U.S. followed a remarkably similar trend, also exhibiting a ratio of 15:2:1. Among other things, these parallel ratios suggest that relative U.S. combat capability has not improved, if the proportion of killed enemy soldiers to killed U.S. soldiers is any measure. The three wars can also be compared from the standpoint of the resulting numbers of total fatalities experienced by the nations pitted against the U.S. The Axis nations of World War II experienced an overall fatality rate (military plus civil) of 5 percent, North Korea one of about 6 percent, and the four Indochinese nations together one of perhaps 4 percent.

Remarkably enough in the light of these several comparisons, total U.S. munition expenditures during the Viet Nam War exceeded those of the prior two wars combined. In terms of the respective U.S. areas of action involved in these three wars, U.S. munition expenditures were in the approximate ratio of 1:5:7. Alternatively, U.S. munition expenditures per enemy soldier killed were in the even more startling ratio of 1:6:18. It would be risky to draw too many conclusions from these summary data. These three wars differed widely not only in their objectives and in the matching of their adversaries, but also in their durations, the nature of their theaters, and other significant features. For example, the World War II figures include the fatalities of two rather different theaters and types of war, the European theater (accounting for perhaps 80 percent of the total U.S. munition expenditures) and the Pacific (accounting for the remaining 20 percent). In turn, the Indochina figures are confounded by lumping South Viet Nam (accounting for 71 percent of the total U.S. munition expenditures for that war) with the rest of the region.

Nevertheless, the only conclusion to be drawn is that the increase in U.S. munition expenditures without a concomitant increase in the level of enemy fatalities reflects the changing nature of the target against which these munitions were directed. In other words, these data suggest a changing military strategy that calls for higher munition expenditures against larger and more ill-defined target areas, and thus for a higher level of environmental damage. The validity of such a surmise is, in fact, substantiated by available information.

The several summary volumes of the U.S. Strategic Bombing Survey of World War II suggest the major Allied air effort during that war was directed against clearly defined military targets on the one hand, and against urban and industrial targets on the other. Specifically, only 31 percent of the World War II air effort was in the form of area bombings, most of which were directed at urban areas.

During the Korean conflict, 70 percent of the U.S. Air Force, almost 100 percent of the U.S. Navy, and 60 percent of the U.S. Marine Corps munition expenditures were directed against ill-defined (usually rural) area targets. A weighted average of these air data comes out to be 70 percent. Although no comparable ground (artillery) data appear to be available for the Korean War, 70 percent of the sea munitions were expended for inland interdiction purposes.

During the Viet Nam War, the proportion of ill-defined area targets rose once again, and almost all the assaults were on rural lands. That means that most of the air and artillery expenditures by the U.S. in Indochina were for purposes of interdiction or harassment. The overwhelming majority of the targets were nebulously described in the military literature as "suspected enemy activity," and a considerable fraction of the strikes were fires aimed at unseen targets. Overall, at least 85 percent of the profligate U.S. munition expenditures in Indochina were spent on this anti-environmental activity.

Along with money better spent on almost anything else, both renewable and non-renewable natural resources are consumed wholesale in war. Even during peacetime maintaining a military posture consumes large quantities of such raw materials. A fact less widely appreciated is that these military uses serve to divert raw materials not only from the civil sector of society to the military one, but also from the poor nations to the rich ones. Additionally, the military use of raw materials draws on stocks that could otherwise be reserved for future generations. Together, these diversions of resources smack of waste and selfishness whose consequences are so great as to call the very notion of a "just war" into question.

But the matter need not be consigned to philosophy, there to be ignored while the business of the world goes on. The extraction or exploitation of raw materials for military paraphernalia and their manufacture into finished products, for example, each adds to the air and water pollution of the world. These effects are measurable and controllable. The economics of warfare can also be calculated: about 6 percent of the combined gross national products of the world's nations is now devoted to military expenditure, so in one sense roughly 6 percent of the world's environmental pollution could be attributed to the military sector of the global economy. On the other hand, were these expenditures not being devoted to military affairs, they presumably would be shifted in large measure to the civil sector of the economy. As a case in point, a recent United Nations study indicates that about 3.5 percent of the annual global consumption of a group of ten major metals—aluminum, chromium, copper, iron, lead, manganese, molybdenum, nickel, tin, and zinc—is devoted to U.S. military purposes. A complete U.S. military moratorium might therefore be expected to reduce the annual global expenditures of these nonrenewable resources by that amount. However, it was further calculated that the U.S. civil economy would as a result of such a cessation expand to account for about 2.6 percent more of global consumption, so the net saving would be only about 0.9 percent.

Worldwide, military expenditures are borne by 135 or more nations; but the 27 richest nations account for 75 percent of the current total, just six nations contribute at least 2 percent each to that total, and only two dominate the scene. Between 1966 and 1975, the world's military expenditures were distributed as follows: the U.S., 31 percent; the USSR, 31 percent; China, 9 percent; West Germany, 4 percent; France, 3 percent; the United Kingdom, 3 percent; and the remaining 153 nations, 20 percent. The combined world military expenditures have remained essentially constant during this past decade on a per capita basis; they have even been declining (at the compound growth rate of −2.67 percent per year) in relation to the sum of the world's gross national products. Nevertheless, in absolute terms, total world military expenditures have been increasing during this past decade at the compound growth rate of 1.68 percent per year, which means they would at this rate double in a little over four decades.

The extravagant wartime use of raw materials has a devasting cyclical effect. Global deficiencies of raw materials, as well as their uneven distribution throughout the world, can lead to unlikely—and thus unstable—alliances, to national rivalries, and, of course, to more war. Raw-material deficiencies become intolerable in part because it takes immense amounts of material and munitions to equip and maintain an army in the field and in part because the raw-material requirements of today's technologically sophisticated weaponry are exacting and can devastate stocks of exotic substances. Throughout history wars have been fought to gain control over one natural resource or another, but never before have so many of them been consumed in the fight itself.

One of the simplest though most fundamental of all environmental resources is the land itself, a commodity that in effect keeps shrinking as the world's population keeps rising. A felt need for space has often been used as one of the justifications for going to war. The need for added *Lebensraum* was one of the major reasons Germany gave for waging World War II. Overpopulation, another way of perceiving the problem, was also at the root of the El Salvador-Honduran War of 1969.

The Lorraine region just south of Luxembourg, one of the rare iron-rich regions of Europe, provides a fine example of the military significance of raw materials. A part of France beginning in 1766, Lorraine was ceded to Germany as one outcome of the Franco-Prussian War of 1870–1871. It reverted to France as a result of World War I, but was reacquired by Germany early in World War II, only to be re-annexed by France at the end of that war, to whom it has since belonged.

Oil is another of the unequally distributed mineral resources of potentially enormous military significance. Oil can pose an especially difficult problem for those nations that must depend completely or largely upon foreign supplies. For example, Germany, which has virtually no oil deposits of its own, was toward the end of World War II substantially hampered in its military efforts by a shortage of oil — hence the half-truth that the Battle of the Bulge was lost because of gasoline shortages. The U.S., which is now about 65 percent self-sufficient in oil, has routinely been using about 7 percent of its total annual consumption for military purposes.

The U.S. has ample domestic supplies of most of the raw materials it uses for military purposes, but by no means all. Some argue plausibly enough that the foreign policy of the U.S. is governed to a considerable extent by its mineral insufficiencies, perhaps more so than by any political philosophy. For example, U.S. relations with South Africa are tempered by its need for chromium, a metal in which the U.S. is only 9 percent self-sufficient, and the newly blossoming friendship between the U.S. and Burundi may be based on the recently discovered deposits in Burundi of nickel, another metal that the U.S. must import.

In any event, some future wars will probably stem from the unequal distribution of the world's natural resources. Most likely, the frequency of such wars will decrease to the extent that lengthy wars of attrition with their voracious appetite for raw materials will give way to more quickly consummated conflicts. Conversely, they will increase to the extent that local and overall shortages of the world's natural resources will be exacerbated by population increases, rising expectations regarding standards of living, and pollution-related losses. Indeed, one Pentagon official recently predicted that "Within the next decade what has been called 'the environment' holds promise of emerging as the most troublesome of all international irritants. Complex enough in a physical sense, the issue grows even more intricate on the political plane through its powerful association with health and survival. National interests that may hitherto have been difficult to define shed their turbidity under an onslaught of new and immediate concerns—the depletion of vital resources, the threats to life-support systems, and the question of continued growth. In this charged atmosphere, options become limited. The policies flowing from them tend to channel nations in directions that make strife, conflict, and collisions all but unavoidable."

It is axiomatic that warfare is detrimental to the environment. Military disruption of the environment during hostilities is especially pernicious because it spills over both the spatial and temporal boundaries of the attack; many of its ramifications are unpredictable, and there is no way to discriminate between combatants and non-combatants in territorial assaults. It is also almost axiomatic that military disruption of the environment is exceedingly difficult to limit or control by legal instruments. Most hostile and many non-hostile military actions result in some level of environmental disturbance, whether intended or not, and establishing the magnitude of disruption is perhaps beyond the power of law. Arguably, then, the most urgently required—and also the most straightforward—arms-control measures from an environmental standpoint are the absolute prohibition of nuclear weapons and the demilitarization and conversion to protected status of ecologically important regions. Determining which regions qualify for such special status will not, of course, be easy. But a start would be to accord such status to those regions that (1) contribute substantially to the global balance of nature, (2) contain intrinsically fragile ecosystems, (3) support unique habitats, or (4) provide the habitat for species in danger of extinction. Beyond these two measures—one absolute and the other a matter of biological interpretation—any military weapon or technique capable of devastating a wide area should be proscribed.

Any necessary restraints on military activity will have to find their basis in ecological, moral, or ethical considerations, each presumably expressed in the form of international legal sanctions. Failing that, it can be hoped at least that consideration for the natural ecology of the different habitats and of the global environment as a whole will deter armed forces from pursuing their more blatant anti-ecological strategies and tactics. Indeed, the immediate integrity of the global ecology will have to depend on such unilateral restraints.

Ecological considerations have until now played little part in civil and military affairs. And to the extent that they intruded upon decision-making processes, they have been subordinated to the belief that humankind dominates the natural global hierarchy. The validity of human supremacy has, however, never been put to the proper test. To date, even the most severe anthropogenic perturbations of the global ecosystem have been modest and transitory compared to what may lie in wait if our intervention continues. Since we have now acquired the capacity to do much more than we could before to upset nature, the world's first true 'eco-disaster' could be the price of our power. However, it is also possible that humankind—with its nuclear weapons and other modern military capabilities—will at last put an end to war. At worst, it will do so by performing some hostile environmental manipulation that leads to a Carthaginian peace. It remains to be seen whether we come to our senses in time to find another way. 🌱

The New Polluter: Giant Sewage-Treatment Plants

Wesley Marx

On September 13, 1979, a shrimp fisherman called California authorities to report that the San Francisco Bay waters near San Jose had turned black and that "everything was dying." By day's end, authorities knew they faced one of the nation's largest sewage spills, and that it had begun eight days before.

Before the giant treatment plant serving one of the fastest growing areas in California have been restored to normal operation (after 38 days), it discharged billions of gallons of marginally treated sewage liberally laced with ammonia, bacteria, and floating matter. The dark brown waters gushed into a part of the Bay that has the weakest circulation. Officials closed 700 acres of waters to fishing, swimming and waterfowl hunting. The sewage shock load depressed oxygen levels and wiped out a commercial shrimp fishery that supplies bait. State fish and game officials predict that the stricken area will take years to recover.

Today, the disaster brings into focus a growing concern over the strategy behind the nation's biggest public works program, the multi-billion dollar effort to clean up water.

The San Jose spill was not triggered by a crude, aging system. It came from the modern $150-million San Jose-Santa Clara Water Pollution Control Plant, with its extensive system of treatment tanks, filter equipment, and water quality laboratory—from the sort of plant the Environmental Protection Agency (EPA) has been pushing in its construction grant program to "regionalize" and upgrade treatment. EPA has already invested some $20 billion in 10,000 projects across the country and expects to spend $20 billion more over the next five years.

Under regionalization, smaller, supposedly inefficient treatment plants are consolidated into one central or super plant facility to achieve that nirvana of public administrators, "economies of scale." Larger plants are supposed to be more efficient, better equipped, and better staffed. EPA exercises formidable power to encourage communities to form regional sewage authorities, including federal funding of 75 percent of plant construction and sanctions against communities that fail to see the wisdom of regionalization.

With its vast scale, impact, and federal financial incentives, the sewage plant program was to the 1970s much as the highway program was to the 1950s and mammoth water projects were to earlier decades. And, as happened with these earlier public works, the question is now arising: are the vast scale, complexity and single-purpose nature of the new plants proving far more unwieldy, costly, and troublesome than smaller locally adapted systems might be?

The San Jose spill was triggered by a breakdown in the biological treatment process used to reduce organic material in the sewage. Such biological processes, which depend on bacteria that can be killed by sewage-flow surges or toxic agents, require careful operation and maintenance (O & M in the trade). In the wake of the spill, the city of San Jose discovered the need for a new staff member—a sewage-plant training instructor—and for engineers to study the plant's reliability. What happened to the purported regionalization benefit of a better-trained and qualified staff?

While EPA funds much of the plant construction, local jurisdictions must assume costs of O & M. These costs can trigger substantial local tax increases—so substantial that beleaguered plant superintendents can find training instructors expendable until a plant "upset" occurs. As an EPA Administrator, Douglas Costle, has observed, O & M "costs are rising rapidly due to inflationary trends in the cost of manpower, energy and chemicals, and the increasing complexity of the plants themselves."

Does regionalization result in federally funded plants that local communities are unprepared or unqualified to operate? EPA's Costle conceded to a Congressional subcommittee that "one-half of the inspected plants . . . failed to meet their original design standards and about 25 percent have severe or chronic operation and maintenance problems."

As the San Jose spill dramatized, one large spill from a central plant can thus match, if not exceed, pollution damage from a series of the smaller, supposedly inefficient plants. Potential single-point shock loads from central plants now haunt Chesapeake Bay, Puget Sound, the Great Lakes, and other water bodies caught up in the drive for regionalization.

The San Jose plant, according to California Regional Water Quality Control Board engineer Harold Singer, had no emergency storage facility to divert the toxic sewage flow during the breakdown. It was not even prepared to properly notify authorities of the spill.

The spill began eight days before the shrimp fisherman called it to official attention. What happened to the official pollution-monitoring system? In language strikingly similar to that used by plant operators of the Three Mile Island nuclear plant during its "upset," San Jose plant officials explained that they thought the problem was only "temporary" and "under control." Plant officials felt the main problem was not so much late notification or spill damage as media "exaggeration" of the spill.

Such tardy notification can deprive health officials of the opportunity to discern immediately potential health threats and prevent people from harvesting potentially toxic marine life. California fish and game official Mike Rugg placed some fathead minnows in a water sample from the stricken San Francisco Bay area. All the minnows died within six to forty minutes.

Civil and criminal sanctions, including fines of up to $25,000 a day, can be imposed for discharge violations and for failure by plant operators to report such violations. The former superintendent for the Little Rock, Ark., treatment plant received a suspended prison sentence in 1978 for submitting falsified reports on plant performance to EPA. The former superintendent of the New Albany, Indiana, Wastewater Treatment Plant was fined $1,500 for filing false discharge-compliance reports. Will stepped-up court action insure more responsible operation of the complex central plants? Perhaps. However, false reporting and failure to report violations reflect tremendous pressures on plant superintendents caught between the technical demands of the large plants and the limits of O & M funds.

The economic bind looming for the regional plants can be expected to raise pressures to relax water quality standards or extend compliance schedules. Part of the reason for that bind, meanwhile, is the fact that while the new plants look modern, they are actually still primitive in approach. They still treat sewage as a waste rather than as a potential resource.

One bright note in sewage treatment has been the success of projects in wastewater reclamation, irrigating dairy pastures, vineyards, football fields, public parks, golf courses, forests, cemetaries, and orchards. Reclaimed water sales can help defray O & M costs. Congress, in the Clean Water Act amendments of 1977, increased funding incentives for reclamation projects.

Can the large central plants shift from disposal to reclamation? Unfortunately, being sited downhill or downgrade to take advantage of gravity sewage feed, they must pump reclaimed water uphill to users, thus raising energy costs. Why not decentralize and locate smaller plants uphill? This alternative is often considered "impractical" because funding has already been committed to the central plant and its massive trunk sewer system. (One large regional authority, the Sanitation Districts of Los Angeles County, has built water reclamation plants in its upper service area.)

Ironically, many innovative advances in water reclamation have been developed by those small, "inefficient" plants that manage to avoid the taxing embrace of the regional sewage authorities. Arcata, in northern California, has wastewater treatment lagoons that nurture salmon and trout smolts (juveniles) to stock public waters. A plant in Oklahoma City uses catfish to control plant growth in wastewater treatment lagoons. The city of Santa Clara, which is not too far from the San Jose plant, is involved in a demonstration project for a low-cost wastewater reclamation system that would operate on-site, where the sewage is generated, such as a housing tract or farm.

Materials Conservation — The Road to Recovery

Richard Munson

While experts—from the Club of Rome to the National Commission on Supplies and Shortages—disagree about the size of the world's stock of resources, all agree that materials are becoming increasingly expensive. As companies are forced to mine and process less rich grades of ore, they will require more energy and more expensive technological methods.

The United States's current troubles with energy could foretell shortages and allocation problems with other resources, difficulties one forward-looking Interior Department official has said will make the energy crises look like "Sunday School picnics." Yet, despite the sky-rocketing prices and the vulnerability of oil supplies, little notice is being paid to those researchers who now warn that the United States will soon experience severe shortages of several essential nonfuel minerals.

Is the nation's dependence on foreign energy and mineral resources growing? According to Dr. V.E. McKelvey, director of the U.S. Geological Survey, "the U.S. now imports, by value, about 15 percent of its total nonfuel mineral supply. But this general statistic obscures the fact that the United States is now dependent on foreign sources for more than half its supply of 20 important minerals, a number of which are critical to some of our basic industries." According to the August 1979 report of the Federal Nonfuel Minerals Policy Review Board, "the future supplies of several important imported minerals critical to the United States and its allies are becoming less secure."

This level of dependence is now causing balance-of-payments problems. In 1978, the U.S. spent $8 billion more for imports of non-fuel minerals than for exports.

While few Americans have forgotten the trouble and expense of obtaining oil and gasoline during the summer of 1979, few realize that the threat of a new embargo of minerals is real. Because the OPEC oil cartel has been so richly successful, industrial nations now fear that other resource-rich nations may follow the example OPEC set. Although skeptical of the power of such actions, *Fortune* magazine admits that three commodities—bauxite, chromium, and manganese—lend themselves to possible "cartelization." Indeed, the eleven members of the International Bauxite Association control 75 percent of world production—a higher fraction than that of world oil production controlled by the Organization of Petroleum Exporting Countries (OPEC). In 1974 Jamaica and Australia, the leading bauxite producers, increased production taxes on U.S. mining companies sevenfold, raising the cost of bauxite from approximately $10 to $25 per ton.

Other international political considerations have also proved capable of disrupting the supply and increasing the cost of imported resources. During 1974 and 1975 a dozen third-world countries nationalized their copper, bauxite, tin, and iron mines. Venezuela, for example, took over several areas that annually supply 15 million tons of iron ore (30 percent of U.S. iron ore imports). According to the U.S. Bureau of Mines, the trend toward nationalization continues. For example, Quebec is now threatening to nationalize its asbestos mines.

Besides the instability of supplies, materials prices will continue to reflect rising energy prices. Using more energy to process less rich grades of ore will exact additional environmental costs. At some point (varying for each mineral), rising expenses will make mining economically infeasible and, for practical purposes, the resources will be exhausted. The traditional method of stockpiling essential materials is only a short-term solution. Over the long term, such disruptions can be avoided only if society accepts substitutes, if technological advances somehow make mining and refining less expensive, or if materials are recycled and conserved.

The Debate

The question of technological capabilities, meanwhile, is a matter of intense debate. Basically, the argument is between those who feel we have (or will develop) technological capabilities to cope with materials supply problems, and those who object to what they call the "blind" faith in technology's ability to solve or circumvent such problems.

Technological development throughout most of this century has been extraordinary. According to one Boston-based business consulting firm, "The addition over time of new reserves of virtually all material has kept up with the extraction rate because of improved mining and exploration technology." According to the master synthesizer, Kenneth

Boulding, who sees the problem in somewhat different terms, the race is between knowledge and population, and the outcome is both uncertain and difficult to predicate on recent history.

Among the less optimistic on this account was the National Academy of Sciences Committee on Mineral Resources and the Environment, which in 1975 concluded that technology can provide only limited solutions while requiring long lead times for implementation. The President's Council on Environmental Quality reached a similar conclusion a decade ago: "Despite spectacular recent discoveries, there are only a limited number of places left to search for most minerals. Geologists disagree about the prospect for finding large, new rich ore deposits. Reliance on such discoveries would seem unwise in the long run."

The evidence on energy conservation strongly supports the logic of materials conservation. After the 1974 energy crisis, for example, several studies showed that Americans waste much of the electricity, natural gas, and gasoline they use. According to the Energy Project of the Harvard Business School, the United States "could consume 30 to 40 percent less energy than it now does, and still enjoy the same or an even higher standard of living."

Waste of our nonfuel resources reflects the same pattern. About 70 percent of all metal produced is used just once and then discarded. The result is enough municipal solid waste to annually fill garbage trucks stretched three abreast from New York to Los Angeles. The cost is staggering: disposal of municipal garbage has become the second largest item in a city's budget, surpassed only by public schools.

The Potential

The potential for materials conservation is significant. According to Denis Hayes, formerly of the Worldwatch Institute, at least two-thirds of the material resources we now waste could be reused, and this approach would not involve important changes in our life styles. With products designed for durability and for ease of recycling, says Hayes, "the waste streams of the industrial world could be reduced to small trickles. And with an intelligent materials policy, the portion of our resources that is irretrievably dissipated could eventually be reduced to almost zero."

Government and industrial representatives in particular have become increasingly interested in large-scale recycling or resource recovery. This cyclical process involves high-technology systems that separate burnable and reusable wastes at a central plant. Unfortunately, the merits of most such systems tend to be exaggerated. Pyrolysis plants, in particular, have been plagued with malfunctions. Moreover, some city officials fear the central facilities are too expensive. And once built, the systems would require at least the same level of waste in order to maximize the return on the sunk investments. The need for waste could serve to discourage conservation.

Some environmentalists believe wastes should be recycled at community source-separation projects. Segregating garbage is the best way to recover wastepaper for recycling, since paper is frequently contaminated when mixed with other solid waste. It is also an attractive way to recycle glass, aluminum, organic wastes for composting, ferrous metals, and some plastics. At least 500 source-separation programs operated in the United States during 1979.

But more important than reusing garbage is another aspect of materials conservation—reducing wastes at their source, *before* they become a problem. Manufacturing more durable goods, reusing materials, and decreasing packaging are all forms of materials conservation that can curtail environmental damage as well as reduce the cost of disposal, mining, and recycling.

To conserve materials effectively, however, the United States and other countries must first re-evaluate those existing laws that encourage the consumption of virgin materials. Depletion allowances are the most offensive policies in this regard since they place secondary goods in uncompetitive market positions. The Treasury Department estimates that, mainly due to the depletion allowance, mineral industries are taxed only about 25 percent of their total net income, compared with 43 percent for other manufacturers. The timber industry receives an equivalent boon through the capital gains tax benefit, by which it is taxed on only 50 percent of its annual income. Originally intended to aid America's young mining companies, these subsidies now encourage the virgin-materials industries to increase production needlessly in order to increase income.

Besides eliminating all depletion allowances, some economists advocate adopting of a severance tax. Noting the uncertainties of the materials supply, Talbot Page of Resources for the Future thinks we should increase the cost of scarce resources so they will be preserved for future generations. Other economists believe that the producers of the nation's waste (rather than the taxpayers) should be charged for the costs of its collection and disposal. Fred Smith of EPA claims that such a "product charge" would encourage industries and consumers to purchase less wasteful products.

Other policies related to resource production and use also need to be reexamined. To the delight of conservationists, Interior Secretary Cecil Andrus wants to change the Mining Act of 1872, which allows private firms almost unrestricted mining on public lands. Moreover, some economists are becoming more critical of the Interstate Commerce Commission's rate policies, which allegedly discriminate against recycled goods in favor of virgin materials.

The best-known examples of materials conservation are returnable beverage containers. Although they dominated the market just ten years ago, returnables have now been almost eliminated by the bottling industry, which has centralized its facilities and adopted throwaways in order to increase profits. Environmentalists are fighting for a "return to returnables." They claim that a five-cent deposit on beverage containers would reduce roadside container litter by 60 to 70 percent; would save 500,000 tons of aluminum, 1.5 million tons of steel, and 5.2 million tons of glass each year; and would save the energy-equivalent of 45.6 million barrels of oil annually. Despite well-financed opposition from the bottling industry, deposit legislation has been approved in Oregon, Vermont, Michigan, and Maine.

Deposits have also been proposed for automobiles, tires, electrical machinery, and consumer durables. In Sweden, everyone who has purchased a car since 1976 has paid a $54 deposit to the government; when the car is returned to a certified scrapyard, the owner receives a refund of $65.

Even without government intervention, many industries are investigating materials conservation. Higher prices caused by shortages or increased mining-and processing-costs have already forced many packaging and container companies to reduce the amount of material used in packaging. The Campbell Soup Co., for example, recently redesigned and marketed a tinplate "drawn and ironed" can for its dog food line. The redesigned can uses 30 percent less material than the old package and the per can cost of manufacture has dropped by 36 percent. According to EPA, if the two-piece "drawn and ironed" can design were used for all canned foods, one million tons of steel and tinplate would be saved each year.

Some environmentalists and economists, however, do not believe that the pricing mechanism is sufficient to prompt Americans to conserve materials and protect the environment. They question whether the marketplace can adequately discourage producers and consumers from imposing social or environmental damage. Some favor a regulatory authority that would impose materials restrictions in advance of manufacture. This approach was taken by the Minnesota legislature in 1973 when it approved the nation's first packaging regulations and empowered the State Pollution Control Board to review all new packaging for its environmental impact. If the agency can show cause, it can temporarily prohibit the sale of wasteful packages within the state.

Easy Targets

Government, industry, and consumers can find the potential for materials conservation virtually wherever they look. If durable goods such as tires and household appliances are redesigned or repaired, the demands on the resource base and on solid-waste disposal mechanisms drop. Tires, for example, are being discarded at the rate of 250 million per year. If all tires were retreaded once, the demand for synthetic rubber would be cut by one-third, tire-disposal costs would be halved, and substantial energy savings would be realized.

Other targets are nondurable goods such as paper tissues, diapers, towels, paper plates, and cups. Many of these single-use disposable products were designed and marketed by industrialists motivated solely by profit. Reducing waste in the nondurable category often means simply returning to the durable, reusable counterparts such as cloth diapers, cloth napkins and towels, china plates and cups.

Thinking Ahead

Despite intense political opposition from those industries that benefit from producing materials in large volumes, materials conservation is beginning to receive increased public support. The Resource Conservation and Recovery Act of 1976, for example, allocates money for cities and states to develop solid-waste management plans that must include, for the first time, waste-reduction efforts. But if integrated planning is not quickly implemented, we can expect in the near future economic disruptions from materials shortages caused by international political developments, price increases, or technological problems. A long-term policy of materials conservation, meanwhile, will demand a fresh examination of those enterprises that concentrate exclusively on increasing sales as a means of increasing profit.

To avoid disruptions similar to those caused by energy shortages, those long-term policies must be developed soon. It's time we avoided, rather than reacted to crises. ☘

IV. ECO-LOGIC

Limits — Absolute and Flexible, Known and Unknown

Kenneth Boulding

The publication of the Club of Rome reports has drawn attention in a dramatic way to the problems that are likely to emerge in the twentieth and twenty-first centuries due to expanding population, the exhaustion of presently known resources, and increasing pollution. The models used by these reports in making their projections are not different in principle from those of celestial mechanics. They rely on a set of interrelated difference equations with constant parameters derived for the most part from past experience. The computer has enabled us to handle large numbers of these equations simultaneously, which would be difficult to do in pencil and paper mathematics, though not necessarily impossible. The computer "spaghetti," that is, a printout in the form of time charts, is a picture that is implied in the assumptions. It tells us what will happen if certain things go on much as they have been going on without change.

Overshoot Systems

The picture these models present is one of a system approaching certain limits on some fairly plausible assumptions. In most of the models it does not approach these limits gradually and gently, but has an "overshoot" followed by subsequent collapse. An overshoot is what happens when a system that is moving toward some sort of equilibrium gathers sufficient momentum on the way and shoots past the equilibrium point, then eventually is pulled toward the equilibrium point again, which it again overshoots, and so on, repeating this in a cyclical movement that is usually convergent to the equilibrium. The oscillations of a pendulum about its lowest point (which is the point of equilibrium) or the twang of a plucked string around its point of ulti-mate rest are good examples of systems of this kind. They are common in the physical world, much less common in the biological world, and by no means unknown though infrequent in social dynamics. In the biosphere the cyclical fluctuations of predator and predatee, which are observed in very simple systems, and the population overshoots of the lemmings, which lead apparently to mass suicide, are interesting examples. In human history there are examples of collapses of societies such as those of the Mayans around 900 A.D. and the Khmers in the 1300s that look in retrospect very much like overshoots. Whether any of the great extinctions that have occurred in the past represent over-shoot patterns, or whether they simply came from subtle changes in the climate or topography, that is, the physical environment to which we all need to be adaptable to survive, we do not really know, though physical environmental change is by far the most plausible hypothesis.

The Explosion of Science and the Closure of Earth

The critical question facing the human race as we look forward into the next century or two is whether we are indeed facing a catastrophic overshoot, whether we can go on expanding the human niche in the face of increasing population, or whether we can move beyond large-scale catastrophe to a high-level equilibrium at the ultimate niche of the human race.

The last 200 or 300 years have been quite unprecedented in the his-tory of the planet Earth. There has been an explosion of human know-ledge and a great expansion of the noosphere. Even 300 years ago the human race was still divided into relatively small groups, each knowing a good deal about its own locality, but very little about the earth as a whole, though this knowledge was growing rapidly. Today, the earth is almost completely mapped. This knowledge is enshrined in globes and atlases in almost every schoolroom of the world. We are now going out into the solar system and we know the topography of the moon and Mars. Even 200 years ago we did not know the structure of physical matter, the elements that are its building blocks. We knew very little about the forms of energy. The first electric power station was built less than 100 years ago. The great period of the application of science to technology occurred during my grandfather's life from about 1850 to 1920. The railroad and the steam engine preceded 1850, but the steam engine owed very little to science. It was really the tag end of the great development of folk technology in the European Middle Ages. From 1850 on, however—perhaps the great exhibition of the Crystal Palace was the signal—there is a great explosion of science-based technology. We get the chemical industry, beginning with analine dyes, which would have been impossible without Dalton, Kekule, and Mendeleev. The elec-trical industry, which begins in the 1880s, would have been impossible without Faraday and Clerk Maxwell. The nuclear industry of the twentieth century would have been impossible without Bohr and Rutherford. Watson and Crick, who discovered DNA, may be the fathers of biological industries yet unborn.

With this explosion of human knowledge there also comes an enormous upsurge in population, partly as a result of increased knowledge of medicine, nutrition, and pest control. The chemical industry probably did more to create the population explosion than any other, simply by the development of chemical controls for malaria. The expansion of human artifacts has been even more spectacular than the population expansion. So far, the artifact explosion has outdistanced the population explosion, and the average output of human artifacts per capita continues to rise, though only a portion of the world's population has really enjoyed this rise.

The Rise of World Inequality

The developmental process of the last 200 years has increased strikingly the disparity between the rich and the poor. We have no national income statistics for the eighteenth century, but it is doubtful whether 200 years ago the richest country had a per capita real income more than five times that of the poorest. In the 1500s, certainly India and China must have had per capita real incomes not very different from Europes. Even in the 1730s, Britain seems to have had a Malthusian equilibrium population of sheer misery and malnutrition aided by gin. Today the difference between per capita income for the richest countries and for the poorest is on the order of 50 to 1 rather than 5 to 1. Rich countries in the temperate zone are 20, 30, 40, 50 times as rich as countries at the bottom of the list like Haiti or Botswana. The reason for this is not exploitation in any simple sense: it is not that the poor countries produce a lot and the rich countries take it away from them. The income differences must be explained mainly by differential development. That is, the rich countries have been getting richer faster and longer and the poor countries have not been getting richer at all. For six generations in the rich countries, income has been doubling roughly every generation: it has gone, say, 100, 200, 400, 800, 1600, 3200. In the poor countries, it has gone 100, 100, 100, 100, 100, 100. The widening gap is again a partial application of the Matthew principle that "to him that hath shall be given"; that is, once the essential development has gotten under way and knowledge has started to increase, it becomes easier to increase it; once capital has started to accumulate, it is easier to accumulate it. At low levels of output, the whole output has to be used just to maintain the society and to keep people alive to reproduce themselves. There is no surplus left over for accumulation of either knowledge or artifacts. Only about a quarter of the human race has participated (to varying degrees) in this process of expanding wealth. About three-quarters of it has not. A quarter, perhaps a third, of the human race has moved toward a kind of world superculture of skyscrapers, automobiles, airplanes, and intercontinental hotels. The rest of the human race still remains close to subsistence.

The superculture is now spread all over the world in urban enclaves. Johannesburg, Singapore, Nairobi, Tokyo, Caracas, and Delhi all have skyscraper skylines. Over most of the tropics, however, cities are merely enclaves. A few miles outside of them, one is back in subsistence agriculture and grinding poverty. The shacks of the *favela* in Rio de Janeiro, the *barrios* of Lima and Caracas, the flimsy huts and the sacred cows that press in on the Delhi skyscrapers symbolize the great gulf between the superculture and the exploding subsistence populations of the poor. There is evidence indeed that economic development in the tropics, with a few exceptions like Singapore and Taiwan, has actually worsened the condition of the bottom 25 percent of the population. As the traditional societies are eroded and traditional skills are made less valuable, the poorer people are unable to make the jump into the factories and the farms of the superculture. The labor unions in the poor countries accentuate this gap, creating a labor aristocracy at the cost of keeping the poor out of it.

The Role of Energy in Developing the "Superculture": Alternatives to Oil and Gas

The development of the superculture is the result of the knowledge explosion, which led not only to new theories and processes, but also to new discoveries, especially of fossil fuels and rich ores. In 1859 the human race discovered a huge treasure chest in its basement. This was oil and gas, a fantastically cheap and easily available source of energy. We did, or at least some of us did, what anybody does who discovers a treasure in the basement—live it up—and we have been spending this treasure with great enjoyment. It has now dawned on us that the bottom of the barrel is no more than a lifetime off. The Arabs put in a false bottom by extracting a monopoly price, and for this we should be grateful, because it has forced us to think about things now that we might not have thought about until it was too late. It is a very fundamental principle of the dynamics of the price system that, if we have something that is plentiful now but is going to be scarce later on, the sensible thing to do is make it expensive now, which will force us into improvements that will save and economize the expensive item, so that by the time it becomes really scarce we will have found means to use it much more efficiently and we will also have found substitutes. One would prefer to do this through the tax system rather than to have the OPEC countries reap excessive monopoly gains as they are doing, but even this is better than having oil remain too cheap, in which case we might not bother to work on finding substitutes and economizing until it were all gone and we would suddenly be in a very severe crisis.

Fortunately, the possibilities both for economizing fossil fuels and for finding substitutes are quite large. Nuclear fission and especially breeder reactors are a possible stopgap, but they are very expensive and dangerous and produce a negative inheritance in terms of atomic wastes of long life. The disposal of these is already a serious problem, and if an attempt were made to make fission and breeder reactors the principal source of energy for the developed societies, and still more for the poor countries, the problem of nuclear waste might become insoluble quite rapidly.

Nuclear fusion is another candidate for a major energy source. There is enough deuterium in the top foot of the oceans to keep us going for perhaps half a million years if we could produce the desired reaction. This would enable us to go on burning up our "spaceship earth" for a long time. The problem in an engineering sense is still not solved, however, and may be insoluble. One is reminded of the alchemist who was trying to find a universal solvent until someone asked, "What are you going to keep it in?" Fussion at ten million degrees is an extremely universal solvent and is hard to contain. The problem may be solved by means of magnetic fields and so on, though we still seem a fair way from it and it may turn out to be very intractable. Furthermore, over a few centuries the released heat could well make the earth uninhabitable. Geothermal energy, that is, from the heat of the earth itself, especially where it is concentrated in volcanic magmas, is already in use in several places such as New Zealand and California. This has its own problems of pollution (for instance, where the heat is pumped up in water, which dissolves minerals along the way). It is, however, a relatively minor potential source of energy.

The last resort, of course, is solar energy, which is very abundant but also very diffuse. The whole biosphere uses much less than one percent of the solar energy that falls on the earth and, if we can get this up to two percent, we would probably be all right for energy for a long time. One source for optimism in this regard is that there are many lines of attack on this problem—mechanical, electrical, chemical, biological—so that it will be a little surprising if none of them work. Other forms of continuous energy can also be expanded. Hydroelectric power, especially in the rich countries, is by now mostly developed, but it contributes only a small amount of the total energy supply. Tidal energy likewise has some potential, but compared with the total energy used even today this is very small.

A promising source of continuing energy is wind, which derives ultimately from solar energy but in some areas is fairly continuous and concentrated. The main problem with wind is its discontinuity and variability. If it can be combined with pumped storage of water, however, this difficulty would be taken care of. Suggestions have even been made for large concrete flywheels to store the energy for use when the wind is not blowing hard enough. If windmills were also tied into a large electric grid, the wind would probably always be blowing somewhere within its range. One could even visualize in windy areas a very efficient windmill on the rooftop pumping water from a tank in the basement to one in the attic, the water then running down to the basement through an efficient small generator, which would provide electricity for all domestic uses. These are technologies that are not remote from human experience. Windmills have been known for nearly 1,000 years in Europe and even longer in China, and if it had not been for the extraordinarily cheap energy provided by fossil fuels, it is likely that this technology would have been developed very substantially in the last 100 years. Even a generation ago almost every farmer in the middle west had a windmill pumping water.

Exhaustion of Materials

The exhaustion of concentrated materials in the form of ores may turn out in the long run to be a more intractable problem than that of energy. Most economic operations increase material entropy (that is, they diffuse concentrated materials); there are a few processes that reverse this and concentrate the diffuse instead of diffusing the concentrated, but these are rather rare and they require large energy inputs that are now coming mainly from fossil fuels, so that at the same time we are concentrating materials, we are also running down our fossil fuel stock. If inexhaustible energy can be obtained from the sun, however, part of this can be used to concentrate diffused materials, both those that have been diffused by human activities in innumerable dumps throughout the world, and those that exist in low concentrations in the rock, the atmosphere, or the oceans. We really do not know how much energy will be necessary to concentrate materials in the absence of natural concentrations of ores. It might turn out to be a large amount.

The human race has indeed been fortunate in that at the time when its knowledge grew to the point where it could utilize fossil fuels and ores, it discovered these things in relatively large quantities. The geological history of the earth might have been different. The metals, for instance, might have been widely diffused through the crust instead of being concentrated in mines. If the earth had not had the extraordinary history of tectonic continental drift, there might not have been any great concentrations of metals as in the Mesabi Range. The fossil fuels again are in a sense an accident of geological and biological evolution that gave the earth large areas of shallow warm seas, which produced the oil-forming organisms and swampy lowlands that produced the carboniferous forests. The earth presumably might have had another kind of history that would not have produced any ores or fossil fuels. If that had been the case, all the knowledge in the world would not have discovered them, and the history of the last 100 years or so would have been very different.

Pollution: The Joint Production of Goods and Bads

Another possible limit to growth is the growth of pollution. Since most processes of production involve joint production in which a number of different things are produced in the same process, again we do not seem able to do only one thing. Even a chemical reaction that produces only a single product, like the burning of hydrogen and oxygen, also produces heat. Many chemical reactions produce two or more products. When we include social products, it would be extremely hard to find any process in social life or in any activity that produces only one product. An automobile factory that produces a particular make of car also produces air pollution and water pollution from the physical and chemical byproducts of the production, and it will also produce a great range of positive and negative social products—jobs for workers, taxes for governments, injuries, perhaps alienation and political dissatisfaction. The list could be extended.

The proportions in which these multiple products are produced are not wholly inflexible and indeed it is always the hope of technology to move toward processes that produce more goods and fewer bads, but there are quite confining limits within which this can be done, and because we want the goods, we put up with the bads.

Pollution therefore is no accident; it is built very deeply into the processes of the world and occasionally it produces great transformations.

Recycling and Segregation

On the whole, the biosphere deals with the problem of pollution by recycling. The excrement of one animal, for instance, is the food of another. The carbon dioxide that animals excrete, plants ingest and turn back into oxygen, which the animals breathe in and use and then again turn into carbon dioxide. Nitrogen passes through plants into the atmosphere, where it is fixed in the soil by nitrogen-fixing bacteria associated with other plants and is again available for protein formation. Carbon is constantly recycled from the atmosphere to the soil, through the biosphere, into the atmosphere and the soil again. Many other elements are recycled in a similar way. The human race indeed is almost the only living being that has developed a linear economy, moving materials from wells, mines, and soil into products that are then distributed into dumps or flushed down to the oceans or burned in the atmosphere. This is obviously a temporary arrangement, but exactly how temporary is a little hard to say. Ultimately, if the human race is to survive, it must develop a cyclical economy in which all materials are obtained from the great reservoirs—the air, the soil, the sea—and are returned to them, and in which the whole process is powered by solar energy. Where the pollution problem cannot be solved by recycling, it can only be solved by segregation—that is, by concentrating the pollutants in some locality where they are not in the way of the human race. We might shoot radioactive waste off into space. We segregate economic waste and garbage in dumps. We may be running out of easily available depositories in the course of the next century or so. It has suddenly dawned on us that neither the ocean nor the atmosphere is infinite. We are now beginning to worry that human activity might produce adverse, irreversible changes in both the atmosphere and the oceans as it has in various places in times past produced irreversible, adverse changes in soils and in water supplies. While not all the deserts are man-made, at least some of them are, and soil deterioration, especially in the tropics, may have been the factor behind the "overshoots" leading to phenomena like the Mayan and the Khmer collapses.

We are worried about the atmosphere because we are putting a lot of previously unknown substances into it—nitrous oxides, carbon monoxide, sulfur oxides, as well as the familiar carbon dioxide. The latest anxiety is over freon, a chemical the earth had never known about before the advent of man. It is used in sprays and refrigerators and is escaping into the upper atmosphere, where it evidently undergoes complex chemical reactions that may destroy the ozone. It is the ozone layer in the upper atmosphere that protects the earth from the dangerous ultraviolet radiation of the sun and, if it disappears, we will be in a bad way. All the evidence is not yet in and the ordinary fluctuations in the ozone content are large enough that it is hard to evaluate what the exact effects of human activity have been, but there is enough evidence to be very worrying.

The increase of carbon dioxide in the atmosphere is supposed to warm it up. This is the greenhouse effect, which we have noticed. The fact that it is not doing so suggests we are still very far from complete knowledge of the earth's systems. The awful truth is that the physical sciences are really very backward, particularly when it comes to dealing with middle-sized systems like the earth. We know a lot about mesons and quasars, but the total system of the earth exhibits a degree of complexity that is very hard to handle with the present apparatus of the physical sciences. We still do not know what really produced the ice ages. The earth is clearly in the grip of very large systems in relation to which human activity is still something of a pipsqueak. Nevertheless, there may be "trigger systems" in which quite small changes induced by human activity could cause very large changes in the end result; and this is frightening.

The more obvious forms of pollution do tend to be dealt with, particularly when they become scandalous enough. We have cleaned up Pittsburgh remarkably and we are cleaning up Lake Erie. The English cities and rivers are far better than they were 40 years ago. The Dust Bowl no longer deposits inches of dust in Chicago as it did in 1934, and though some of this may have been a long stretch of good luck in the weather, some of it is due to changes in agricultural practices. I sometimes scandalize my young friends by telling them that I have lived through a period of great improvement in environment. On the other hand, the things that are worrying are the unknowns, the trigger effects, and the novelties. Perhaps the most disturbing thing about human activity is that it has introduced large numbers of new chemical and radioactive substances into the earth with which the biosphere never had to deal before. There are no bacteria, for instance, that know how to eat nylon and dacron. These substances are here to stay. They may not cause much damage; on the other hand, it is a bit alarming to find that nylon fragments from fishing nets are getting into the digestive systems of a good many marine animals, and it is not altogether clear that they will know what to do with it. We should be careful of delusions of grandeur on the part of the human race, because we are still a very small influence. But we must also be on the lookout for the invisible dangers, where our small activities may turn out to have large effects.

The Necessity for Population Control

The ultimate outcome of the present dynamic may depend more than anything else on the ability of the human race to control its own population. We are in a period now of uncontrolled population growth, which has followed from the improvement of food supplies, the improvement of health, and the decline in mortality, especially infant mortality. This all follows from general easing of the conditions of life, which the great expansion of human artifacts has produced. The human population has been expanding for a long time, as we have seen, despite relatively brief periods of contraction such as those following the fall of the Roman Empire, following the Black Death in 1349 in Europe, resulting from the Thirty Years War in Germany, or resulting from the Mexican and Russian Revolutions of the twentieth century; but these have usually been temporary and the losses are very soon regained once conditions improve. It is a rare period of decline that is not made up in a generation or two, simply because of the enormous power of exponential growth.

In the last 200 years or so, there have been two great surges of population. The first was the European population from about the middle of the eighteenth century, and was largely a result of improvements in nutrition, originating in technical improvements in agriculture. This explosion of European population led to the settlements of the Americas, Australia, New Zealand, South Africa, and Siberia by European populations. The indigenous populations in the areas of European immigration often declined, and in most cases were very small to begin with, though often with a subsequent recovery as in the Americas. The European population explosion diminished substantially after about 1880, and in the twentieth century populations of European origin have been expanding relatively slowly.

In the tropics the great population explosion begins about 1950, with the introduction of DDT and the control of malaria, producing a spectacular decline in the death rate, especially because it is virtually equivalent to an increase in the birth rate. There was even some rise in birth rates as populations became healthier. The result has been a population expansion at rates of 3 percent and over per annum, which means doubling every generation. This kind of rate of increase was prevalent in the American colonies in the eighteenth century, but then these populations had an enormous land area, which they were in a position to occupy, and which could support with the European-type techniques a very much larger population than it had before the European expansion. Now, however, we are having the same kind of population increase without any great empty spaces. The formerly empty spaces of the world are now all full, with a few possible exceptions. The present population explosion is taking place in areas that are either already very crowded like South Asia, or tropical Africa. We are now therefore having a population explosion in a very confined space, and this bodes ill for the future.

The High Probability of Demographic Catastrophe

There is no acceptable solution to the population problem short of bringing the birth rate down to the death rate. There is an unacceptable solution, which is to bring the death rate up to the birth rate. The forces that underlie human fertility, however, are a considerable mystery. We do not really understand, for instance, even in the United States why fertility was so high between 1947 and 1961 and why it has fallen so dramatically since. It is to the point now indeed where native-born Americans are close to being an endangered species, in that they are no longer reproducing themselves, though this may not last. Even at the present fertility rate, it would take a very long time for Americans to become extinct! In a country like India, which has made a determined effort to reduce the birth rate, these efforts have not been very successful. A brillant essay by Mahmood Mamdani suggests why in the Indian village with sharp class and caste distinctions the only hope of the poor peasant for rising in the world is to have about four sons who can enable him to expand his holdings, with perhaps one or two going to the city to send back remittances, and so on. It is hard to have four sons without also having four daughters on the average, and this leads to a great population expansion which is catastrophic for the society.

We have here almost a classic example of the failure of the "invisible hand"—that is, a situation in which the rational private interest is directly opposite to what is necessary for the long-run public good. A catastrophe that will make the Irish famine look like a minor episode, in which perhaps over a relatively short period 100 million people will starve to death, is by no means impossible in south Asia. The potentialities for demographic disaster in tropical Africa and Latin America are perhaps a little further off than they are in south Asia, but these parts of the world are now on a course that will either be changed or lead to catastrophe.

Mankind—Turning Point or Lifeboat Ethic?

The second Club of Rome report, "Mankind at the Turning Point," by Mesarovic and Pestel, concludes that if a major demographic catastrophe in the tropics were to be avoided, there had to be almost immediate reduction of the birth rate in the tropics on a large scale and there also had to be very substantial transfers of economic goods from rich countries to poor, an order of magnitude larger than the present flow of investments and foreign aid. Unfortunately, neither of these events seems to be very likely. The expansion of grants from the rich to the poor ones depends first on the development of an increased sense of community (that is, a stronger world integrative structure). In the second place, it depends on the perception that these grants will be efficient. The perception of the efficiency of grants is a very important element in their supply. If by giving up $1, I can benefit another by $100 or even possibly save another's life, I am very likely to do this. If by giving up $1, I only benefit the recipient by 10 cents, I am very unlikely to do it.

Unless grants from the rich to the poor countries can be tied to an effective method of population control, they are likely to be ineffective and may simply increase the ultimate sum of human misery and the size of the eventual disaster. On the other hand, up until now we have simply not devised any social technique for tying grants to birth reduction. There are very good reasons for this failure. Grants are often perceived as degrading to the recipients. There is always a status gap between the recipient and the donor. Grants in the form of gifts are usually handed down the social scale, though if they are in the form of tribute obtained through threat, as they sometimes are, they may go from the poor and lowly to the rich and powerful. Furthermore, procreation is regarded rightly as one of the most private and sacred aspects of human life, and to turn it into an object of exchange or even reciprocity is deeply repugnant in most cultures. We can see the moral dilemma in extreme form if we postulate that the method of control is infanticide; are we going to offer $1,000 for every dead baby? That, I think, would carry rationality almost to the point of Jonathan Swift's "modest proposal."

The appalling moral dilemmas of the present situation are reflected in the "lifeboat model" of Garrett Hardin. If we have a lifeboat with 20 people in it and enough food for only ten to survive until land is reached and if they all share the food, none will survive, and for every one thrown overboard up to ten, the better the chances are that the rest will survive. The question is: "Who will be thrown overboard and who will decide?" The most obvious solution is a lottery; perhaps the most just solution is that the virtuous and deserving should survive. The less virtuous should certainly be thrown overboard, although this again raises the question, "Who will decide?" The most probable solution, unfortunately, is that the most powerful will survive. If indeed we are in this scenario in the world (and we cannot be sure that we are not), the inference is that the powerful temperate zone will simply let the tropics sink. The abandonment of the European empires may indeed be a prelude to an abandonment of responsibility. Independence might be construed as simply prying the clutching fingers of the old colonies off the gunwhale of the lifeboat.

The Limits of Human Organization

The last 100 years or so have shown us that something better than classical civilization is possible, though we may have some doubts as to whether it is sustainable. In other words, some systems have a rather low evolutionary horizon, which they soon reach. A feeling prevalent in post-Roman Europe even as late as the early eighteenth century was that civilization had reached its peak in the West, at any rate in Greece and Rome, and had been declining ever since. Cycles of rise and fall are frequently observed by philosophers of history, though the complexity of interaction of different segments of society destroys any simple pattern. Nevertheless, it is a very interesting question whether once a society has reached the limits of a given system it can stay there in a stable equilibrium, or whether a process of decline does not inevitably set in as the impetus gained from rising is lost. Many systems seem to exhibit what might be called a "balloon pattern" of rising to some kind of ceiling, but then losing buoyancy and sinking slowly but surely below the maximum point.

The problem of the limits of the integrative system is very puzzling and in the long run may be very important. We are pretty sure we have not reached these limits in general. Nevertheless, we do run into partial and local limits. This happens, for instance, when a marriage breaks down or when there is a civil war or revolution, or even when there is widespread apathy and the lack of developmental activity of all kinds, which seemed to characterize Portugal for nearly three centuries. The rise and decline of the morale or the "nerve" of a society is an extremely puzzling phenomenon, and yet a tremendously important one. It is a great harbinger of change.

We know something about the limits to growth. What do we know about the limits to love? The limits to community? The limits to benevolence? The limits to the grants economy? The limits to dedication? The limits to freedom? The limits to justice? The answer is very little. We hope these limits are a long way from where we are now.

It is important to realize, however, that no limits are absolute. The evolutionary process is one in which existing limits have constantly been transcended because of the evolutionary process itself, first in the growth of complexity in the genosphere (genetic material as it spreads over the earth's skin in the form of eggs, sperm, and the genetic components of cells) and now in the growth of complexity in the noosphere (the totality of the cognitive content of the human nervous system and its extensions).

The classical economist saw economic development as the race between capital and population. We might broaden this to see it as a race between increasing knowledge and increasing scarcities. For the last 200 or 300 years, knowledge has been winning hands down. The ultimate limits, however, are the limits to knowledge. These we obviously cannot know. For this reason the future must always remain mercifully uncertain. ✤

Environmental and Human Limits to the Exercise of Power

David Ehrenfeld

Problems inherent in the development and use of technology pose severe constraints on our exercise of power. At the same time, ecological realities impose further, albeit sometimes overlapping, constraints. The most direct of these is that few biological systems in the world, either individual organisms or groups of organisms, have evolved any mechanisms for coping with large, surplus inputs of concentrated energy in their immediate environments—energies of the sort that man now has readily at his disposal. We ourselves provide a good example of this: although we have numerous biochemical and physiological ways of detoxifying and excreting a host of different poisons, we have no mechanism for expelling excess energy. If we eat too many calories we get fat, to our own detriment. Poisons have been with us, especially in plant materials, for as long as we have existed, but surplus energy is a new phenomenon.

Many ecological systems are fragile and are especially vulnerable to our energetic interference. They are fragile either because they have evolved in extremely stable environments (rain forests, coral reefs, and old deep lakes), or because they are "preoccupied" with some overwhelming environmental force (tundra, deserts, or steep mountain slopes). As an example, a single cross-desert motorcycle race may alter and largely destroy five hundred square miles of desert plant community. We think that the damage will last for a century or more.

A second ecological constraint is time. Natural plant and animal communities change their structures and species compositions over time—the process is known as succession. We can modify the process, derail it, but we can hardly ever accelerate it in a predictable way. Most of our energetic environmental activities bring succession back to earlier stages, and it is the earlier stages that are dominated by organisms in conflict with people—the weeds, the pests, and the vermin. Thus we can destroy the labyrinthine structure of a forest soil in milliseconds with a bomb or in hours with a bulldozer, yet it will not be coaxed back again before decades of slow successional change have prepared the way for its return. In the meantime we must live with the bamboo, the imperata grass, the bramble thickets, or whatever. As another example, in North America ragweed is a member of the earliest of successional plant communities; it flourishes in recently disturbed soil, but if left alone will disappear after one or two summers, to be replaced by goldenrod, aster, and blackberry. If it is pulled up forcibly, however—preferably by a power tiller—conditions will be ideal for return of more ragweed at the next opportunity. Nature provides the best of paradoxes.

Irreversibility is the third ecological constraint. It seems difficult for the modern humanist, committed to the dominant world belief that the human mind can prevail over any obstacle, to grasp the significance of the many irreversible processes that we have stirred up in living systems. The tendency is to deny that anything so final, so thoroughly beyond our control, can occur. But we are causing irreversible changes all the time. Species are extinguished wholesale, and no genetic prowess will ever bring them back. Deserts are substituted for garden spots and rich grassland—a few thousand years ago the Sahara was a fertile place, and more recently the parched, cracked earth of parts of modern Iraq was the cradle of our agricultural civilization. Perhaps the deserts are not permanent, but compared with the time scale of human civilizations, they can be regarded as such. "Desert-makers" is truly as appropriate a title for humans as "tool-users."

The popular idea of "clean fusion power" is a myth that encompasses every environmental delusion and folly of which the humanistic attitude is capable. It beautifully illustrates the importance of recognizing the limits of power. For even if we accept the dubious and unprovable assumption that fusion reactors will pose no radioactive, explosive, or thermal threat to people and environments, what will happen to the unlimited, cheap fusion power after it leaves the power plant and transmission lines? If a source of power is to be called "clean," the judgment can only be made if all of the consequences and effects of the power have been traced—from the time of its generation to the time the last kilowatt has been dissipated as irrecoverable heat. "Impossible to trace," mutters the physicist or engineer. But not really—we already know what will happen to that power.

It will be used to manufacture more snowmobiles, which will destroy more of the winter vegetation of the north, and diminish the dwindling privacy and quiet that northern dwellers once enjoyed during the months of snow. Granted, snowmobiles will save some lives; but even this is a mixed blessing, because snowmobile accidents will take more lives than are saved.

It will be used to make more laser bombs and surface-to-surface missiles and Rome plows and anti-crop defoliants.

It will be used to provide more electric outdoor billboards, which will help accelerate the destruction of the meaning of language.

It will power the pumps of tube wells in the world's dry grasslands, thus permitting more cattle to be grazed, and more deserts to be formed.

It will help the Soviets turn their Arctic rivers southwards, thus greatly reducing the flow of fresh water to the Arctic Ocean, increasing its salinity, lowering its freezing point, and perhaps, in consequence, changing the weather of the world, although we don't·know in what direction such a change would be.

It will be used to produce more synthetic nitrogen fertilizer, which will be used to fertilize the "miracle crops" developed for "Green Revolution" agriculture. This, in turn, will mean that massive irrigation will be necessary for proper growth, which in dry areas will lead to the buildup of toxic salts in the soil—one of the roads to desert formation. It will mean that agriculture will continue to be a capital-intensive enterprise, because Green Revolution crops can only give heavy yields with the aid of expensive (and destructive) insecticides, herbicides, harvesting and cultivating machinery, drying ovens, etc.; and this further means that the twin processes of concentrating land holdings in the hands of the few who control the money supply and creating a landless peasantry will continue. It means that the soil, most valuable of all resources, will still be mined, in effect, rather than nurtured and preserved. It means that the allure of the fertilized, high-yielding "miracle crops" will still cause traditional farmers to abandon their precious local varieties of grains, vegetables, and fruits, some of them thousands of years old and perfectly adapted to the climate, pests, and diseases of the regional environment—and it is these local varieties, tens of thousands of them, that constitute the entire genetic heritage of agriculture, the hope of the future. It means that crops will still have to be grown in massive, "efficient" monocultures in order to turn a profit in the face of the heavy capital investment, and this means that they will continue to be exceptionally vulnerable to insect pests and diseases.

It will be used for the construction of more levees, diversion canals, flood walls and the like, thus reducing the incidence of minor flooding, but further encouraging the human settlement of flood plains and increasing both the likelihood and destructiveness of major floods, as happened along the Mississippi River in what C.B. Belt, Jr. has called "the man-made flood" of 1973.

All this and much more will be the fate of fusion power after it leaves the transmission lines. The adjective "clean" cannot be applied to such a train of consequences, and reserving it solely for the power plant portion of the system is a bit like certifying the water of a sewage- and chemical-polluted river as fit for drinking because the rain that falls upon its watershed is pure and sweet.

Never before has delusion been such an important part of our lives and plans. Because we cannot comprehend the entire value and variety of the human experience, we simplify it, proclaiming certain isolated features—"engineered" features—to be the best. In this spirit, T-cyto-plasm corn became the best, because it reduced the need for much labor in the production of hybrid seed. Yet we were taken by surprise when after planting almost the entire corn acreage of the United States in this one variety, we lost 15 percent of it—more than a billion dollars' worth—in a single outbreak of a fungus to which it was particularly susceptible. T-cytoplasm corn is indeed an immensely useful invention, but why is it that we seem incapable of appreciating our own clever- ness and recognizing our limitations at the same time?

The case of krill is another example. We have finally developed ways of harvesting these abundant little crustaceans from Antarctic waters (although the energy cost of this technology is exorbitant). But why do we gloat? Krill harvesting and processing devices used to be free for the taking—they were called "whales"; they ate the krill and turned it into whale meat. Now the whales are nearly gone, and progress has led us to the point where we must take the krill for ourselves at great expense. Is this, in fact, a triumph? More delusions.

"Anthropomorphic gremlins," catchy labels that let us think we un- derstand or control a situation, frequently can be seen popping in and out of our delusions. Take the case of "stack scrubbers," which are "pollu- tion control" devices. They do indeed remove many pollutants from smokestack gases. In exchange, many release sulfuric acid into the air in large quantities. The very rain that falls on industrial, populous coun- tries is now highly acidic, and 60 percent of the acid content is sulfuric acid. Aquatic animals such as certain fish, frogs, and salamanders are born, if they are born at all, with acid-induced birth defects; some major plant diseases are acid-enhanced; the acid rain etches and destroys stone buildings; and even the growth rates of forests in eastern North America and Scandinavia may have been slowed by the acid contamination. This is "pollution control."

Nor should we have delusions that if we sneak up on Nature with a smile, muttering the right charms and incantations—"biological control," "natural insecticide," "mulch"—we will catch her unaware and in a good mood. The gentle methodologies of the counter-culture are a vast improvement in our relationship with Nature, a long stride forward in these retrogressive times. But there are those who bring the old arrogant expectations to these new or resurrected methodologies, who still seek the eternal free lunch that is never really forthcoming. We can use radiation to produce sterile male screwworms by the millions, and release them into the environment to waste the reproductive efforts of the females. How long this will work we do not know; already there are indications that the sterile males may no longer be competing as well as they once did for the females' favors. These mass-sterilized males are probably defective in various ways, and the few females who do manage to reproduce may be passing on to their daughters the means for choosing properly between normal and sterile mates. In a contest between evolution and human brains it is not wise to bet on brains.

"Natural" insecticides such as rotenone also have their uses. But rotenone poisons fish, is responsible for some human allergies, kills desirable as well as undesirable insects, and only remains effective for a day or two. Similarly, mulches of hay or leaves are easy and effective ways of controlling weeds and conditioning the soil. Mulches also, however harbor rats and mice, promote the growth of molds, and shelter plant insect pests from cold or heat.

The grand delusion of our "space age" is that we can escape the earthly consequences of our arrogance—evade the limits to our use of power—by leaving the mother planet either for a little ersatz world of our own making or for distant celestial bodies, some of them as yet undiscovered. This is an immature and irresponsible idea, that having fouled this world with our inventions, we will somehow do better in other orbits. However, if one sees humanism for what it is, a religion without God, then the idea is not so strange: space with its space stations and space inhabitants is just a replacement for heaven with its angels. Even the idea of immortality is there, fuzzy like everything else in this imaginary humanist domain—for if one looks closely at the writings of the futurologists and the would-be space pioneers, one finds hazy references to relativity and time warps, ways of making immense journeys of many light years' distance without aging, except perhaps with reference to the people left behind on earth. Space is nothing more than a watered-down heaven for modern unbelievers. Only now we have located heaven more precisely in the solar system than in the days when Dante wrote about paradise.

Maybe the least important of the criticisms of space colonies is that they won't work; they cannot possibly survive for very long, at least with living inhabitants (though the debris from them might). There have been numerous specific criticisms of specific design features, but these are not of concern here. One only needs to look at the general concept of a space colony in order to see the functional problems.

On July 13 and 14, 1977, the electricity supply of the City of New York failed completely, resulting in a "blackout." Imagine if a blackout were to take place on a space station, if power were lost for twenty-four hours. When this happened in New York it was unpleasant, even dangerous. But New York exists in an essentially hospitable environment for man: during a crisis there is no need to manufacture day and night, air, or gravity; water continues to flow downhill out of most taps, and temperatures will not reach lethal limits. If the situation deteriorates one can, if necessary, drive or walk away. On a space station, the only alternative to complete control is death. Yet we know of no complex, managed situations on earth in which humans have been able always to maintain perfect control, regardless of built-in redundancy. In fact, the more complex the system, the more the "down time." And space stations are much more complex than copying machines or computerized elevators.

We are thoroughly familiar with this troublesome aspect of man-made complexity—Murphy's Law (if anything can go wrong, it will) is an accepted fact of contemporary life—yet we are always incredulous when things do go awry. The following example is taken from an article by Wallace Turner in the New York Times; the quotation is attributed to a spokesman for the operators of the Trans-Alaska Pipeline, speaking after an explosion had occurred on the line:

> "We had this system designed so there would never be volatile fumes in the air, and we had it designed so there would never be an open ignition source," Mr. Ratterman said, standing on a hillside with reporters and looking down at the twisted steel and smoking machinery that had been the pumping house. "But as you can see, we got both volatile fumes and ignition, and we got them at the same time."

"Human error" usually receives the blame for malfunctions in our mechanical world, as if this somehow absolved our inventions. But where there are humans there will always be human error; nor are machines any more reliable in our absence.

Perhaps all of the loose talk about "spaceship earth" has corrupted our thinking. The earth is really not like a spaceship, save for the facts that they both travel in space and both have limitations of certain resources. There the similarity ends—the "life-support systems" of earth are vast, complex, poorly understood, very old, self-regulating, and entirely successful. In fact, the term "life-support systems" is a misnomer when applied to earth, a product of an engineering rather than an ecological mentality. On earth, the life and the "life-support systems" are not separable, they are part of the same whole. In a space station the "life-support system" would indeed be separate. It would also be in need of constant regulation and management. Like any "machine" built to exacting engineering standards, it would work most of the time, and occasionally it would fail. It would fail not just because of our inadequate understanding of ecology and of "life-support systems," but because it is a machine, and sooner or later all machines fail. When the failure is minor and of short duration, the space colony will survive, and when it is serious and long-lasting the inhabitants of the colony will die—unless, of course, they can go home to Earth. One can tell that most of the space enthusiasts have never been serious gardeners. If they had been, they would not be so fatuously optimistic about the future of life in barren space, where Earth and Nature will not be available to correct their mistakes. Some day we may be foolish enough to commit our hopes and resources to space stations and galactic explorations. The space travelers will leave with enthusiasm and amid great fanfare. And they will not return.

We will hear much, in the years to come, from the advocates of space travel, and some of it will sound like this: "What if Columbus had been afraid to set sail in his ships, or the Polynesians on their frail rafts? Where is the dauntless human spirit of exploration in these craven times?" But the ocean, terrifying as it can be, is not space—we came forth from this ocean and contain its water and salts within our very cells, and it is surrounded by inhabitable land and covered with breathe-able air. Alien as the ocean may seem to some of us, it is part of our heritage; the outer darkness of space is not. We have paid the evolutionary price of billions of deaths to adapt to this world, beginning before the days when our ancestors were tiny invertebrate animals swimming in the sea. Every birth and survival in our line has been a testimonial to the goodness of fit between human beings and the environment of our home planet. We cannot reproduce more than the palest of copies of that environment elsewhere, terribly imperfect and unreliable; and our survival in such clumsy fabrications will be equally imperfect and unreliable, a transient affair. Like species of large animals colonizing very small islands, we will arrive, live fitfully for a while, and go extinct. Ecologists have developed rate equations that describe this process—maybe we will get a chance to apply them to ourselves in space.

The main point, as I said, is not that we will be unable to get our space colonies to work. It is rather the strategy of our foolish efforts to do so, our eager acceptance of schemes that Mumford, with his characteristic wisdom, has called "technological disguises for infantile fantasies." George Wald, writing in the *CoEvolution Quarterly*, has directly illuminated the tragedy:

> What bothers me most about Space Colonies—even as concepts— is their betrayal of what I believe to be the deepest and most meaningful human values. I do not think one can live a full human life without living it among animals and plants. From that viewpoint, urban societies have already lost large parts of their humanity, and their perversion of the countryside makes life there hardly better, sometimes worse . . . .
> So that my point is that the very idea of Space Colonies carries to a logical—and horrifying—conclusion processes of dehumanization and depersonalization that have already gone much too far on the Earth. In a way, we've gotten ready for Space Platforms by a systematic degradation of human ways of life on the Earth.

People in space are diminished people, out of their ancient, inherited, and supremely beautiful context. And like anything ripped from context, there is no point to them.

There is a fundamentalist lesson to be learned from these examples. We have been reading the old biblical story of the expulsion from the Garden of Eden too carelessly of late; like fundamentalists, we must pay more attention to detail. For was not the Garden of Eden described as a better place than the world outside after the fall? And was it not the clear implication of Genesis that all the new-found skills and knowledge that the fateful apple could provide were imperfect? The serpent was lying when he said, "Ye shall be as gods"; indeed we now know that we will never live in such a state of grace again.

I have not examined in any depth the techniques of self-deception that are in common use to support humanistic assumptions. These techniques include the use of mathematical models that make their own inappropriate assumptions about nature (assumptions of linearity, generality, continuity, importance values, randomness, etc.), the clever methods of extrapolation from a poorly described present to an unknowable future, the elaborate statistical ways of weighting or ignoring or accentuating evidence in order to preserve an appearance of objectivity while arranging the desired answer, the crediting or discrediting of certain classes of perception, and many others. Instead, I have relied on the idea of "end-product analysis," which is to say that it is fair to judge a process by its results even when one does not understand all of the intrinsic theory, mechanisms, and defects involved. In fact, when we are dealing with our own future, it is not only fair but necessary.

On the basis of these end-product analyses I have concluded that there are many types of limits to the knowledge and power that human beings can muster for any purpose, at least four of which warrant a brief review.

First, there is the limit imposed by our inability to know the future, to make accurate long-range predictions. This is a theoretical and inalterable limit based on the great complexity and uncertainty of the interacting events that will determine the future, and on the catalytic influence on the future of seemingly minute and trivial happenings in the present.

Secondly, there is a limit imposed by the consequences of prior failures of our assumptions of control. These take the form of expanding waves of technological pseudo-solutions to the problems that technology has itself produced, and the worsening secondary and tertiary problems resulting from the pseudo-solutions—all hastening the time of a final paralysis and collapse of further efforts to keep the situation under a facsimile of control.

Thirdly, there is the limit—an especially frustrating one—that is described by the maximization theory of von Neumann and Morgenstern, which says in effect that in a complex world we cannot work everything out for the best simultaneously. This third limit is why evolution has proven more reliable than our substitutes for it. Evolution is slow and wasteful, but it has resulted in an infinity of working, flexible compromises, whose success is constantly tested by life itself. Evolution is in large measure cumulative, and has been running three billion years longer than our current efforts. Our most glittering improvements over Nature are too often a fool's solution to a problem that has been isolated from context, a transient, local maximization that is bound to be followed by mostly undesirable counter-adjustments throughout the system.

Fourth is the limit inherent in my own version of the "uncertainty principle." This is seen in the growing realization that our ability to seek technical solutions to certain kinds of problems grows along with our capacity to augment and multiply these kinds of problems—that we do not solve problems as we acquire new technologies because new technologies simultaneously make our problems worse. Thus, our technology has given us new research methods to fight the endless fight against cancer, while the same technology is making cancer itself more widespread and more common.

There are other limits that I have only hinted at: those imposed by vanishing resources and by the exhaustion of the capacity of ecological systems to withstand excessive interference without radical change or disintegration. Finally, there is the perversion of our control technologies to evil purposes.

In the face of all this, it is especially difficult to understand the boundless optimism of people who have a knowledge of what is now happening to the world. How can those who appreciate the ecological realities of contemporary life embrace the unwarranted optimism of a humanistic cult whose efforts to redesign the world in our own image have given us a lengthy string of ever-worsening failures? The overwhelming trend of the humanist-dominated present is towards more ruined soils, more deserts, more children with anomie, more shattered societies, more violence, more weapons whose horror surpasses imagination, more techniques of autocratic suppression, and more mechanisms for isolating human beings from one another. How is it possible to extract from this present reality a toil-less utopia in which technology is "the partner of man's creativity"?

Those who are ignorant of the present state of the world have a faith in humanism that is much easier to comprehend. Perceiving our power, but not its consequences, they are free to project their fantasies upon a magical future. Orwell wrote, "Power worship blurs political judgment because it leads, almost unavoidably, to the belief that present trends will continue." This is also true for forms of judgment other than political. Here we have the "futurologists," who have been mesmerized by our brief surges of power into believing that it all will continue— because we have left a golf ball and the autograph of a president on the moon we shall be able to build hanging gardens in space and populate them with a happy multitude. But no matter how strong the tide, there comes a time when it reaches high water and recedes. Even as the futurologists write, our power surges are being paid for, in a thousand ways and in a thousand places, although there is no one capable of summing the costs. ❦

Technology as Legislation

Langdon Winner

The ecology movement, consumerism, future studies, the technology assessors, students of innovation and social change, and what remains of the "counter-culture" all have something to say about the ways in which technology presents difficulties for the modern world. But as diverse as the approaches and perspectives are, the issues themselves can be sorted into two broad categories.

In the first domain, far and away the most prominent, the focus comes to rest on matters of risk and safeguard, cost and benefit, distribution, and the familiar interest-centered style of politics. Technology is seen as a cause of certain problematic effects. Once this is appreciated, the important tasks become accurately predicting and anticipating changes in order to alleviate risk, adequately evaluating the costs that will or could be incurred, equitably distributing the costs and risks so that no group gains or suffers more than the others, and shrewdly evaluating the political realities bearing upon social decisions about technology.

Under this model the business of prediction is usually meted out to the natural and social sciences. Occasionally, some hope is raised that a new art of science—futurism or something of the sort—will be developed to improve the social capacity of foresight. The essential task is to devise more intelligent ways of viewing technological changes and their possible consequences in nature and society. Ideal here would be the ability to forecast the full range of significant consequences in advance. One would then have a precise way of assigning the risk of proceeding in one way rather than another.

The matter of determining costs is left to orthodox economic analysis. In areas in which "negative externalities" are experienced as the result of technological practice, the loss can be given a dollar value. The price paid for the undesirable "side effects" can then be compared to the benefit gained. An exception to this mode of evaluation can be seen in some environmental and sociological arguments in which nondollar value costs follow the form Leibniz suggested for the solution of all rational disputes: "Let us calculate." Taking this approach one tends to ask questions of the sort: How much are you prepared to pay for pollution-free automobiles? What is the public prepared to tax itself for clean rivers? What are the trade-offs between having wilderness and open space as opposed to adequate roads and housing? Are the costs of jet airport noise enough to offset the advantage of having airports in the middle of town? Such questions are answered at the cash register, although the computer shows a great deal more style.

Once the risks have been assigned, the safeguards evaluated, and the costs calculated, one is then prepared to worry about distribution. Who will enjoy how much of the benefit? Who will bear the burden of the uncertainty or the price tag of the costs? Here is where normal politics—pressure groups, social and economic power, private and public interests, bargaining, and so forth—enters. We expect that those most aware, best supplied, and most active will manage to steer a larger proportion of the advantages of technological productivity their way while avoiding most of the disadvantages. But for those who have raised technology as a political problem under this conception, reforms are needed in this distributive process. Even persons who have no quarrel with the inequities of wealth and privilege in liberal society now step forth with the most trenchant criticisms of the ways in which technological "impacts" are distributed through the social system. A certain radicalism is smuggled in through the back door. The humble ideal of those who see things in this light is that risks and costs be allotted more equitably than in the past. Those who stand to gain from a particular innovation should be able to account for its consequences beforehand. They should also shoulder the major brunt of the costs of undesirable side effects. This in turn should eliminate some of the problems of gross irresponsibility in technological innovation and application of previous times. Since equalization and responsibility are to be induced through a new set of laws, regulations, penalties, and encouragements, the attention of this approach also aims at a better understanding of the facts of practical political decision-making.

Most of the present work with any true influence in the field of technology studies has its basis in this viewpoint. The ecology movement, Naderism, technology assessment, and public-interest science each have somewhat different substantive concerns, but their notions of politics and rational conduct all fit within this frame. There is little new in it. What one finds here is the utilitarian-pluralist model refined and aimed at new targets. In this form it is sufficiently young to offer spark to tired arguments; sufficiently critical of the status quo to seem almost risqué. But since it accepts the major premises and disposition of traditional liberal politics, it is entirely safe. The approach has already influenced major pieces of legislation in environmental policy and consumer protection. It promises to have a bright future in both the academic and the political realms, opening new vistas for "research," "policy analysis," and, of course, "consulting."

On the whole, the questions I have emphasized here are not those now on the agendas of persons working in the first domain. But for those following this approach I have one more point to add. It is now commonly thought that what must be studied are not the technologies but their implementing and regulating systems. One must pay attention to various institutions and means of control—corporations, government agencies, public policies, laws, and so forth—to see how they influence the course our technologies follow. Fine, I would not deny that there are any number of factors that go into the original and continued employment of these technical ensembles. Obviously the "implementing" systems have a great deal to do with the eventual outcome. But in what technological context do such systems themselves operate and what imperatives do they feel obliged to obey? The hope for some "alternative implementation" is largely misguided. *That* one employs something at all far outweighs (and often obliterates) the matter of *how* one employs it. This is not sufficiently appreciated by those working within the utilitarian-pluralist framework. We may firmly believe that we are developing ways of regulating technology. But is it perhaps more likely that the effort will merely succeed in putting a more elegant administrative facade on old layers of reverse adapted rules, regulations, and practices?

The second domain of issues is less easily defined, for it contains a collection of widely scattered views and spokesmen. At its center is the belief that technology is problematic not so much because it is the origin of certain undesirable side effects, but rather because it enters into and becomes part of the fabric of human life and activity. The maladies technology brings—and this is not to say that it brings only maladies—derive from its tendency to structure and incorporate that which it touches. The problems of interest, therefore, do not arrive by chain reaction from some distant force. They are present and immediate, built into the everyday lives of individuals and institutions. Analyses that focus only upon risk/safeguard, cost/benefit, and distribution simply do not reveal problems of this sort. They require a much more extraordinary, deep-seeking response than the utilitarian-pluralist program can ever provide.

What, then, are the issues of this second domain? Some of the most basic of them are mirrored in the theory of technological politics. This model represents the critical phase of a movement of thought, the attempt to do social and political analysis with technics as its primary focus. But these thoughts so far have given little care to matters of amelioration. In the present formulation of the theory, I have deliberately tried to avoid dealing in popular remedies. It is my experience that inquiries pointing to broad, easy solutions soon become cheap merchandise in the commercial or academic marketplace. They become props for the very thing criticized.

For better or worse, however, most of the thinking in the second domain at present is highly specific, solution-oriented, and programmatic. The school of humanist psychology, writers and activists of the counterculture, utopian and communal living experiments, the free schools, proponents of encounter groups and sensual reawakening, the hip catalogers, the peace movement, pioneers of radical software and new media, the founders and designers of alternative institutions, alternative architecture, and "appropriate" or "intermediate" technology — all of these have tackled the practical side of one or more of the issues of technological politics.

Much of the work has begun with a sobering recognition of the psychological disorders associated with life in the technological society. The world of advanced technics is still one that makes excessive demands on human performance while offering shallow, incomplete rewards. The level of stress, repression and psychological punishment that rational-productive systems extract from their human members is not matched by the opportunity for personal fulfillment. Men and women find their lives cut into parcels, spread out, and dissociated. While the neuroses generated are often found to be normal and productive in the sociotechnical network, there has been a strong revolt against the continuation of such sick virtues. Both professionals and amateurs in psychology have come together in a host of widely differing attempts to find the origins of these maladies and to eliminate them.

Other enterprises of this kind have their roots in a pervasive sense of personal, social, and political powerlessness. Confronted with the major forces and institutions that determine the quality of life, many persons have begun to notice that they have little real voice in most important arrangements affecting their activities. Their intelligent, creative participation is neither necessary nor expected. Even those who consider themselves "well served" have cause to wonder at decisions, policies, and programs affecting them directly, over which they exercise no effective influence. In the normal state of affairs, one must simply join the "consensus." One consents to a myriad of choices made, things built, procedures followed, services rendered, in much the same way that one consents to let the eucalyptus trees continue growing in Australia. There are some, however, who have begun to question this submissive, compliant way of life. In a select few areas, some people have attempted to reclaim influence over activities they had previously let slip from their grasp. The free schools, food conspiracies and organic food stores, new arts and crafts movement, urban and rural communes, and experiments in alternative technology have all — in the beginning at least—pointed in this direction. With mixed success they have sought to overcome the powerlessness that comes from meting out the responsibility for one's daily existence to remote large-scale systems.

A closely related set of projects stems from an awareness of the ways organized institutions in society tend to frustrate rather than serve human needs. The scandal of productivity has reached astounding proportions. More and more is expended on the useless, demeaning commodities idealized in the consumer ethos (for example, vaginal deodorants), while basic social and personal needs for health, shelter, nutrition, and education fall into neglect. The working structures of social institutions that provide goods and services seem themselves badly designed. Rather than elicit the best qualities of the persons they employ or serve, they systematically evoke the smallest, the least creative, least trusting, least loving, and least lovable traits in everyone. Why and how this is so has become a topic of widespread interest. A number of attempts to build human-centered and responsive institutions, more reasonable environments for social intercourse, work, and enjoyment, are now in the hands of those who found it simply impossible to continue the old patterns.

Finally, there is a set of concerns, evident in the aftermath of Viet Nam, Watergate, and revelations about the CIA, that aims at restoring the element of responsibility to situations that have tended to exclude responsible conduct. There is a point, after all, where compliance becomes complicity. The twentieth century has made it possible for a person to commit the most ghastly of domestic and foreign crimes by simply living in suburbia and doing a job. The pleas of Lieutenant Calley and Adolf Eichmann—"I just work here"—become the excuse of every man. Yet for those who perceive the responsibility, when distant deeds are done and the casualties counted, the burdens are gigantic. As Stanley Cavell and Nadezhda Mandelstam have observed, there is a sense in which one comes to feel responsible for literally everything. Evils perpetrated and the good left undone all weigh heavily on one's shoulders. Like Kafka's K. at the door of the castle, the concerned begin a search for someone or something that can be held accountable.

I admit that I have no special name for this collection of projects. *Humanist technology* has been suggested to me, but that seems wide of the mark. At a time in which the industrialization of literature demands catchy paperback titles for things soon forgotten, perhaps it is just as well to leave something truly important unnamed.

The fundamental difference between the two domains, however, can be stated: a difference in insight and commitment. The first, the utilitarian-pluralist approach, sees that technology is problematic in the sense that it now *requires legislation.* An ever-increasing array of rules, regulations, and administrative personnel is needed to maximize the benefits of technological practice while limiting its unwanted maladies. Politics is seen as the process in representative government and interest group interplay whereby such legislation takes shape.

The second approach, disjointed and feeble though it still may be, begins with the crucial awareness that technology in a true sense *is legislation.* It recognizes that technical forms do, to a large extent, shape the basic pattern and content of human activity in our time. Thus, politics becomes (among other things) an active encounter with the specific forms and processes contained in technology.

Central to all thinking in the second domain is the idea that *technology is itself a political phenomenon.* A crucial turning point comes when one is able to acknowledge that modern technics, much more than politics as conventionally understood, now legislates the conditions of human existence. New technologies are institutional structures within an evolving constitution that gives shape to a new polity, the technopolis in which we do increasingly live. For the most part, this constitution still evolves with little public scrutiny or debate. Shielded by the conviction that technology is neutral and tool-like, a whole new order is built—piecemeal, step by step, with the parts and pieces linked together in novel ways—without the slightest public awareness or opportunity to dispute the character of the changes under way. It is somnambulism (rather than determinism) that characterized technological politics—on the left, right, and center equally. Silence is its distinctive mode of speech. If the founding fathers had slept through the convention in Philadelphia in 1787 and never uttered a word, their response to constitutional questions before them would have been similar to our own.

Indeed, there is no denying that technological politics is, in the main, a set of pathologies. To explain them is to give a diagnosis of how things have gone wrong. But there is no reason why the recognition of technology's intrinsic political aspect should wed us permanently to the ills of the present order. On the contrary, projects now chosen in the second domain bear a common bond with attempts made to redefine an authentic politics and re-invent conditions under which it might be practiced. As a concern for political theory this work has been admirably carried forward by such writers as Hannah Arendt, Sheldon Wolin, and Carole Pateman. In the realm of historical studies it appears as a renewed interest in a variety of attempts—the Paris Communes of 1739 and 1871, nineteenth-century utopian experiments, twentieth-century Spanish anarchism, the founding of worker and community councils in a number of modern revolutions—to create decentralist democratic politics. In contemporary practice it can be seen in the increasingly common efforts to establish worker self-management in factories and bureaucracies, to build self-sufficient communities in both urban and rural settings, and to experiment with modes of direct democracy in places where hierarchy and managerialism had previously ruled.

Taken in this light, it is possible to see technology as legislation and then follow that insight in hopeful directions. An important step comes when one recognizes the validity of a simple yet long overlooked principle: *Different ideas of social and political life entail different technologies for their realization.* One can create systems of production, energy, transportation, information handling, and so forth that are compatible with the growth of autonomous, self-determining individuals in a democratic polity. Or one can build, perhaps unwittingly, technical forms that are incompatible with this end and then wonder how things went strangely wrong. The possibilities for matching political ideas with technological configurations appropriate to them are, it would seem, almost endless. If, for example, some perverse spirit set out deliberately to design a collection of systems to increase the general feeling of powerlessness, enhance the prospects for the dominance of technical elites, create the belief that politics is nothing more than a remote spectacle to be experienced vicariously, and thereby diminish the chance that anyone would take democratic citizenship seriously, what better plan to suggest than that we simply keep the systems we already have? There is, of course, hope that we may decide to do better than that. The challenge of trying to do so now looms as a project open to political science and engineering equally. But the notion that technical forms are merely neutral and that "one size fits all" is a myth that no longer merits the least respect. ☙

Enough is Enough — The Economic Concept of Sufficiency

Herman Daly

There are two basic errors that are often made in thinking about economic growth in the future. One is the error of *wishful thinking* (assuming that because something is desirable it must somehow also be possible). The other is the opposite error of *technical determinism* (assuming that just because something is possible, it must somehow also be desirable). Traditionally, technologists have tended toward the error of technical determinism, and moral reformers have been prone to wishful thinking. But this is no longer so clearcut, if indeed it ever was. Today we find technologists passionately and wishfully committed to their unproven technical dreams. Is the nuclear power industry, for example, characterized more by technical determinism or wishful thinking? Social reformers on both the Left and the Right are often so committed to their visions of social justice via abundance (a world of middle-class American consumers in a classless society?) that they eagerly accept every promise of cornucopian technology from nuclear power to genetic engineering and space colonization, revealing a degree of blindness to the social consequences of technology that becomes indistinguishable from technical determinism.

These errors can be avoided. Fortunately, not everything that is desirable is impossible, and not everything that is possible is undesirable. There *is* overlap, but we must make sure that economic growth does not push us out of the intersection—that in chasing the desirable we do not crash headlong into the boundary of the possible, and that in following the technical impetus toward "the effecting of all things possible" we refrain from crossing the boundary in the other direction.

The Ecological Necessity of Limiting Economic Growth

Much is heard today about the problem of running out of accessible *nonrenewable* resources. Actually, the more basic problem is with *renewable* resource systems and the destruction of their capacity to reproduce. A reduction in the sustainable yield capacity of a renewable resource system, such as forests, fisheries, grasslands, and croplands, is a far more serious matter than the depletion of a nonrenewable resource. The latter is, after all, inevitable in the long run. The former is not inevitable (except in the astronomical long run). Any permanent reduction in renewable carrying capacity means fewer or less abundant lives will be lived in the future.

Although renewable resources are the crucial ones to protect, their destruction is not independent of the rate of use of nonrenewables. There are two ways in which the too-rapid depletion of nonrenewables contributes to the destruction of renewables. First, high rates of depletion result in high rates of pollution of air and water that directly threaten biological resources. Second and more importantly, rapid use of nonrenewables has allowed us to reach and sustain temporarily a combined scale of population and per capita consumption that could not be sustained by renewable resources alone. As these nonrenewable resources run out, the danger is that we will try to maintain the existing scale and rate of growth by overexploiting our renewable resource base, thereby reducing carrying capacity, and consequently, the total quantity and quality of life ever to be lived on earth.

For a sustainable economy two things are necessary: one is a renewable resource base, the other is a scale of population and per capita consumption that is within the sustainable yield of the renewable resource base. We have a resource base of forests, fisheries, grasslands, and croplands on which mankind has lived almost entirely until the advent of industrialization some two hundred years ago. We are still dependent on these natural systems, but we have increased their short-run productivity with subsidies of nonrenewables and fossil fuels and minerals.

Even with the aid of such large subsidies, the global per capita productivity of each of the four natural systems has likely peaked and begun to decline, according to data compiled by Lester Brown of the Worldwatch Institute. Forest productivity, as measured by cubic meters per capita per year, peaked in 1967 (at 0.67 cubic meters). The productivity of fisheries, as measured by kilograms of fish caught per year per capita, peaked in 1970 (at 19.5 kilograms). For grasslands, we look at annual per capita output of wool, mutton, and beef. Wool peaked in 1960 (at 0.86 kilograms), mutton in 1972 (at 1.92 kilograms), and beef in 1976 (at 11.81 kilograms). Croplands productivity, as measured by kilograms of cereals per capita per year, peaked in 1976 (at 342 kilograms). Of course, trend is not destiny, and conceivably some of these peaks will be surpassed, especially the most recent ones. But it is sobering that these levels of productivity were attained in the first place only with the aid of large fossil fuel and mineral subsidies to mechanization, irrigation, fertilizers, insecticides, and transport. It is difficult to believe that existing levels of output per capita can be maintained, much less surpassed, as we deplete the easily available petroleum and as world population continues to grow.

Mankind is the only species that does not live entirely on the budget of solar energy income. All other forms of life live off the produce of the surface of the earth, where current sunshine is captured by plants. Only man digs "for riches couched and hidden deep in places near to hell," as Ovid puts it. Our rapid consumption of energy capital to supplement our energy income (that is, our consumption of not only today's sunshine, but also the stored sunshine of paleozoic summers) has thrown us out of ecological balance with the rest of creation. To the extent that we overexploit natural systems and reduce their capacity to trap the energy of sunlight, we are in effect consuming tomorrow's sunshine as well as today's and yesterday's. This does *not* mean that all terrestrial minerals should be left in the ground "close to hell," or that mankind should renounce industrialization. But there are limits to how fast such exhaustible resources should be used, and we are in danger of reducing the carrying capacity because we have used mineral wealth too rapidly and built up a scale of population and per capita consumption that is too large to be sustained by our renewable resource base. If, as our minerals subsidy is depleted, we persist in trying to maintain the present scale (or rate of growth!) on the basis of renewable resources alone, we will diminish carrying capacity and future life. To some extent this may already be unavoidable, but if we cannot avoid some destruction of life support systems, we can at least minimize it.

Faced with this situation, we can either define our sustainable-yield biophysical budget and live within it (allowing technology to devote itself to increasing the efficiency with which we use the given throughput) or we can devote technology to increasing the total throughput, with no recognition of a limited biophysical budget. The first response is the one proper for stewards of creation. The second response is that of modern Promethean paganism and modern growth economics. The latter view further assumes that all the world will follow the U.S. into the age of high mass consumption in which, as W.W. Rostow has said, "Growth becomes its normal condition. Compound interest becomes built, as it were, into its habits and institutional structure." Such a vision, implicit or explicit, underlies most of the economic development theories and policies of today. But it is a wishful thought. As Nobel laureate chemist and underground economist Frederick Soddy pointed out long ago: "You cannot permanently pit an absurd human convention such as the spontaneous increment of debt (compound interest) against the natural law of the spontaneous decrement of wealth (entropy)."

The starting point in our thinking about economic development should be that a U.S.-style high mass consumption economy for a world of four billion people is impossible to achieve, except, perhaps, very briefly. Even less possible is an ever-growing standard of consumption for an ever-growing population.

As a simple intuitive demonstration of this "impossibility theorem," consider the following. If it requires roughly one-third of the world's annual production of mineral resources to support that 6 percent of the world's population residing in the U.S. at the standard of consumption to which it is thought that the rest of the world aspires, then it follows that present resource flows would allow the extension of the U.S. standard to at most 18 percent of the world's population, with nothing left over for the other 82 percent. Without the services of the poor 82 percent, the "rich" 18 percent could not possibly maintain their wealth.

But, it will be objected, the answer is simply to increase total world resource flows! By how much would such flows have to increase to bring world per capita levels up to U.S. per capita levels? By a factor of about six or seven, it turns out. But this refers only to current production. According to an analysis by Harrision Brown in *The Scientific American,* to supply the rest of the world with the average per capita accumulation or "standing crop" of industrial metals already embodied in existing artifacts in the ten richest nations would require more than sixty years of production of these metals at 1970 rates.

Neglecting the enormous problem of capital accumulation, for how long could the biosphere sustain even the sixfold increase in the throughput of materials and energy? Existing throughput levels are already damaging life-support capacity, so a sixfold increase would be highly destructive. Furthermore, the sixfold increase is a gross underestimate not only because it neglects the problem of past differences in accumulation between rich and poor that must be made up, but also because it neglects diminishing returns. A sixfold net increase implies a much larger gross increase as we are forced to use poorer grade ores from less accessible places and to dispose of ever larger quantities of waste. And it is the gross throughput that affects the environment.

Recognizing the long-run aggregate biophysical budget constraint is imperative. Equally imperative is the discipline to keep the scale of population and per capita consumption within the biophysical budget. The ecological necessity of limiting economic growth at some level is irrefutable, and the evidence that current levels are unsustainable is persuasive. The only way around the obvious conclusion that economic and demographic growth must be limited is through faith in technological miracles. But even if such miracles seem to be possible in the future, does not common sense require that we limit the growth of scale while waiting for the second coming of Prometheus?

The Moral Necessity of Limiting Economic Growth

From the impossibility theorem just discussed it follows that the total number of person-years of industrially developed living is limited.

It is limited by the pattern of geologic concentrations of minerals in the earth's crust and by the capacity of complex ecosystems to absorb either large quantities (or exotic qualities) of waste materials or heat. Once we recognize this condition, a number of important and difficult ethical questions arise.

How will the limited number of person-years of developed living be apportioned among nations? Among social classes within nations? Among generations? To what extent should present luxury be limited to permit more lives in the future? To what extent should sub-human life be sacrificed in exchange for more person-years of developed living? If a man is worth many sparrows then we must take it for granted that a sparrow's worth is not zero. How many sparrow-years are worth one person-year? How many sparrow-years are worth the difference between one person-year of luxurious living and one person-year of frugal living? Should the burden of scarcity be made to fall more heavily on the present or the future? On the standard of consumption or on numbers of people?

Probably the main value of such questions lies more in their tendency to inspire humility rather than in any prospects for an answer. But they cannot be ignored. Already leaders of overdeveloped countries seem to be saying that the burden of scarcity should fall more heavily on numbers, especially of the poor. Let the poor, they say, limit their populations. The leaders of the underdeveloped countries seem to believe that the burden should fall on the high consumption of the rich. Let the rich, they say, limit their per capita consumption. Both sides seem willing to pass as much of the burden as possible on to the future and on to sub-human life. Let the future have fewer people, reduced per capita consumption, and fewer sub-human species.

The old Marxist class conflict between capital and labor has been softened by rapid economic growth. Struggle over relative shares is less intense when the absolute income of each class is increasing. But growth based on rapid resource depletion constitutes exploitation of the future. To the extent that we refrain from exploiting the future we sharpen the class conflict within the present generation. Ethical questions of fair distribution within one generation must be considered simultaneously with questions of equity between generations. In this three-way struggle, the future has the great disadvantage of not yet existing. But it must be of some weight in a democratic society that future people greatly outnumber present people. If the present is to consume less for the sake of the future, then the rich of the present must bear most of the burden. All that can reasonably be asked of the poor is that they limit population growth while continuing economic growth up to a sufficient, not luxurious, level. The rich must limit population growth also, and reduce per capita consumption from luxury to sufficiency.

Rather than vainly attempt to calculate how many person-years of future life are worth one Cadillac or how many sparrow-years are worth the difference between one person-year of luxurious living and one person-year of frugal living, we might here reconsider an old rule of right action that has played a large role in economics—the utilitarian or Benthamite rule of "the greatest good for the greatest number." That, in turn, means considering three problems associated with the dictum.

First, how do we define "good"? In applying the rule, economists have substituted measurable "goods" for the unmeasurable "good." The rule has become "the greatest production of goods and services for the greatest number." Debatably, for poor societies such a reduction of good to goods may be defensible. But for an affluent country, such a reduction is absurd. Secondly, how do we avoid the problem of "double maximization"? Only one variable can be maximized at a time: an increase in product can be had in exchange for a reduction in numbers, and vice versa. Bentham's dictum contains one too many "greatests." For one of these "greatests" we must substitute "sufficient." Which of the "greatests" should be substituted? Thirdly, how do we define "number"? Does it refer to the population alive now (or at some future date) or to the cumulative number ever to live over time? Usually it is taken as those currently alive, even though Bentham may have thought in terms of cumulative number ever to live. We might also ask whether the number should count subhuman species in some appropriate way.

One way to meet these objections is to reformulate the general rule of right action: *sufficient per capita product for the greatest number over time.* In this reformulation we define number as number over time and suggest some appropriate consideration for subhuman life, but beg the question of defining "appropriate." We retain the economists' substitution of goods for the good in the interest of operationality, but apply to it the condition of "sufficient" rather than "greatest." Since production cannot be considered "the good," it should not be maximized. Production is clearly a good thing up to a point, but beyond some sufficient level, further production no longer contributes to the good and even begins to detract. By substituting "sufficient" for "greatest" we avoid the logical fallacy of double maximization and recognize that goods represent a greatly reduced form of "the good."

But why should number over time be maximized? Is such maximization more important than the quality of life? No. The maximization of numbers is subject to the prior constraint of sufficient per capita product. Sufficient for what? Sufficient for a good life. But once sufficiency is met, why not maximize numbers ever to live? Life is good, isn't it, if one has sufficient resources to enjoy it? The other possible reformulation would have been "greatest per capita product for a sufficient number over time," but that doesn't work because per capita product is such a reduced form of the good that it does not merit maximization, and we cannot know what is a sufficient number of people ever to live.

The dictum "sufficient per capita product for the greatest number over time" is no magic philosopher's stone for solving the difficult questions raised earlier, but it does seem a better principle of right action than "greatest per capita product for the greatest number now." (The latter principle sins against both logic and Christian ethics, and probably against Jeremy Bentham as well.)

Up to now, the concept of sufficiency has played no role in modern economic theory, even though it leads to the basic question of philosophy and religion: "What is a good life?" In its quest to become a positive science, economics has stifled this question and attempted to cut free from all religious and philosophical issues that could not be solved deductively or empirically. With consideration of the good life thus ruled out, there was no possibility for the issue of sufficiency to arise. Therefore learned people concerned themselves ever more strenuously with satisfying their appetites, without raising the ever more obtrusive question of whether the appetite itself was excessive. Although appetites can be excessive only in relation to sufficiency, the concept of sufficiency remained undefined because its definition would require some reference to the taboo concept of a good life. This is ludicrous, but it happened. However difficult or utopian it may appear to be to introduce sufficiency into economic theory and practice, it is even more utopian to think that economics can get along without the concept.

Sufficiency—an Economic Concept

An important step toward getting the concept of sufficiency into economics would be to recognize a long-run aggregate biophysical budget constraint—something like the ecologists' notion of permanent carrying capacity. It would refer to that level of throughput that the ecosystems of a country could supply to the economy on a sustainable-yield basis and to the level of waste products the ecosystem could absorb in a sustainable way.

In symbolic terms, if we let B represent the long-run aggregate bio-physical budget constraint, and P represent the population, then B/P is per capita resource use, and the budget equation is

$$B = P \cdot \left(\frac{B}{P}\right)$$

If the total (B) is fixed by the ecosystem's sustainable capacity and the ratio (B/P) is set by considerations of sufficiency, then P will be determined. There is clearly a trade-off on the demand side: a larger per capita consumption implies a smaller population and vice versa. Since human populations have variable standards of per capita consumption, human population size must be as much determined by standard of consumption as by aggregate resources.

What does this equation tell us about our environmental limits? First, the real biophysical budget must be recognized and given a financial counterpart—either a depletion quota or a national severance tax. (The need to limit population has long been apparent and many schemes suggested, so that issue will not be pursued here.) Secondly, population policy and resource policy go hand in hand: they must be made together. Thirdly, we need an institution for limiting the inequality in per capita resource consumption. Simple minimum and maximum limits on individual income would restrict inequality without implying a jealous quest for flat equality.

Sufficiency has still not been defined. The argument here is simply that the concept is necessary and that even the vaguest definition is better than none. E.F. Schumacher attempted a definition of sufficiency along lines proposed by St. Ignatius Loyola. The goal of man is salvation. Man should make use of the resources of the rest of creation just so far as they help him to attain this goal, and should withdraw from their use just so far as they hinder him. That may be more a restatement of the problem than an answer, but at least it focuses our attention in the right direction.

In the United States, we have some withdrawing to do. We must limit our resource consumption for our own spiritual welfare as well as for ecological reasons. Probably it will be enough of a challenge for now to stop growth in our resource consumption scale, which is sufficient now, if justly and wisely used. We will never seek greater justice and wisdom in resource use as long as we believe that the total can grow forever at compound interest and submerge all inequalities in a sea of absolute abundance. ☘

Human Ecological Planning

Ian McHarg

While ecology has traditionally sought to learn the laws that obtain for ecosystems, ecological investigation has not extended beyond the study of biophysical systems to the study of environments affected by human beings. Yet, what systems remain unaffected by man? Indeed, studies of the interactions of organisms and environments are likely to reveal human dominance. Redressing that gap, "human ecological planners" have begun to study the interactions of organisms (including man) and the environment (including man among other organisms).

Creating a human ecology involves extending and integrating existing scientific disciplines, a process with a precedent in ecology, which has been used to integrate the biosciences. If we extend ecology via ethology we introduce the subject of behavior as an adaptive strategy. If we further embrace ethnography and anthropology, we can study human behavior as adaptation. If, finally, we annex medical anthropology and epidemiology we can close the cycle by examining the natural and human environment in terms of human health and well-being.

When "planning" is linked to human ecology, the primacy of goals and their measurement is modified. Goals take on not only a human, but also a regional face. Viewed through the lens of "human ecological planning," the region is a physical, biological, and cultural entity wherein opportunities and constraints are manifest in every realm. Geophysical and ecological regions are identified as cultural regions in which characteristic people pursue characteristic means of production, develop characteristic settlement patterns, and have characteristic perceptions, needs, desires, and characteristic institutions for realizing their objectives. These needs and desires are in turn matched against resources—physical, biological, and cultural. In short, planning takes place in the context of a particular group's value system.

Fit and Not So Fit

All living systems apparently tend to oscillate between two extreme states. One is syntropic-fitness-health, and the other is entropic-misfitness-morbidity. The evolution of matter in the universe is what Buckminster Fuller has called "syntropic." Put simply, the order and complexity of the *products* of evolution are greater than the order and complexity of the *ingredients*. Consider photosynthesis, the most notable example of syntropy. Given continuous energy in the presence of carbon dioxide and water, the chloroplast creates glucose, a higher level of order than the ingredients. So it is in the evolution of life forms in general: successive forms represent increased capability.

Fitness has two definitions, each complementary. Sir Charles Darwin stated that "the surviving organism is fit for the environment." Much later Dr. Lawrence Henderson augmented this proposition by showing that the actual world consists of countless environments, all exhibiting fitness for appropriate organisms. These two propositions can be linked into an evolutionary imperative: every organism, system, and institution is required to find the fittest environment, to adapt that environment and itself in order to survive. An environment is fit for an organism to the degree to which it meets the organism's needs as found. (The corollary is that the environment is fit to the extent that it minimizes the need to import and employ energy and time to modify the environment and itself to survive.)

All creatures, as individuals, species, or ecosystems, aspire to survival and success. They realize this aspiration through adaptation, which has three modes: the physiological (including mutation and natural selection, which are used by all life forms) the innately behavioral (which is shared by animals and man), and the cultural (which is uniquely human). Until recombinant DNA is employed, physiological adaptation will remain beyond voluntary control; and by definition innate behavior resists manipulation. But cultural adaptation is a mode apart, the most plastic instrument for surviving and succeeding voluntarily.

While the verb "to fit" applies to the active selection of environments, adapting those and the self, the noun "fitness" has another meaning. It implies health—the ability to cope with or solve problems and the ability to recover from insult or assault. In terms of evolutionary biology, health is the capacity to adapt, and fitness and health are linked more profoundly than common word usage suggests since both are "syntropic." More than that, the quest for health and fitness is itself actually health-giving!

These etymologies and linkages bring us finally to planning. Of all the means of cultural adaptation — language, religion, symbolism, art, philosophy, etc. — the one most directly connected to the evolutionary imperative of finding fit environments and adapting them, of accomplishing syntropic-fitness-health, is planning.

How Do We Plan Well-Being?

Theory produces an objective; method, a means of achieving that objective. In the case of planning for human health and well-being, this means describing regions as interacting physiobiocultural systems, reconstituting them as resources (and hence, as social values), considering the attributes of these systems as either costs or benefits for prospective consumers, and selecting the "maximum benefit-least cost" solution. Such modelling, quantitative at best and descriptive at least, enables us to forecast the consequences of altering our physical and cultural environment and to prepare for those we want or can't avoid.

The first objective of the method, which is based on the assumption that each region has unique attributes and potentialities, is to construct a model that shows a particular region's physical evolution, biophysical evolution, and cultural history. Mapping physical evolution involves the laws and findings of meteorology, geology, hydrology, soil science, and physical oceanography. To model the biophysical evolutionary dimension we must call on botanists and zoologists, plant ecologists, animal ecologists, limnologists, and marine biologists. Human evolution requires anthropologists (physical, cultural, and medical), ethnographers, and those economists, sociologists, and political scientists capable of taking the ecological view. The final participant is the planner — the problem-solver willing to try to synthesize the work of the rest.

One World, A Layer Cake

Since science has divided this "one world" into discrete disciplines, planners are required to accept this situation even as they strive to unite all the discrete perceptions into a description of a single interacting system. The trick is to array the data in a way that is true to history and the laws of causality. To do so, human ecological planners build a "layer cake" representation of the region. They place the oldest evidence on the bottom and superimpose new, consequential layers.

The oldest evidence, bedrock geology, is the bottom layer. We ask the geologist, mindful of meterological history, to reconstruct regional geological history. Upon bedrock geology, surficial geology is added. We next ask a geomorphologist to add his more recent data and explain physiography in terms of bedrock and surficial geology. The next scientist, a groundwater hydrologist, interprets the prior data to explain historic and contemporary phenomena. A surface water hydrologist follows. Together they describe hydrological processes, contemporary phenomena, and tendencies. The next layer is the domain of the soils scientist. He too is required to invoke the data contributed by the other scientists to explain the processes and phenomena within his realm, paying due heed to the effect of life forms historically. The plant ecologist comes next. He draws on geology, meteorology, hydrology, and soil science to describe plants in terms of communities occupying habitats. He recapitulates vegetational history to explain the existing plant communities and makes way for the limnologist (who populates aquatic systems using a similar method) and, finally, the animal ecologist (who constructs a history of wildlife and explains the contemporary populations and their environments).

The next task is to populate the region with inhabitants. To explain folk-work-place, we wish to know who the people are, why they inhabit the region, why they are where they are, and why they are doing what they are doing. Here, ethnographic history comes in. We begin with the biophysical representation of the region before the advent of western man, an anthropological model. While a region may be described as an interactive biophysical system, at the same time it is a social value system. And the perceptions of the inhabitants (or the observers), as well as natural history and the available technology and capital, determine what constitutes a "resource." Identifying resources—minerals, lumber, wildlife—locates the means of production and the utilization of resources—all of which are determined by natural history. In turn, the means of production indicates appropriate skills—fishing, mining, lumbering, farming. Historically, Americans who share an occupational identity and an ethnic and religious identity tend to have similar perceptions of themselves, characteristic land uses and settlement patterns, and characteristic public and private institutions to promote and enhance their success and well-being. (The agents of change in this process are, of course, technological breakthroughs and major social events such as wars and immigration.)

Now the layer cake has aboriginal inhabitants, plants, animals, and people, their settlement patterns, land uses, and transportation corridors. The next land-use map should portray colonial settlement in a way that accords with then-current perceptions and technology and that explains the differences from the original map in terms of resources, technology, and social events. For example, the age of sailing entailed the colonization of the eastern U.S. seaboard, the search for safe harbors, and the search for estuarine and river systems that permitted the penetration of the interior. The Hudson, Delaware, Christiana, Susquehanna, Potomac, and James rivers provided safe harbors, but penetrating the interior posed serious problems since the main rivers and their tributaries had waterfalls. All of the waterfalls occurred on the same geological phenomenon, the interface between the crystalline Piedmont and the Coastal plains. So at this point, on each of these rivers, settlement occurred—Albany, Trenton, Philadelphia, Wilmington, Baltimore, Washington, and Richmond. (New York was a special case—a granite island located in the drowned tidal estuary.)

Cannons and shot provide another illustration of how our layer cake explains the past (as well as predicts the likely consequences of future events). In revolutionary times, iron for cannon and cannon balls was obtained from bogs, which were abundant in the coastal plain of New Jersey and scarce elsewhere. The progression from bogs to bog iron to foundries to settlements is plain—so with grist and saw mills, ports, harbors, fisheries, and farming. Each successive map shows changes responsive to new options presented by technological innovation or impelled by social events, revolutions, war, or immigration.

The top layer of the cake shows current land use, and it is gravid with meaning. It shows that people are who they are, where they are, and doing what they are doing for good reasons. Moreover, they are not reticent to describe themselves in economic, ethnic, occupational, religious, and spatial terms, and that is what human ecological planners invite them to do. When this people-place description, called "consensual mapping," is compared to "natural" regions and features, we see a great conformity between human nature and nature.

Consensual mapping leads to the next task—ascertaining the needs and desires of the population, especially those subjective values that constitute "fitness" and "misfitness." For this purpose, it turns out, interviews with a small sample of people from each group under study suffice.

At this stage formal politics is obviously important, but informal institutions receive even greater attention. Voluntary associations— conservation groups, fraternal organizations, voluntary fire companies, parent-teacher associations, the League of Women Voters, and the Shell Fisherman's Association—reveal their values, positions on issues, membership, financial capabilities, and public relations strategies. This analysis, combined with one of kinship, reveals the social system as a complex network with a mosaic of overlapping constituencies, each having characteristic needs and desires, with varying capabilities of realizing them through the market and through private and public institutions.

Values Count

Once the data are ordered and comprehensible, human ecological planners must make either assumptions or predictions about the size and composition of the population at _future_ times. This prerogative is usually the economist's. The economy of the region is reviewed historically and, in conjunction with assumptions made about the national and regional economy, predictions of growth or decline are made for population, employment categories, and public facilities. Taken into account are anticipated levels of private investment and fiscal expenditures by government at all levels.

In addition to these other maps, one other is usually prepared. It is called "Protection." On it, human ecological planners can locate and identify all hazards to life and health from floodplains, hurricane zones, seismic areas, and the like. This map also reveals areas that can be made hazardous by human intervention—the withdrawal of water, gas, oil or minerals, for example. It also locates all rare, endangered, scarce, or valuable species of plants and animals, as well as all buildings, places and spaces deemed historically, scenically, or scientifically valuable.

Once we have modeled the natural region as an interacting system in which values repose, we can search for fit environments for all users, present and prospective. This requires a two-part process. First we must interpret the data maps, identifying opportunities and constraints for all prospective land uses. At this point, say, the geology map might be interpreted for seismic activity, landslide hazards, fault zones, economic minerals, and compressive strength, while the physiography map will reveal such features as elevation.

The sum of all the legends on all the maps—the whole layer cake—constitutes the sum of attributes considered in the allocation process. Since any single phenomenon can be an opportunity for one user and a constraint to another, the users must now be identified explicitly (by the team's anthropologists). Then, all the relevant attributes in every data set are compiled in terms of opportunities and constraints for that land use. The region is then shown as a gradient of maximum suitability (fitness) for each and every land use—agriculture by type, industry by type, etc. At this point human ecological planners can synthesize all the optima for all prospective land uses, showing the intrinsic fitness of the region for all existing and prospective uses, and they can identify locations where more than one land use can (or cannot) coexist compatibly with another.

This procedure can help government planners evaluate the intrinsic "health" of a region. Even more important, it can help them *allocate resources using the value system of the constituencies that inhabit the region.* Truly democratic, ecological planning seeks to fit consumer and environment, and thus, is itself health-giving. Success in such planning or fitting should reveal itself in healthy communities, with physical, biological and social systems in dynamic equilibrium.

Human ecological planning may seem beyond the financial or human resources of most communities. Yet, what could be more important than health and well-being, or more worthy of personal, familial, and institutional resources? A natural inventory and ethnographic history provide us with some sense of the impact of our intervention in evolution and with direction in our collective quest for health and well-being. ❦

V. RENEWABLE ENERGY

The Transition to Renewable Resources

Barry Commoner

The resources that have supported rising standards of living are rapidly becoming scarcer. As a result, developing countries cannot afford development, industrialized countries face serious economic disruptions, and international competition for diminishing resources threatens world peace. The solution to the physical problem is self-evident—a gradual replacement of nonrenewable resources with renewable ones. However, superimposed on this monumental problem is an overriding issue: rich nations and privileged classes have the power to determine the course of the transition to renewable resources, which may therefore take place at the expense of poor nations and poor people in rich nations.

Solving the problem in an equitable manner means avoiding a number of traps, including the temptation to substitute philosophy for fact and to submerge the discussion in a sea of aphorisms. Because the technical aspects of the problem seem relatively simple, it is particularly tempting to reduce the more difficult social and political issues to biological ones, cloaking partisan political aims in pseudo-objectivity. But considering the basic facts about resource renewability scientifically as a series of propositions is perspective-giving.

1. *The availability of all other resources depends on the availability of energy.* The resources needed to produce goods and services can be divided into two main classes: matter and energy. Since matter cannot be destroyed, it is essentially renewable. The amounts of the different elements on earth—such as carbon, oxygen, nitrogen, and the various

minerals—are constant, but the accessibility of many mineral resources is reduced as they are used. The spontaneous chemical and physical changes that occur in such use—for example, the scattering of substances—can be reversed, but only by expending energy. Thus, all mineral resources are fundamentally renewable if we are willing to expend energy on them. The practical example is the conservation of gold and other precious metals. Nearly all such metals mined over the course of human history are still available in useful form. Because they are highly valued, great care has been taken to avoid scattering them and, where necessary, to recover them. Nothing prevents us from treating iron or copper in the same way. Theoretically at least, material resources can be renewable, provided energy is available. So the overall problem comes down to the renewability of energy.

2. *While energy is indestructible, its ability to do work is not.* Energy is useful only as it yields work, and work can be obtained only when energy flows from one place to another. In the process of yielding work, the ability of energy to perform additional work is always reduced. The First Law of Thermodynamics tells us energy is itself indestructible, but the Second Law says that its ability to do work—its only value—is nonrenewable.

3. *Work (and therefore energy) is essential to the production of all goods and services.* The Second Law of Thermodynamics tells us that only work will make something happen that will not happen by itself. Since all the goods and services that meet our needs—houses, shoes, bread, automobiles, telephones, and telephone messages—do not happen on their own account, all of them require that work be done and energy made to flow. Thus, everything that is produced and all economic value depends on the use of energy to generate work.

4. *The availability of energy depends on its price, which in turn depends on the renewability of energy resources.* We have an energy crisis because nearly all the energy sources on which modern production systems rely (96 percent in the U.S.)—oil, natural gas, coal, and uranium—are nonrenewable. Because these fuels were laid down only once, their deposits are limited. Inevitably, as a nonrenewable energy source is depleted, the cost of producing it—and therefore its price—rises faster and faster as more is produced and less and less accessible deposits are exploited. Thus, unlike the production of other goods (in which increasing production usually *decreases* production costs), as the total amount of energy produced grows, the cost of production *increases*.

The exponential rise in the cost of producing a unit amount of a nonrenewable resource such as oil reflects the strong interaction between the acts of finding and producing oil and the structure of the "crop" of accessible oil fields that remains to be found. When exploitation of the U.S. oil resource began in earnest at the turn of the century, the largest, best-yielding, most accessible fields were the first ones found and tapped. Production costs then were only a few cents per barrel. But soon those fields were exhausted and it became more costly to find and exploit the next best ones. At first, when the costs were reckoned in pennies per barrel, the gradual rise was hardly noticeable. But now, after nearly 100 years of exploitation, the cost per barrel is reckoned in tens of dollars, and the annual increase in cost is correspondingly large. Like the rate of growth of a 100-year-old bank deposit at compound interest, the rate of growth of oil production costs has become spectacular. Oil will not necessarily become physically totally depleted, but it will become too costly to produce. We will not exhaust the oil but our ability to pay for it.

5. *There is no substitute for energy in the production system.* Like raw materials, labor, and machines, energy is an essential ingredient in the production of goods and services. When the cost of a particular factor of production rises, it is likely to be replaced by a less costly one. In the case of energy, can such substitution halt the exponential rise in price? Buffalo robes provide an unlikely clue. During the decade 1880–90 when the once-vast U.S. herds of buffalo were destroyed, the price of a buffalo robe increased about tenfold. Although as a species, buffalo are an irreplaceable resource, viewed as a source of food and clothing they are replaceable. The exponential rise in the cost of buffalo robes prompted people to substitute less costly sources of food and apparel, incidentally saving the species from extinction.

However, energy is different: there is no substitute for it. Whether provided by fuel-fed machines, by beasts of burden, or by people, work must be done in every production process, and work is generated *only* by the flow of energy. The labor of people or animals can substitute for inanimate forms of energy, but only for certain limited production processes. Practically speaking, unless we are willing to forgo most of the advantages of modern industrial and agricultural production and transportation, we must use some non-living sources of energy. Unlike the buffalo, energy cannot be replaced in the economy.

Viewed thus, the present exponential rise in the price of oil and the other nonrenewable fuels on which we depend is not likely to end. The conventional explanation for the rising price of oil is that, angered by U.S. and European support of Israel in the war with Egypt and Syria in October 1973, OPEC cut back oil production, inducing a world-wide shortage that enabled the cartel to quadruple the price of oil in six short months. In fact, the real reason for the increase originates in the United States, not in the Arab nations. In 1973, the Arab oil ministers were well aware that OPEC's largest customer, the U.S. oil companies, had announced a year earlier that the price of oil produced in the U.S., which had remained essentially constant for 25 years, would need to begin rising exponentially. In response, the OPEC oil ministers followed the normal business practice—that goods ought to be priced at what the market will bear—and raised their own price. The Arab-Israeli War only provided a convenient excuse. Thus, contrary to conventional wisdom, the escalating price of energy, which is the only real evidence of an energy crisis, originates not with the greed and hostility of Arab shieks—however real that might be—but with the inevitable economic outcome of the depletion of oil in the United States.

6. *The rising price of energy is a powerful inflationary force.* Because energy is used in producing all goods and services, when its price rises, the cost of everything else is driven upward. Before 1973, U.S. commodity prices rose about 2 percent a year, after 1973 they took off, going into double-digit figures in 1974. Since 1974, they have run at more than 10 percent a year. And consumer prices have not been far behind. The present disastrous rate of inflation is the main symptom of the energy crisis.

7. *Energy-driven inflation places a particularly heavy burden on the poor.* A notorious evil, inflation reduces purchasing power, lowers the demand for goods, depresses production and so leads to unemployment. The prices of goods that are particularly dependent on energy—among them housing, synthetic fibers, and food—are affected most by the rising price of energy. Thus, the heaviest burden is on poor families, which spend a much larger part of their budgets than other families to buy necessary energy intensive items. According to the analysis of 1976 consumer expenditures by the Exploratory Project for Economic Alternatives, the poorest 10 percent of U.S. households spent nearly 30 percent of their income on energy purchases, while average families spent 7.4 percent, and the wealthiest 10 percent spent only 4.2 percent in that way. As the price of energy keeps rising, emergency funds are needed to help the poor buy fuel for heating.

8. *The rising price of energy tends to hamper new industrial investments.* Since 1973 the price of energy has been rising at a rate unprecedented in the U.S., and this high *rate of increase* in energy costs inhibits new capital investment. Between 1950 and 1970, when energy prices were stable, the entrepreneur could count on energy price forecasts in predicting the operating costs of a new enterprise. But with price rises rapid enough to add a new element of uncertainty, the risk that a new investment will fail is increased. Many business commentators have identified such uncertainties as a major cause of the present slowdown in the rate of investment—a slowdown that means that plants are not built and job opportunities are lost.

9. *The present energy system wastes capital.* The availability of capital and the willingness of investors to risk it in new productive enterprises is essential to the economy's health. And the connection between the flow of capital and the flow of energy is close. Present forms of energy production are extraordinarily capital-intensive—that is, relative to the economic value of their output, energy production demands much more capital than other productive enterprises. As a result, the energy industry is particularly vulnerable whenever it becomes difficult to raise investment capital. This fact explains what otherwise might seem an anomoly: energy projects that are especially capital-intensive (nuclear power plants for example, and synthetic oil

and shale oil projects) are often abandoned or delayed even when energy needs are great.

Various ways of producing energy differ considerably in their capital productivity—that is, in the yield per dollar of capital invested. A recent analysis by the American Gas Association shows, for example, that to deliver one quad of energy per year to residential or commercial users, an electric power plant system would require more than twice the investment required for systems based on natural gas. For industrial use the disparity is 3 to 1. In general, the present emphasis on electric power and on producing coal and synthetic fuels promotes the waste of investment capital.

Considered together, these propositions tell us that although the energy crisis arose because present energy sources are nonrenewable, it is expressed not in the reduced production of these sources but in their exponential rise in price. In this sense, the energy crisis is fundamentally an *economic* crisis. In an industrialized country such as the U.S., the escalating price of energy places a growing burden on the poor and has become a chief reason for increasing difficulties with inflation and unemployment. In the world economy, the developing nations occupy a position analogous to that of poor people in the industrialized countries.

The resulting economic difficulties can only be resolved by switching from nonrenewable sources to renewable ones, the cost of which will become stable with time. Such a transition must begin at once if we are to avoid the catastrophic economic effects of further escalation in energy prices, so we must choose now between the two possible existing forms of renewable energy: nuclear power supported by a breeder reactor system (which would extend the availability of nuclear fuel to perhaps 1500 to 2000 years) and solar energy.

The nuclear/breeder alternative would involve grappling with enormously risky and as yet unmanageable problems related to radioactive wastes. It would also involve accepting a growing danger of proliferation of nuclear weapons, military control of power installations, and huge capital expenses. Finally, it would involve isolating energy sources from control of energy users, which means that economic and political dominance by whatever agency controls these sources is a distinct possibility.

In contrast, the solar alternative is environmentally benign and in no way endangers peace. Solar energy is universally distributed and its use in most cases involves no economy of scale. It is equally efficient in whatever size is most appropriate to the task, so large units of capital are therefore not essential to going solar and solar energy can be controlled by the user.

Usually, suggesting that the immediate introduction of solar energy could begin to solve the energy crisis brings the response that this is something for the distant future. But this is a tragically false perception. The fact is that most solar energy technologies are already in hand and can be introduced at once for various uses at economically competitive costs, as the following propositions make clear.

1. *The cost of producing solar energy will not escalate, but will remain stable as production expands.* Unlike oil, natural gas, coal, or uranium, solar energy will never run out (or at least not in the next few billion years). It is thus not subject to diminishing returns—which means that its price, instead of escalating like the price of present energy sources, will be stable, will even fall, as the cost of solar devices declines. By stabilizing the price of energy, the use of solar energy reduces the threat of inflation and eases the task of planning investments in new productive enterprises, thus relieving two of today's worst economic problems—inflation and unemployment.

2. *Solar energy is available everywhere, but the availability of its most accessible forms varies from place to place.* The use of solar energy does not depend on any single technique. Everywhere the sun shines solar energy can be trapped in collectors and used for space heat and hot water. In some places, the most available form of solar energy may be wind (which is driven by the sun). In agricultural areas, solar energy will be available in the form of the organic matter photosynthesized by plants: manure, plant residues, or crops grown to be converted into methane or alcohol. In forested areas, waste wood, or even wood grown for the purpose, can be transformed into heat. And wherever the sun shines, photovoltaic cells can be used to convert solar energy directly into electricity.

3. *The necessary solar technologies are available now.* Solar collectors are used all over the world, and about 80 years ago were common in Florida and California. Small windmills used to dot the farm landscape, methane plants now operate in hundreds of thousands of Indian and Chinese villages, alcohol produced from grain was used extensively in a gasoline mixture to run cars and trucks during World War II, and photovoltaic cells now power satellites and remote weather stations. Solar energy needs to be stored during the night or over cloudy periods, but a variety of storage options exist to meet that need: batteries, tanks of alcohol or methane, silos full of grain, standing timber, or even piles of manure.

4. *Some solar technologies are already economically competitive, and all will eventually become competitive relative to nonrenewable energy sources.* Since the cost of solar energy is fixed only by the cost of the equipment, which will fall in price as experience is gained and production increases, solar energy's cost will inevitably equal that of the exponentially more costly conventional alternatives and then each year become cheaper relative to them. Estimates of when and how are thus worth examining. Those made by the Solar Energy Task Force of the Federal Energy Administration in 1977 (now part of the Department of Energy) follow.

Solar heating. In most of the central U.S., it would today pay a householder who uses electricity or oil for space heat and hot water to replace about half of it with a solar collector system, if the government would provide low-cost loans. Even borrowing all the necessary funds at 8 percent interest with a 15-year amortization period would cut the average annual heating bill by 19–20 percent.

Photovoltaic electricity. Beginning immediately for the more expensive installations such as gasoline-driven field generators, within two years for road and parking lot lighting, and within five years for residential electricity in the Southwest, photovoltaic units can compete economically with conventional power. All that is required to achieve this remarkable accomplishment is to invest about $0.5 billion in the purchase of photovoltaic cells by the federal government. This would allow the government to order about 150 million watts capacity of photovoltaic cells and industry to expand its operations sufficiently to reduce the price of the cells from the current price of $10/watt (peak) to $2-3/watt in the first year, to $1/watt in the second year, to $0.50/watt in the fifth year, and to invade the huge market for electricity.

Methane and alcohol production from organic matter. While methods of commercializing these sources of solar energy have not yet been worked out by the Solar Energy Task Force, current independent efforts, especially by farmers, show that commercialization is feasible. Public works funds can be used to rebuild urban garbage and sewage-sludge disposal systems so that they generate methane, which can help meet a city's energy demand. In certain farm operations—such as a dairy with 200 or more cows or a farm raising 5,000 or more chickens—it is already economical to replace current manure-disposal systems with methane generators that produce electricity to drive farm machinery and heat to warm the barns. In Midwestern states, farmers are organizing to produce alcohol from grain and other agricultural products, which is being sold as "gasohol" (10 percent alcohol and 90 percent gasoline) to drive cars, trucks and tractors. Gasohol is an excellent substitute for unleaded gasoline, the short supplies of which (due to inadequate refinery capacity) cause the intermittent lines at gas stations.

5. *The economic feasibility of solar energy depends on how it is integrated into conventional energy systems.* The economics of providing space heat can be optimized by integrating the conventional and solar sources into a single system that is more flexible than either a purely solar or a purely conventional system. When sunshine is plentiful, the system derives all the needed energy from the sun. When sunlight is scarce (or the temperature is low) the system can operate on conventional fuel. This flexible, albeit complex system, is able in the first situation to substitute cost-free sunlight for expensive fossil fuel and in the second, to substitute fossil fuel for a costly expansion of the solar system. The key to the economic feasibility of the combined system is that it is *integrated*—its solar and conventional parts are fitted together so as to use the system's dual capabilities when each of them gives the most favorable results.

6. *The economic feasibility of solar energy also depends on integration with the energy-using process of production.* The high cost of storage is a major reason for the relatively large capital costs involved in solar technologies. This cost can be sharply reduced by incorporating the solar source into an energy-*using* system that itself has a built-in storage capability. Thus, if a photovoltaic system is used to provide power for an electric car which must have a battery in order to operate, the high cost of storage normally needed in a photovoltaic system is shared. In the same way, an industry that finds it useful to equip its workers with battery-operated hand tools to spare them the hazards associated with long electric cords would find photovoltaic electricity particularly economical. Again, integration—this time between energy source and energy-using task—is the secret to successful economic introduction of solar energy.

These considerations show that to be economically successful a solar technology should not be considered as an isolated piece of equipment. It is a mistake to develop a solar technology autonomously and then judge it (with respect to its economic efficiency) against some other, equally isolated, conventional technology. Indeed, solar energy will be commercially successful only if it is introduced as an integral part of an overall system of production, when it improves the economic efficiency *of the production system as a whole.*

7. *The present energy system must be modified to facilitate the solar transition.* Existing energy and production systems on the whole are so faulty that the chances of successfully fitting a new solar technology into them is small. Here we have a "bootstrap" problem. The solar transition requires a transformation of *both* the energy system as a whole and of its constituent technologies.

This problem can be solved by recognizing two facts. First, the purpose of introducing solar energy is not to satisfy some cultural longing, but to accomplish an *economic* purpose. Secondly, certain non-solar steps can be taken to achieve the same purpose, which will so alter the overall structure of the energy system as to facilitate the introduction of solar energy. This is the basis for a realistic solar transition. An essential feature of a solar transition is the replacement of existing *energy-using* devices that are incompatible with a solar source with comparable devices that can be operated on either a conventional or solar energy source. An oil- or coal-burning heating system poses a good example of such incompatibility: producing an equivalent fuel, capable of being used in such a system, from a solar source is likely to be difficult. In contrast, a heating system that burns natural gas can operate either on that fuel or on a solar fuel—methane produced from organic wastes or crops. Such a system would be an essential bridge between the conventional energy system and its solar replacement. In the same way, decentralized operation and high thermodynamic efficiency will also aid the development of the solar system.

8. *Cogeneration of heat and electricity from natural gas plays a* *crucial role in the solar transition.* In conventional electric power plants, at least two-thirds of the energy available from the fuel is wasted, being emitted into the environment as heat. Cogeneration, in which this wasted heat is put to use, is an ideal transitional process. The economic advantages of cogeneration have thus far been exploited for fairly large industrial and commercial installations. But cogeneration also lends itself to use on a very small scale—a single house—if need be.

The Fiat Company of Italy recently put on the market a small cogenerator for a single-family home—a four-cylinder auto engine that drives an electric generator and supplies heat for space heating and hot water. It will run on gasoline, methane, natural gas, or alcohol. The unit can convert 66 percent of the energy input into heat and 26 percent into electricity; only 8 percent is lost. (A conventional home furnace converts 40 to 65 percent of input energy to space heat.) For producing electricity alone, it is almost as efficient as a central electric generating station. Widescale use of units like those Fiat manufactures would save both energy and utility costs. In addition, it would create jobs in the auto industry and in maintenance and repair work, decentralize energy production and establish a base for efficiently introducing solar energy.

Ideally, the size of the cogenerator should be matched economically to the size of the task. Thus, in rebuilding an urban neighborhood, it might pay to include a small cogenerator that would provide all the rehabilitated buildings with space heat, air conditioning, and electric power—probably selling some electricity to the utility as well. In this way, increased electric capacity would be automatically linked to new demand, the costly overcapacity inherent in existing centralized systems could be avoided, and the introduction of solar energy would be made that much easier. Here for the taking is not only an answer to rising utility bills, but also relief from the feeling of helplessness that tends to overwhelm consumers when they confront the giant utilities.

Adopting a cogeneration system helps speed the transition to solar energy. Three different sources of solar energy can be readily introduced with relatively small changes in the system itself. Solar collectors can be readily introduced by feeding the heat that they collect into the system's existing heat storage and transfer system, and panels of photovoltaic cells can be installed to provide a good part of the needed electricity. At the same time, methane from a solar source can be substituted for at least part of the natural gas that fuels the cogenerator. In the U.S., this could reduce the amount of fossil fuel now used to supply the residential and commercial sector by 87 percent.

Fundamental to such schemes is natural gas. Because cogenerators must be close enough to residential and commercial consumers to efficiently supply them with heat, cogenerators must be compatible with an urban environment. Only a cogenerator fueled by natural gas, which releases only carbon dioxide and water when it is burned, can meet this requirement. Natural gas is also the only fossil fuel that can be replaced by a solar fuel—methane generated from organic matter—with no change in the energy-using equipment. Using natural gas, the essential bridging fuel, therefore facilitates the gradual introduction of solar energy without excessive disruptions and costs. (In Chicago, the gas utility is already buying methane produced from manure at a cattle feedlot in Oklahoma at $1.97 per 1000 cubic feet. The solar methane is being pumped into the Texas-Chicago natural gas pipeline and delivered to Chicago consumers as a very small proportion of the gas that they are now burning in their furnaces and kitchen stoves.) For these reasons, natural gas is the essential "bridging fuel" in the solar transition.

9. *U.S. fossil fuel resources are sufficient to sustain a gradual transition to solar energy.* The U.S. could, over a 50-year period, accomplish a gradual transition from our present nearly total dependence on nonrenewable fuels to a nearly total use of solar energy—but only if the available supplies of conventional fuels, especially natural gas, are sufficient to sustain this transition. In such a transition the present use of coal, oil, and nuclear power could over the 50 years be reduced to zero, and oil imports could be eliminated in 20 years. But the present annual consumption of natural gas (about 20 trillion cubic feet) would need to be increased to about 35 TCF over the first 25 years. It could then be reduced, over the next 25 years, to about 5 TCF.

No natural system could be *completely* solar until it had enough excess capacity to allow for storage. The output of a national solar system would depend on the weather. We could not afford to run out of energy in a bad year, so a standby energy source is essential. Again, natural gas is the leading candidate since it could be quickly produced from capped-off wells, distributed in the pipelines used for solar methane, and burned without need for technical adjustments in the equipment that uses the latter.

These ideas seem strange when viewed against the common conception that we are "running out" of oil and natural gas. Of course we are "running out" of these fuels; this has been true ever since the first barrel of domestic oil was taken out of the ground in 1859. The relevant questions are how much remains to be produced, at what price, and whether remaining supplies can sustain the transition to solar energy.

Making this calculation, it is all too easy to get the wrong answer by asking the wrong question. For our purposes, the main question is not how long the *known*, already-found resources of fuel will last, but rather how long the much larger *findable* resources will last. While speculations vary, recent data from the U.S. Geological Survey indicate that the potential resources of domestic oil in the U.S. could supply the nation's needs (at the present rate of consumption) for about 70 years. Similarly, the Petroleum Industry Resource Foundation contends that the world supply of oil is probably enough to meet present world demand for about 30 years. Thus, oil supplies are quite sufficient to sustain a 50-year transition to solar energy, in which the present rate of oil consumption would be gradually reduced to zero.

The single most crucial question is whether the potential supply of natural gas is sufficient to serve as the "bridging fuel" in a solar transition. Evaluating the potential supply in the U.S., industry experts recently estimated that annual production would rise from the present level of 20 trillion cubic feet to 35 TCF by the year 2000. The total size of the resource is estimated at 900-1300 TCF from conventional sources and 5,000-10,000 TCF from the new, deeper sources. The newer gas can be produced at a price of about $4-5 thousand cubic feet — a price that conventional gas is expected to reach within a few years. Clearly, we have enough of this crucial fuel available to support a 50-year solar transition described here and some left over to serve as a standby fuel for many years or until solar methane production creates a surplus for storage.

Applied sensibly, solar energy can be efficiently used on whatever scale is appropriate—from a solar water heater in a single dwelling, to a neighborhood power plant in an industrialized city. All of the sensible forms of solar energy—solar collectors, windmills, fuels from organic matter, and even photovoltaic cells—can be efficiently applied at whatever scale matches the need. There are, of course, *unreasonable* forms of solar applications that imitate the huge, centralized design of present conventional sources. Centralized solar electric power stations for example, or the proposed solar power satellite are unreasonable because they ignore one of the crucial differences between conventional and solar energy sources. The former have a large economy of scale, so that the efficiency of a large centralized plant can support the extra cost of the necessary transmission network. But solar installations have no economy of scale (that is, the efficiency of solar devices is independent of their overall size) and do not produce savings that can support the network needed in connection with centralized plants.

Finally, we must return to the overriding economic, social and political issue of poverty. How does this relate to the foregoing considerations? Some advocates of solar energy believe that the only way to encourage the introduction of solar energy is to raise the price of conventional energy even faster than at present. The reasoning is that the sooner the cost of conventional energy overtakes the high cost of a solar installation, the more people will be encouraged to make the solar investment. The trouble is that this inducement will work only with those people who possess the capital needed to meet the high initial cost of a solar installation (which is about $15,000 to heat a typical one-family home)—that is, the rich. Meanwhile, the poor, who cannot afford to go solar, would be burdened by an unnecessary increase in the already high cost of conventional energy. This scheme is Robin Hood's in reverse: it would take from the poor and give to the rich. It would force both the poor people in a single country such as the United States, and the poor countries of the world, to bear the economic burden of a solar transition.

The answer lies in social action that would govern the production and pricing of energy in the interest of carrying out the solar transition in an equitable manner. Here I reflect a political point of view that is not shared by every energy analyst. I believe that the global transformation to dependence on renewable resources—the solar transition—ought to be designed to end poverty, within nations and among them. This ought to be the great purpose of transforming the world economy from its present, catastrophic dependence on nonrenewable resources, to the balance and stability that is endowed by the endlessly renewable global resource—the sun. ☥

Solar Energy and Conservation — Pragmatic Energy Choices

Robert Stobaugh and Daniel Yergin

Solar Energy

Except for those who believe in an electrified world using fusion power, there is general agreement that eventually a transition will have to be made from oil, gas, coal, and uranium to what is called solar energy. The term "solar" covers many diverse sources, their common thread being that they are all renewable, depend ultimately on the sun, and, in the case of burnable materials, have come into existence on the earth "recently," in the last century or so (in contrast to fossil fuels).

At the present time, all forms of solar energy account for only one million barrels per day of oil equivalent in the U.S. energy balance — and this only if one includes hydroelectric power under this heading. And in the conventional forecast for the late 1980s, this amount is predicted only to double.

The amounts allocated by the government to solar energy research and development have increased substantially, as have the attention and effort by private companies. But the policy direction of the government's research effort is open to serious question, and private solar industry remains in the difficult first phase that characterizes the initial diffusion of innovation.

---

*The section on Solar Energy is based primarily on the work of our colleague Professor Modesto A. Maidique in *Energy Future: Report of the Energy Project of the Harvard Business School.*

Far too much of the present research program is directed at "big solar"—expensive high-technology projects that mimic the space and nuclear programs. There are two prominent examples. One is the "power tower," which would use acres of mirrors to focus light in order to heat water to boiling; it accounts for a fifth of the government's entire solar research and development budget. The other is the orbiting satellite which would beam the sun's energy back to earth, and whose supporters have attempted to obtain large-scale funding.

While the various forms of big solar differ in many ways among themselves, they have certain important features in common: they fit in well with the traditional mode of federal budgeting for technological development; they are highly uncertain as to their practicality; they are likely to be very expensive, with current cost estimates highly speculative; and they may well encounter severe environmental problems. Unfortunately, federal solar policy favors these programs at the expense of "small solar"—the decentralized forms of renewable energy that can deliver a sizable contribution in this century.

Of these, the foremost are those related to space and hot water heating, and the consumption of "biomass"—organic matter, primarily from plants—for all forms of burning.

In terms of quantitative contribution, solar space and hot water heating can make its greatest impact—in the next decade at least—through the so-called active systems, which involve mechanical moving parts. The most common form today is the solar panel designed to catch and concentrate the sun's rays, to heat air, water, or some other medium flowing through pipes, and to convey the heat, with the aid of fans or pumps, to where it is needed.

The potential for active solar heating is vast because it is well suited to most new residential and commercial buildings and to about one-third of the nation's 55 million dwellings. It had formerly been thought that it would take decades for passive solar heating—designing buildings to take advantage of the environment—to make a major impact, because of the slowness with which the building stock turns over. But recent evidence indicates that passive solar heating can also be effectively retrofitted onto existing structures on a substantial scale and in a much shorter time.

In 1975, one could still have only speculated about the possibilities for a solar heating industry. Today it is a vibrant, growing industry. Sales, including installation, increased tenfold in three years, from $25 million in 1975 to $260 million in 1977. The development of the industry and the market potential permit one to be increasingly optimistic about solar energy.

But yet, in absolute terms, the industry remains small and fragmented. The key problem is to help the diffusion of innovation occur at a more rapid rate, and this requires mechanisms to help overcome a series of economic and institutional obstacles.

The most important is the question of payback, how fast a building owner will recover his investment. Research seems to indicate that about a five-year payback is required. Currently, solar heating has about a twelve-year payback. But, of course, that is measured against other energy sources that are sold to consumers at prices heavily subsidized (by price controls) and some of which bear heavy externalities.

Other major obstacles include building codes, financing, "the right to sunlight," quality control, distribution, and the relationship to utilities. That last is a most important consideration. Some proponents of solar power are making a serious error in trying to keep utilities out of solar energy instead of encouraging them to enter the business of "delivering" solar energy by taking the responsibility for installing and financing (perhaps owning) solar units. Wide diffusion of solar heating will have a major impact on the utilities, and if they feel threatened and so oppose it, then large-scale implementation of solar could be delayed for a long time.

The other major near-term renewable source is biomass—organic matter from plants and animals. Biomass can be burned, or it can be converted into a gas or liquid fuel. Considered as biomass, for instance, municipal solid waste can be converted from a major disposal problem into a significant energy source, rivaling the present contribution of nuclear power. But the main source of biomass energy in the near term will probably be wood, forest wastes and other plant products. That potential can be augmented through the development of fast-growing energy crops. The equivalent of three million barrels per day of oil might be obtained from burning forest wastes and wood without relying on sophisticated forest management techniques and new tree species, but such a high level will take many years, perhaps several decades.

Rapid expansion of the use of solar energy requires, at this stage, major additional support from government. If such support were forthcoming, we believe that it would be reasonable to project by the late 1980s a supply from solar sources equivalent to four mb/d of oil, roughly twice the current Department of Energy forecast.

This projection does not assume any dramatic technological breakthroughs becoming available on a production basis during this time frame. The most obvious such possibility has to do with photovoltaics, that is, small cells of silicon that convert sunlight directly into electricity. We omit photovoltaics not because we are skeptical, for we are not, but rather to underline the potential of existing technologies that do not require a major breakthrough. Photovoltaics may well be on the edge of such a breakthrough. They are made through the same processes used to manufacture semiconductors and integrated circuits. The early photovoltaic cells used to power orbiting satellites worked satisfactorily, but were also extraordinarily expensive. Although costs have since dropped to less than one-half of one percent of initial levels, a major refinement of cells is still required to make photovoltaics competitive with commercial fuels. This is a reasonable prospect, however, very much in line with what happened to semiconductors. And that, obviously, could radically transform the energy supply picture in the United States.

Conservation

For various economic and political reasons we have outlined in *Energy Future*, the prospect for major increases in domestic energy supplies from the four conventional sources—oil, gas, coal and nuclear energy—is bleak. Today, domestic production from these four sources accounts for the equivalent of 27 million barrels of oil per day. Over a period of ten years or so, that 27 mb/d could perhaps be stretched to 32 mb/d, and supplemented by an additional four mb/d from solar-related sources. But during that period, according to the current forecasts of the Department of Energy, consumption requirements could rise to the equivalent of 51 mb/d of oil by the late 1980s, even on the Department's assumption that by then we shall have achieved a saving, through conservation measures additional to those in use in early 1978, estimated at the equivalent of three mb/d of oil. The need for imported oil would still be 14 mb/d, a level we believe to be economically and politically untenable.

Today, Americans are conservation-conscious to a degree that would have been unthinkable a decade ago. A great many Americans are aware that the United States now uses much more energy per capita and per unit of GNP than other advanced industrial countries that enjoy as high an average standard of living. And considerable progress has been made on a few fronts: the increased gasoline mileage of new automobile production—now slated to rise to an average of 27.5 miles per gallon by 1985—may in itself be saving two mb/d by the late 1980s, as compared to what consumption levels would be if the gasoline mileage of new cars had stayed at pre-1974 levels. But since automobiles will continue to be central to American life, there is a need for post-1985 performance standards that will allow automakers to find flexible ways to reach a higher goal of perhaps 50 miles per gallon.

But it is also true that on many major fronts we have hardly begun to practice serious conservation. In American industry, the range for further energy savings remains very broad—from better housekeeping, to recovery of waste heat and materials, to major technological innovation. Altogether, according to one recent study, it may be possible to reduce industrial energy use in economically justifiable ways by more than a third through familiar conservation methods, without any breakthrough.

One of the major methods is cogeneration, the combined production of heat and power. Today there are two independent energy delivery systems in the United States. One is composed of utilities, in which electricity is centrally produced and steam is released as waste into the air or lakes and rivers. In the second system, companies generate their own steam for heating and industrial processes. Almost half of all energy consumed by industry is used to produce steam. Cogeneration integrates these two systems at industrial sites, using only about half as much energy as is needed to produce the steam and electricity separately. There is nothing fancy about the technology. It is quite common in Europe and used to be in the United States. Today, however, major institutional barriers stand in its way—such as how electricity generated by an industrial firm can be incorporated into the regulated utility system.

For while there are notable examples of effective energy saving in U.S. industry, the overall record could be improved considerably. One of the most thorough independent analyses shows that five out of the eight most energy-intensive industries actually increased their energy use per unit of output since the embargo.

There are many reasons for the relatively slow pace of energy saving. One is the confusion over energy prices and about whether there is an energy problem. Many firms have discovered that energy prices do not affect market share or profit margin because they can be passed on to consumers. The regulatory system impedes cogeneration. Many executives are confused by the twists and turns of government policy. One of the principal obstacles, it now appears, is the high rate of return that many firms demand for conservation investments—30 percent after taxes, or in some cases twice that required for strategic investments. The rather small tax credits in the National Energy Act are insufficient to overcome this critical obstacle, which is probably retarding industrial energy conservation more than anything else. A more stimulative policy that encourages investment could be very effective.

The same kind of broad potential exists in the building sector. Almost 40 percent of American energy consumption goes for space heating, hot water, air conditioning, and lighting in homes, commercial structures, and factories. Prior to 1973, energy consumption had been a subject increasingly neglected in buildings: in New York City, for instance, the sealed, glass office buildings put up in the late 1960s used twice as much energy per square foot as those put up in the late 1940s. Since 1973, "energy-conscious design" has begun to work its way into the repertoire of architects and construction companies. But even with the push of new standards, the effects of energy-conscious design will take a decade or more to be felt, as the building stock turns over very slowly.

The real opportunity in the building sector is "retrofit"—changes in equipment and structure that "button up" buildings, that is, improve thermal and lighting efficiency. The possibilities are considerable. IBM, for instance, which set out in 1973 to reduce energy consumption by ten percent in 34 major locations around the country, was surprised to discover that it actually cut its energy consumption by 39 percent by 1977. "Nothing very technical or profound" was required.

Real-world experience proves that major savings are also possible in the residential sector. Studies across the country indicate that 20 to 50 percent reductions in energy use in the American housing stock are possible with relatively simple efforts. And a five-year study of a New Jersey town by researchers from Princeton University showed that a 67 percent reduction in annual energy consumption for space heating in residences was possible with a relatively simple package. "With patience, groups of small and tiny fixes can be put together into large assemblies that overall can produce impressive results," they concluded. "It does not appear to be impossible, in fact, that under present technology and economic conditions, space heat in houses could be a minor rather than a major consumer of fuel."

All this suggests a major realm of possibility. Retrofit is occurring in the United States, but at a much slower rate than is possible or desirable. The main reason is the lack of stimulative government programs. Until 1978, the United States had no major national retrofit programs, despite the fact that the United States has one of the most inefficient housing stocks. The problem is that the American building stock is highly decentralized. Home-owners are very poorly informed, have only limited access to capital, and do not know whom to trust. Strong positive incentives are needed. The National Energy Act contains minor inducements, but the required level of encouragment has been missing.

This sector analysis demonstrates the wide flexibility possible for energy use in the United States. Its extent was underlined in the recent report of a panel on energy futures assembled by the National Academy of Sciences, which looked at four different plausible and carefully constructed scenarios for future energy demand in the United States. The results were extraordinary—that in the year 2010 "very similar conditions of habitat, transportation, and other amenities could be provided" in the United States using twice the energy consumed today or, alternatively, using almost 20 percent less than used today. And this is with continuing economic and population growth. The fundamental conclusion is "that there is much more flexibility toward reducing energy demand than has been assumed in the past."

How much, then, might a really intensive conservation effort reduce the predicted level of energy demand in the United States, by the late 1980s, of roughly 51 million barrels per day in oil equivalent? Our best guess is that if the government—Congress as well as the executive branch—were to approve and get behind realistic programs of subsidies and incentives, the result could be savings on the order of eight million barrels per day of oil equivalent, which would be five mb/d more than the results of increased conservation now forecast by the Department of Energy, reducing total energy consumption to 46 mb/d of oil equivalent.

We are confident that such further savings in energy consumption in the United States can be achieved without affecting predicted levels of economic growth. Indeed, mounting evidence strongly suggests that energy conservation is itself a form of productive investment, yielding much more rapid and substantial real changes in the energy balance of the nation than almost any given investment in energy production. Furthermore, it can actually stimulate employment, innovation and solidly based economic growth.

But "conservation energy" is not so simple to recover as it might seem. Unfortunately, it is a diffuse source, and it has no clear constituency in the way that oil, gas, coal and nuclear do. Public policy must be its champion, and many different strategies will be needed. If we had decades, then the market alone, working through gradual rises in prices, would be sufficient. But the decades are not there. For conservation to make the kind of contribution it should in the relevant time span, there must be found an adroit mixture of signals—of price, regulation, incentives, and information. Only in that way can conservation actions become as economically attractive to individual decision-makers as they are to the society at large.

The American system is particularly responsive to incentives, and that is where public policy has been particularly loath to intrude. Up to now, the failure of public policy has been its inability to assess the true prices and true risks of conventional alternatives, and its consequent inability to measure against them the costs of incentives that will promote conservation.

Balancing the Energy Budget

The balanced program we believe should be pursued to meet U.S. energy needs in the late 1980s without increasing the amount of oil we import is not an "either-or" program. On the contrary, it presupposes every reasonable effort to increase domestic supplies of conventional fuels, including:

1. The leasing of offshore oil and gas properties, under strict environmental regulations, and in a manner to promote rapid development.

2. Eventual decontrol of all oil and gas with incentives for newly found oil and gas and for oil obtained by using enhanced recovery methods to recover petroleum remaining after normal recovery methods have been used.

3. Government assistance for technologies that could provide new supplies—such as coal gasification and liquefaction, and extraction of shale oil. But the synthetic fuels program should avoid highly inflationary super-crash programs that might lock us into using uncertain technologies too early.

4. A major attempt by the government to find an acceptable method to dispose of spent fuel from nuclear reactors and to insure reactor safety.

Unless measures such as these are pursued, there might be very little, if any, increase above the 27 million barrels a day of oil equivalent from the four traditional sources. Indeed, there could be an absolute decline, potentially making the United States far more dependent on imported oil than current forecasts indicate. But whether the four domestic sources increase somewhat, remain constant, or decline, the broad choice before the United States is the same—increased dependence on imported oil, or a transition to a more balanced energy system in which conservation and solar energy play large roles.

The attentive reader may; at this point, be bothered by what seems a paradox of our argument. On the one hand, we say that conservation and solar energy are the most effective alternatives to imported oil. Yet, on the other, the thrust of our argument is to point out that they suffer from the least momentum and the weakest advocacy. Do not the very difficulties faced by conservation and solar, some may say, undercut our argument?

The answer lies in clarifying the handicaps under which conservation and solar energy labor. To begin with, they run against the force of habit, the familiar patterns of energy production that have been associated with the great period of postwar economic growth. Second, conservation and solar do not now have a fair chance in the market to compete with imported oil and other traditional sources. The subsidies caused by price controls that encourage consumers to use oil, gas, and electricity run into tens of billions of dollars yearly. Moreover, many of the conventional sources carry potentially great external costs that are not reflected in prices. Indeed, these costs tend to be seriously underestimated. Studies, for instance, often equate the health costs of pollution with lost wages plus medical expenses. Presumably, in such a formulation, it "costs" society very little for a non-working wife to contract lung cancer from air pollution if she dies quickly, so that large medical bills are avoided.

Third, conservation and solar lack the constituency of the conventional sources. A solar constituency is beginning to develop, but it is still quite small, and is often disregarded because it is considered a fringe element. Conservation has virtually no constituency. As the former assistant Federal Energy Administrator for Conservation observed, "The oil companies and utilities are busy talking up how much they need to produce. But no one's out there wholesaling conservation by the ton and barrel."

Fourth, conventional energy sources generally depend upon centralized production by highly competent firms. In the past, it has proved much easier to generate electricity in a central power plant and then distribute it over wires to the population. Large firms will continue to play an important role in energy production. But conservation and solar energy involve much more decision-making and action at the point of end-use of energy. They involve a move away from a producer-dominated system to a more balanced one, in which consumers play an important, rather than passive, role as well. But that, in turn, means that energy decision-making becomes highly decentralized, involving millions and millions of actors, often poorly informed, without easy access to capital or to the requisite skills, and for whom energy is only one of a myriad of concerns, rather than the central organizational focus. To reach these actors, indeed, represents a problem, but the California experience with financial incentives for solar installation indicates that it is possible. What is needed are government policies that reflect an adroit blend of pricing, incentives, regulations, and information.

An ever-more-regulated system is not the answer to the problems posed by energy. But if the market is to resolve the problems, its distortions must be corrected so that all energy sources, including conservation and solar, will be able to compete on an equal footing. Without a transition to a more balanced energy program, the market system itself in the years ahead will inevitably become increasingly constrained by regulation and disruption. Although both incentives and sanctions have a role to play in the process of equilibration, the emphasis should be placed on incentives. The carrot makes for better politics and more acceptable change than does the stick.

The last point is crucial, because a politically acceptable program that can make a significant contribution to a solution of the energy problem is better than one that might theoretically solve it altogether but which has no chance of being adopted.

In sum, our conventional energy production—oil, gas, coal, and nuclear—may be thought of as an already well-explored producing region. We favor continuing and augmenting production in that terrain. No reader should mistake our commitment there. But, in terms of allocating resources and effort for further major increments of energy, the evidence strongly indicates that the nation would be better served by concentrating its exploratory and development "drilling" in the highly promising but still largely untested acreage of conservation and solar energy. ❦

Soft Energy Paths
(A Talk)

Amory Lovins

Until maybe a couple years ago there was a broad consensus in industry and government (remnants of which still linger here and there) that the energy future ought to be like the past, only more so, and that the energy problem is simply where to get more energy of whatever kind to meet projected demand—lumping together all the different uses and kinds of energy, treating them as homogenous, not asking what kind of energy and what it will be used for, but just saying we will need so much total energy in the year X.

Ours has been essentially a policy of Strength Through Exhaustion: that is, we push very hard on all of the depletable fuels we can find—coal, oil, gas, uranium, and presumably there is some oil shale in the U.S. version. But the important thing that is not obvious is that these increasingly scarce fuels are converted faster and faster into premium forms of energy, fluid fuels and especially electricity, in ever larger, more complex, more centralized plants.

There are a lot of reasons that this sort of policy does not work. Some are logistical. Some are political. Some are straightforwardly economic; and they show up immediately if you ask how much capital you have to invest to build new energy systems of different kinds in order to deliver energy to final users at a given rate. As we go from the traditional direct-fuel systems on which our economy has been built to North Sea or Arctic oil and gas and synthetic fuels made from coal or from oil shale, the capital intensity goes up about tenfold. And as you go from those, in turn, to central-electric systems, power stations, and electric grids, the capital intensity goes up about another tenfold. It is that roughly hundredfold increase in capital intensity that makes it impossible for any major country outside the Persian Gulf to use these big high technologies on a truly large scale—large enough to replace today's oil and gas. They are just so expensive they are starting to look rather like future technologies whose time is past.

They are, however, exactly the systems on which the "hard energy path," as I call it, relies for most of its growth. If you run out the numbers for the United States or for most other countries, you find typically that just the first ten years of that sort of "hard" program would require you to put into the energy sector its present quarter or so of all discretionary investment in the whole economy, plus about two-thirds of all the rest—which means you would not even have the money left to build the things that were supposed to _use_ all that energy. The further up this sort of curve you went, the heavier the burden would become. You cannot suddenly start putting ten or a hundred times as much capital as before into each unit of energy-supplying capacity and not have serious problems getting the capital to put to those uses without running out somewhere else.

In fact, that is just the beginning of the problems with this sort of policy. The energy system itself would provide a lot of electricity (you would have that coming out your ears, and it would probably give you quite a lot of gas if the gas plants work), but you would still be seriously short of liquid fuels to run vehicles because of slow and imperfect substitution. Even worse, out of all this enormous energy growth over the 50-year period shown, more than half would never get to the final users because it would be lost first in conversion and distribution before it ever got delivered. Putting billion dollar blocks of capital into things that take ten years to build would tend to make inflation worse, utility cash flow unstable, and energy prices obviously much higher. We are talking now about synthetics delivered at, say, $30 to $60 a barrel, which is a lot higher than OPEC oil; and indeed these energy systems would take so much capital that other sectors would be starved. For every big power station we build, for example, we would directly and indirectly lose the economy around 4,000 net jobs just by putting disproportionate capital into energy and not having it left to make workplaces elsewhere.

It appears, then, that this approach to the energy problem would make our economic problems worse, rather than better. But at the same time it would create some serious political problems that may be even more important in the way we actually make energy decisions. For example, just getting these resources into the energy sector—which the market has always been unwilling to do—would require a strong central authority, something like an Energy Mobilization Board and an Energy Security Corporation acting outside the market. Presumably, once you built these big complex energy systems, you would need big complex bureaucracies to run them and to say who could have how much energy at what price. Because these systems are centralized, they automatically give the energy and the side effects, or social costs of getting it, to different groups of people at opposite ends of the transmission lines, pipelines, or rail lines, so that the energy goes to Los Angeles and New York, while the side effects go to Colorado, Montana, Alaska, Georges Bank, and Appalachia. It's a very old story, except that there are now over 60 so-called "energy wars" going on in this country between, for the most part, politically weak rural people and the "slurbians" at the other end, as represented by the energy-siting authorities, because agrarian people do not want to live in a "zone of national sacrifice" for the benefit of somebody several thousands of miles away.

Another disturbing political feature of this sort of future is that it is very vulnerable to disruption, whether by accident or by malice. The electric grids, in particular, and the gas grids can be turned off by just a few people. In England, where I have lived for the past twelve years, we're turned off now and then because relying on energy systems like this does basically alter the power balance between large and small groups in society. If you don't like being turned off, you may need stringent social controls. It is also very hard just to make democratic decisions about technologies with compulsory perceived hazards that are exotic or disputed or unknown or maybe even unknowable; and governments trying to make decisions like that are tempted to substitute "we the experts" for "we the people" That makes the experts feel good for a while, but it may also lead to a loss of legitimacy, as we have seen in the nuclear business. Over all of these domestic political problems (which are certainly serious enough) looms a larger threat of nuclear violence and coercion in a world where, we are told, a few decades from now we are supposed to have some tens of thousands of bombs' worth a year of strategic materials like plutonium running around as an item of commerce within the same international community that has never been able to stop the heroin traffic.

Now these are some of the simple, first-order, direct side effects of this approach to the energy problem; and if you fiddle with the numbers a bit and you have a little less demand or a little more of this and that and a little less of something else, it doesn't really make all that much difference to the basic problems. But our analysis cannot stop there because these problems, in turn, interact with each other to make new, higher-order side effects that together suggest that the cheap and abundant energy at which this policy is aimed is not cheap at all; we just pay for it everywhere else: in inflation, unemployment, insecurity, and so on. I would like to spin out this argument because many of us who should know better still tend to think of energy too much in isolation.

Suppose we think energy ought to be cheap, so we continue to subsidize it to the tune of over $100 billion a year to make it look cheap, and we pay that out of the other pocket, so maybe we don't notice so much. If we think the energy looks cheap, we will continue to use it wastefully and to import lots of oil, which is, of course, bad news for Europe and Japan, and disastrous news for the Third World. That much is pretty well known. But then we have to earn the money to pay for all that oil; and traditionally, we have done that in three main ways. One is to run down our domestic stocks of commodities. That is inflationary. It leave big holes in the ground. It leaves the forest looking sort of moth-eaten. The second way we earn the oil money is to export weapons. That is inflationary and destabilizing and immoral. The third way is to export a lot of things like wheat and soybeans, which turns the midwestern land markets upside down, probably puts up our food prices, and certainly makes us mine the soil and mine the groundwater. (The last I heard there was a dumptruckload of topsoil passing New Orleans every second—9 tons per acre per year average—25 in parts of the Midwest.) Then we turn around and sell some of the wheat to the Russians and divert some of their investment from agriculture into military activities, so we have to raise our own military budget. That is inflationary. We have to do that anyway to defend the sea lanes to bring in the oil and to defend the Israelis from all those arms we just sold to the Arabs. (I guess if you follow that argument very far, the best kind of Middle Eastern arms control might be American roof insulation.)

Then because the wheat and soybeans are looking important to our oil balance of trade, we feel driven to engage in ever more energy- and water- and capital-intensive chemical agribusiness, which "does in" a lot of the natural life-support systems, so we feel driven to use still more fertilizer, pesticides, herbicides, desalination, irrigation—you name it, we are doing it, to the point of mining Pleistocene groundwater in west Kansas at twenty times the recharge rate. Anyway, the upshot of all this is that the soil gradually burns out, dries up, blows away, washes away, loses interest—but who cares? At 10 percent discount rates, soil in 50 years isn't worth anything.

Meanwhile, back in the cities where people are not so aware of the problem because the energy looks cheap, we have been substituting it disproportionately for human skills, displacing people with black boxes. The economists call this "increasing productivity"—by which they mean increasing *labor* productivity, and specifically, the labor productivity of the people who have not yet been displaced: the others do not count in this statistic. We are then told that we need energy to fuel the economic growth—that we need to employ the people whom we have just put out of work by this process. In any case, when we displace people with energy-intensive black boxes, we are increasing poverty, inequity, alienation, and crime. We then try to spend money on things like crime control and health care, only we cannot because we spent the money already on the energy sector, which is contributing to the unemployment and illness at which those investments are aimed.

At the same time, we drift gradually toward a garrison state at home, trying to protect ourselves from some of these homemade vulnerabilities. Abroad we are not addressing rational development goals; in fact, we compete with our trading partners to see who can export the most reactors and weapons and inflation to the Third World. These things all encourage international distrust and domestic dissent, which bring on further suspicion and repression. Meanwhile, we are burning all these fossil fuels, putting a lot of çarbon dioxide and other guck into the air (synthetics make that a lot worse), and thus running the risk of destabilizing world climate, on which marginal agriculture depends—for example, in the monsoon belt and in the Midwestern breadbasket on which by this point everyone is depending for exported food. Meanwhile, we are also spreading bombs all over the place.

If you start to add up these kinds of side-effects and ask how they interact with each other, what the third-order effects look like, and what kind of world this would be like to live in, then it becomes clear that you would not really want to live there and that if, as proponents of this view keep telling us, there is no alternative to it, then the human prospect is indeed bleak. We might as well all go home right now. In that world, the only useful skill to have is knowing how to dig a very deep hole and pull it in after you.

There is, however, a quite different way to look at the energy problem—a way that makes more sense and leads in a nicer direction. I will call it a "soft energy path." Its main technical elements are using much more efficiently the energy we have and, through the intelligent transitional use of fossil fuels, getting to eventual reliance wholly on "soft technologies." These two paths differ not only in how much energy we use and not only in our choices of equipment, but most importantly, in their very different implications for the political structure of our society. These hard and soft paths also reflect two quite different views of what the energy problem is. In the hard path there is a tacit assumption that the more energy we use, the better off we are, so energy is elevated from a means to an end in itself—as if people want more electricity because they could eat it, rather than because it is nice to have lights and motors do work. In contrast, in the soft path how much energy we use to accomplish our social goals is considered a measure not of our success but of our failure—just as, if you wanted to get to some place, the amount of traffic you had to endure to get there would be no measure of how well off you are, but it might be a measure of our failure to have a sensible settlement pattern in which you are already near where you want to be. Then too, the energy problem that a soft path is addressing is not just where to get more total energy to meet projected lumped-together aggregated demands. One starts instead at the other end of the problem by asking, "What are the many different jobs we are trying to do with the energy?" That is, what are our *heterogeneous* end-use needs? And how can we meet those needs with a minimum—with, if you like, an elegant frugality—of energy, supplied in the most effective way *for each task*. This approach is really using the criteria of good engineering—economy of means and the right tool for the job. Yet it leads to a somewhat unconventional view of what kinds of new energy supply make sense.

Let me take the three elements of the soft path in turn. Starting with the question of "end-use efficiency"—how much work can we wring from each unit of energy delivered to us? The conventional wisdom says that by insulating our houses better, designing better appliances, better cars, and better machinery in factories, we can save something like 20 to 40 percent of our energy and be just as well off, and indeed, that this saved energy is cheaper than new energy. That much is pretty well known. However, the conventional wisdom is wrong. It comes from not looking carefully enough at how great the opportunities are for using energy more efficiently through what are called "technical fixes"—that is, technical measures that are now economic by normal criteria, use today's (or quite often, 1870's) technologies, and have no significant effect on lifestyles. These are conventional measures such as better insulation, more efficient cars, and the like, except that if you look *very* carefully at the best state-of-the-art right now, you find vastly more opportunities for saving than anybody knew were there. This is something we have learned only very recently. One of the first people to show this was Gerald Leach, who with his colleagues in England did a big study for the Ford Foundation that showed in quite a ratproof way (looking carefully at more than 400 sectors of British energy use) that if you use energy more efficiently to do the same jobs, using conservation measures that are cheaper than present cheap North Sea gas, you can triple the energy efficiency of this country. You could do three times as much work and have three times the GNP using the same amount of energy as now, or actually a little bit less.

A colleague of mine has since dug into the numbers even more thoroughly. He wanted originally to find out what would happen if you used conservation measures that, although perhaps not cheaper than North Sea gas, are cheaper than synthetic gas or the new power stations we would otherwise have to use to replace the North Sea oil and gas that we are going to run out of. He found twice as much saving—a factor of six. We have assumed here a tripling of the British Gross Domestic Product. (I happen to think that is spherically senseless— that is, it makes no sense no matter which way you look at it—but I am going to assume it anyway to save argument.) And yet at the same time the total energy used to triple economic activity in the conventional heavy-industrial sense, drops by half, just through technical fixes. We have since had similar results from a number of other countries, for example, West Germany, which is already considered more energy-efficient than the United States. The lesson is that when we start looking at hundreds of individual little energy uses throughout the economy, the opportunities for saving add up in ways we never expected.

Of course, there has also been very rapid technical progress. We now know, for example, how to make an economically and aesthetically attractive house, in essentially any climate, that doesn't take any energy to heat. We know how to make cars that are five times as efficient as the average American car, and we can do a lot better than that without pushing technology very hard.

Let me take as my text for a moment your refrigerator, because it is a nice graphic example. Around the end of World War II your refrigerator motor was probably 80- or 90-odd percent efficient and it sat on top. Nowadays the motor is maybe 50 or 60 percent efficient, probably because the price of electricity to your house has dropped severalfold since then; and the motor sits underneath, so the heat goes up into the box. Therefore, your refrigerator probably spends about half of its effort taking away the heat of its own motor. Over the years manufacturers began to skimp on the insulation. It got thinner and thinner because they tried to make the inside pretty big compared to the outside. (I guess if you gave them a little longer, the inside would be bigger than the outside.) And because of that and because it is designed so that when you open the door all the cold air falls out, it frosts up, so your refrigerator probably has in it a lot of electric space heaters that go on now and then to defrost it. And then it probably has electric heaters around the door to keep the gasket from sticking because manufacturers cannot be bothered to use a Teflon coating. Then the heat gets pumped out the back into a kind of radiator, which is usually pressed right into that thin insulation to help the heat get back inside as fast as possible. In addition, the refrigerator is probably installed next to your stove or dishwasher, so when that goes on, it goes on. It is really hard to think of a better way to waste energy. Now if you design the thing properly, it will keep the same amount of food just as cold, as conveniently, using only a sixth as much electricity as now. There is an extra capital cost for the factor of six, and you get it back in about three years from your electricity savings—highly cost effective. These kinds of measures can be found, of course, throughout the economy, not just in the household, and they add up to a very large saving indeed.

I am not assuming here the need for any significant changes in how we live, where we live, or how we organize our society. I am assuming traditional industrial growth for people who think that is a good idea. If you happen to think that today's values or institutions are imperfect, as I am told some people do, then you are welcome to assume some mixture of technical and social change that would make this all easier, but I have not done that. I have tried to keep my personal preferences separate from my analytic assumptions. I suspect that I have even *under*estimated the scope for purely technical savings in energy.

Clearly, if our long-term energy needs are going to level off and come down a bit, rather than zooming upward, then we could do a lot more a lot faster with soft technologies than we used to think we could. I define soft technologies by five specific properties. First, such technologies are diverse: there are dozens of different kinds, each one used to do what it does best, not as a panacea. They are renewable; they run on sun, wind, water, farm and forestry wastes, not on depletable fuels. Third, they are relatively simple and understandable from the user's point of view—but of course, they can still be technically very sophisticated. My calculator, for example, is a very high-technology gadget. I do not quite know what goes on in there; I do not think I could make one; but what I care about as a user is that to me this is a tool, not a machine. I run it, it does not run me. It is something I can make up my own mind about. It is not some arcane giant lurking over the horizon, and I am not initiated into its mysteries. So that is the kind of social criterion I have in mind under this third point.

Fourth and fifth, soft technologies supply energy at the appropriate _scale_ and _quality_ for our range of end-use needs. These are very important points that I want to amplify in turn, so let me start with scale.

We have often been told that energy systems must be enormous to be affordable, and there are often some real economies of scale in construction. There are also, however, some real diseconomies of large scale that we just have not properly counted before. For example, if you make a refinery, gas plant, or power plant bigger and more centralized, then you have to pay for a bigger and costlier distribution network to spread out the energy again to dispersed users. That distribution network can be awfully expensive. It is typically about half the investment in the electric system, for example. If you were an average residential customer for electricity in 1972 or for gas in 1977, then you were paying about 29 cents of your utility-bill dollar actually for energy, and the other 71 cents for getting it delivered to you. That is a diseconomy of centralization. Secondly, some of the energy gets lost along the way. It may not be a big amount; it might be about 5 or 10 percent, but it adds up. Thirdly, we cannot mass produce, say, power stations the way we do cars. If we could, they would cost at least ten times less than they do, but they are too big to handle in that way. By the same token, we cannot conveniently use total-energy systems—use waste heat and save a lot more money that way—and we cannot integrate energy and agricultural systems very well.

There are also some direct diseconomies of scale. A look at a sample of half of all the thermal power stations commissioned in the United States in a recent two-year period reveals that as the plants get bigger, the fraction of the time that they do not work also gets bigger: it goes up from about 10 to about 35 percent, for very good technical reasons that are not going to go away. But it is actually even worse than that because if one of these thousand-megawatt stations dies on you, it is embarrassing. It is like having an elephant die in the drawing room and having a thousand-megawatt elephant standing by to haul the carcass away. Now suppose that instead of paying for all that so-called "reserve margin," you built several smaller plants of only a few hundred megawatts each. Because there are several of them, they probably would not all fail at the same time, so you would not need to plan on as much loss of capacity at once, thus you do not need as much reserve margin;

and in a typical grid, for that reason, if you switched to a smaller plant size, you could do the same job just as reliably with about a third less new capacity. Congratulations! You just saved $300 million. And if you went to say 10- or 15-megawatt units at the substation, quite dispersed, you could often get by with only a third as much new capacity to do the same job.

So there are some direct diseconomies of large scale in unreliability and reserve requirements. There are also some indirect effects that show up if we calculate how much capital we have to invest in various plant sizes to install a kilowatt of new capacity. According to classical economy-of-scale theories, the bigger plant should be cheaper per kilowatt. But there is something funny going on because it is actually costing us less to install the kilowatt in a small plant than in a very big one. I suspect—and there is a lot of evidence emerging on this now—that that is because the small plant is so much *faster* to build that it protects us from cost escalation, interest payments, changes in regulatory requirements during construction, technical changes, and especially the uncertainty in future demand. It is a sad story: in the United States, investor-owned utilities' forecasts of demand one year ahead over the past five years have been high, with a margin of error that averaged two and one-half times the actual load growth. Not a very good forecasting record. If you do that and you are locked into things that take ten years to build, before you know it, you are bankrupt. You have all these plants sitting there and you cannot sell what they produce, so you are stuck. Then the less people use, the more you have to charge. Whereas if you have plants with short-lead-times, then you have a much lower-inertia investment program that protects you better from that kind of uncertainty.

These are some pretty obvious diseconomies of scale, but there are some more subtle ones that are probably even more important; however, they are harder to quantify, so some people do not count them so much. For example, there are all the political side effects I mentioned earlier. I would especially note military vulnerability: there is no point in having an army if a few people can come turn you off. That is called national insecurity. Then there is increased local, social, and environmental stress around the site of the big plant. That means it is harder to get a site to build the plant, so when the utility, oil company, or coal company can get a license to build that plant, it will probably want to put as much capacity on the site as possible. But that makes the plant a worse neighbor than it would have been, so there is a political reaction to that, and it becomes harder to get the next site, so the transaction costs go up exponentially. We are well into that loop—it is called various siting councils. It then becomes possible to make truly large mistakes. We are also encouraging oligopoly because small business cannot make big machines. Furthermore, what we are doing is less relevant to the needs of most of the people in the world. The technologists themselves have less personal responsibility and scope for innovation, and policy tends to pass into the hands of big promotional constituencies. Anyway, as Freeman Dyson points out, big technologies are less fun to do and too big to play with, so technologists cannot be as innovative as they would be with smaller, simpler things that a lot of people can tinker with. It is with simpler technologies that most of our progress has come from in recent years.

Now all these effects are real and important; but if you like to count only what is easily countable, as I fear many people do, then you will probably want to stick to the first five. Let me just stick to the first two—the costs and losses of distribution, and do a little economics.

I was brought up as a normal, healthy technotwit, and I always assumed that, although soft technologies were nice, they would cost more. But then I started shopping around for the best technologies of every kind, seeing what was actually available, how much it cost, and how well it worked. I then used these real cost and performance data to calculate how much whole energy systems cost to deliver new energy to final users at a given rate, like a barrel of oil per day. So this is again a measure of capital intensity. You have already seen the steeply rising capital intensity of the hard technologies, and the lower capital intensity of energy-saving measures is pretty well known. But I have found something rather surprising about the soft technologies—they are actually cheaper than hard technologies that do the same jobs.

For example, suppose you have a house. The cheapest, easiest, quickest thing to do with it is retrofit it to the teeth, plug up the square yard of holes in it, insulate it very heavily—what is now called superinsulation. And you have to do it right, but it can certainly be done, even to existing houses. (Swedes in particular have very good techniques for retrofit.) You can even make the house essentially air-tight and ventilate it with a heat exchanger. You can recover waste heat from the greywater going out of the house and use that to preheat water going into the water heater. It costs money to do all these things; however, it is cheaper than not doing it. Your payback will still be some years, but as energy prices rise, you will be very happy you did it. If you do a really good job, you will not need any heating when you get through because you will be heated by people, windows, lights, and appliances, even if you live where it gets cold. If you still want some heat—if perhaps you did not do quite as thorough a job as that—then, as many of you have found out, the cheapest way to get it is to stick a greenhouse on the south side of your house. That heats better than flat plates and costs a lot less. It is also nice to sit out there among your tomatoes in February. If you do not want to do that, you can put in a seasonal-storage active solar heating system, and if you do it for district heating on a neighborhood scale, it is a very good deal—it competes with $8 a barrel oil right now.

If you do not want to do that, you can use a 100 percent active solar heating system just for your house. And yet, if you shop carefully, that fancy solar system added to an efficient house will cost you less than half as much capital as you would otherwise have to pay to build a very efficient nuclear-powered heat pump system to heat the same house. And it would probably cost you less than a synthetic gas and furnace system to heat the same house. And so on; whether you are talking about space heating, high temperature heat for industry, making farm and forestry wastes into liquid fuels (alcohol and pyrolysis oil), or making electricity, you find that although the soft technologies are not cheap, they are in general cheaper than not having them. They may or may not be cheaper than present oil and gas—some are, some are not; what matters is that they are a lot cheaper than what you would *otherwise* have to use to replace present oil and gas (synthetics, for example).

Now you notice that I am comparing all these alternatives with each other. You will not find any Department of Energy publication that does this. DOE's analysts like to play a little shell game with costs. The way it works is that they take things they like to build (like different kinds of power stations and synthetic fuel plants) and compare their costs with each other. Then, when it comes to the things they have not historically been so excited about, like conservation and solar, they will compare those costs not with the competing hard technologies, but instead with the historically cheap (and heavily subsidized) oil and gas, which we are running out of and which all of these things are therefore meant to replace. So the Department says oil costs us, depending on where it comes from, say $10 or $20 a barrel ($20 to $25 for imports), and we will therefore reject as "uneconomic" the more expensive kinds of soft technology—some kinds of biomass fuels and solar heat that might come in at $20 or $25 per barrel equivalent—because they might cost more than the oil. But at the same time, we are asked to put zillions of dollars of our money into subsidies for synthetic fuels at $30 to $60 a barrel, or nuclear electricity at $100 a barrel. That is just nuts (or more formally, that leads to a misallocation).

Clearly, what we ought to be doing is comparing all our investment opportunities *with each other*, not some with each other and some with the cheap oil and gas. And when we do that, we find that the cheapest things to do are the efficiency improvements, then the soft technologies, then (quite a way after that) the synthetic fuels, and worst of all the central electric systems. Our national energy policy has, of course, taken it in reverse order—worst buys first. We are now in Phase 2; we have gone from power stations to synthetics. We have not yet discovered the relatively cheap ways to do it.

The more fundamental question here is not what class of energy supply system to build—hard or soft—but of what kind of energy to supply with it. If you decide not to build a new power plant, that does not mean you should go out and look for another way to deliver big blocks of electricity. That is not the point. What you are looking for is how best to do the jobs that you would have done with the oil and gas if you had them in the first place— and it was because they were becoming scarce that your utilities told you you had to build more power plants to use coal and uranium. So what are we really trying to do with the energy? This concerns the fifth and most important part of the definition of soft technologies—that they should supply energy of the right _quality_ for each task. In the United States, for example, it turns out that 58 percent of our "delivered energy" needs are for heat, mainly at low temperatures. Another 34 percent is for portable liquid fuels for vehicles. Only 8 percent is for the special, premium uses that need electricity and that can give you your money's worth out—because electricity is very special expensive stuff that can do difficult kinds of work, and costs more accordingly. You will be lucky to get new electricity at less than 6-plus cents per kilowatt-hour delivered. But that is the equivalent on a heat basis to buying oil at over $100 a barrel. (That is 3.5 to 4 times the early 1980 OPEC oil price). You would not want to heat your house with something that costs $100 a barrel (about $2.40 a gallon). If you were going to use it to run motors, electronic devices, lights, smelters—special uses like that that really need electricity—you might be willing to pay that price. But those special uses, which are only 8 percent of all our delivered energy needs, are already taken care of: we supply today not 8 but 13 percent as electricity, with more on the way. Where does the extra 5 go? It is already going where more electricity would have to go if we made more: namely to low-temperature heating and cooling. That is a waste of such special energy. You cannot get your money's worth out of it. Trying to is like using a forest fire to fry an egg, or cutting butter with a chainsaw!

Our energy supply problem is thus overwhelmingly—92 percent—a problem of heat and of portable liquid fuels for vehicles. But more electricity is too slow and much too expensive to be a rational response to that problem. So arguing about what kind of power station to build is really missing the point. It is like debating the best buy in mansions when all you need or can afford is a little apartment. (Of course, arguing about what kind of synthetic fuel to use to heat your house is equally the wrong question. You do not need a special fuel that you can carry around with you to do something easy like producing heat at 60 or 70 degrees.)

Let me illustrate why it is so important to get straight what the energy problem is. Some of you have probably seen what is called a "spaghetti chart," a gadget used by energy planners to describe the energy flows in a country. You draw a chart that has going into it on the left-hand side all the different primary fuel inputs—oil, gas, coal, etc.—and on the right are listed the different things you use energy for, like making steel and running cars and heating houses and so on; in between are the different kinds of energy flow by different conversion processes to different destinations, so the chart looks like a big tangle of spaghetti. Energy goes every which way.

A few years ago in France, the energy conservation people in the government started at the right-hand end of the chart, asking "What is the best way to heat a house?" They looked at a particular end-use task, and they decided the worst way to perform that task was with electricity. So they had a big fight with the utility, which they won, and as a result, electricity use is to be discouraged and if possible phased out for heating in France because it is such a waste of money and fuel. Meanwhile, down the street the energy supply side of the French Government said, "Here is some oil going into our energy system. We want to replace that oil. Oil is energy. We need another kind of energy. Nukes give us energy. We will build nukes." But they did not ask where the energy was going to go after that. So they proceeded in opposite directions. These two conflicting views of the nature of the French energy problem have just collided in the middle. In 1979, the planners realized that the only way that they can sell most of that planned nuclear electricity is for electric heating, which they had agreed not to do. Our utilities here have been working themselves into just the same position. So when we talk about whether the energy problem is supplying more total energy or meeting end-use needs in the best way for each task, that is not an academic distinction; it affects concretely what we actually go out and buy.

Now suppose that the United States were to supply electricity only for the tasks that require it, and to do those tasks efficiently. In that case, we could live just as well as now, with no significant changes in lifestyle using less than a third as much electricity as we use now. If we did that, we would not need *any* thermal power stations; we would do very nicely with present hydro, small scale hydro, and a modest amount of wind. If we did that, we could largely eliminate the costs and losses of converting energy. And if we supplied it in the right scale for each task, we could largely eliminate the costs and losses of distributing the energy because it would already be where we wanted it. Those two kinds of losses, conversion and distribution, take up most of the growth in the hard energy path. The amount of primary energy (the fuel that you pour into the hopper) zooms up, but the amount of delivered energy that gets to you hardly goes up at all, because the difference is lost in conversion and distribution. On a soft path, in contrast, by matching the supply to the need, we gradually squeeze out most of those losses; and meanwhile, because we'd be wringing several times as much work out of each unit of energy that was delivered, the "delivered function"—the goods and services—(or, if you like, the GNP) we got out would actually end up a good deal higher than in the hard path, even though we were using less energy. We'd be doing more with less.

We've had in recent years extraordinary rapid technical progress with a wide range of soft technologies. As I've shown in some technical papers elsewhere, if you take the best soft technologies now in or entering commercial service—that is, things that are already here and that we don't need to wait for—and if you add them all up and use each one to do what it does best, there are more than enough to meet essentially all long-term energy needs, even for countries like Japan or Denmark. I'm not assuming here the availability of any cheap solar cells, although I think they'll be here before we know what to do with them. I'm not assuming we will have things that are not now on the market. What I'm assuming is the best present art in passive and active solar heating, solar process heat for industry, the conversion of farm and forestry wastes (not special crops) to liquid fuels to run efficient vehicles, present hydro, the readily available small-scale hydro, and a bit of wind—some for electricity, more for water pumping, heat pumping, and compressing air to run machines. Used to advantage, these add up to more than enough. And yet, even though we've got them, it will take a long time to put them all in place. It might take about fifty years because it takes that long to do anything in the energy system—it's so big and sluggish. So we will certainly need, meanwhile, to buy that time by briefly and sparingly using fossil fuels to build a bridge. And we ought to use them in clean ways, as we know how to, that are designed to plug in the soft technologies as they come along. For example, we can have a clean coal-fired district heating system that is later converted to solar district heat using the same plumbing. If we do that, we can get by on less oil and gas, with only a modest and temporary expansion of coal-mining and no significant Western stripping. We would thus be constructing this very different sort of energy future not by wiping the slate clean, but by starting where we are and doing different things from now on. We wouldn't be abolishing technologies, but rather saying that they have an important place that they have filled up, and we can take advantage of the ones we have without multiplying them further. It's not an anti-technology program. It involves very exciting technical challenges. But those challenges are of a different and, to some people, an unfamiliar kind: making things that are sophisticated in their simplicity, not in their complexity.

I set up these two paths as a vehicle for ideas, and I want quickly to run through some comparisons between them. As I have already suggested, the soft path is cheaper—about three times cheaper in what you finally pay for your energy services. It is also much less demanding of capital, because not only is it less capital intensive, but on it you turn over your money faster, and hence, need less working capital.

A soft path is also quicker. That is, for each dollar invested it gives you more energy, money, and jobs back faster, because the things you are building take less time to build; they sell spontaneously into a big consumer market, like that for CB radios or snowmobiles, rather than requiring delivery to a specialized market like power plants; and there are many different kinds of soft technology, each held back by different problems that are largely independent of the others. Passive solar is held back by the need to retread architects and builders; micro-hydro is held back by regulatory hassles, and so on. And because those are separate problems, these separate, slowly growing sources can independently add up by strength of numbers to very rapid total growth.

It's not the same as putting your bets on monolithic technologies like those needed to produce synthetic fuels and nuclear power which have the same problems everywhere at once. For the same reason, the risk of technical failure is much lower when you spread it among dozens of simple things known to work than when you put all your eggs in a few baskets like big coal-gas plants and oil-shale plants (and breeders, which aren't here and may or may not work).

The soft path is environmentally much more benign. It hedges our bets on the climatic problems (like carbon dioxide build-up), getting us out of the whole fossil-fuel burning business as fast as possible. The soft path is also compatible with not only urban and industrial societies but also with modern development concepts.

Another important geopolitical side effect of the soft path is that it gives us a very strong political lever for stopping the proliferation of nuclear weapons. But the last comparison I want to make between the paths—the one that really defines the difference between them—is politics, because each path entails difficult political problems of very different kinds: on the hard path, problems like centrism, vulnerability, technocracy, inequity; and on the soft path, less familiar problems like pluralism—how do we get used to doing with billions of individual choices in a market that we would otherwise do with a few big projects run from Washington? That may be a rather difficult adjustment for central managers, but there is no energy future free of social problems. You have to choose which kinds of problems you want.

There's no free lunch; but some lunches are cheaper than others. The social problems of a soft path are a lot more tractable, and get easier as we go rather than harder. In fact, the social and economic advantages of a soft path are so great that if we let them show themselves, it would largely implement itself through existing market and political processes.

To get that ball rolling, we ought to do three things. The first and most difficult is to clear away, mainly at a state and local level, a long messy list of what are called "institutional barriers," or in economist's jargon, "market imperfections," (silly rules and habits that keep people from using energy in a way that saves money). For example, we have obsolete building codes and mortgage regulations, restrictive utility practices, inequitable access to capital, architectural fee structures that encourage inefficient buildings, and split incentives. (For example, why should your landlord stuff up the cracks around the window if you pay for the heat? Or why should a builder make a better house that costs a little more if you are going to pay for the heat later and all the builder wants is to sell a cheap house in the first place:) These are difficult problems. If we're not smart enough to solve them, however, I think we won't be smart enough to solve the much more formidable political problems of a hard path.

Second, mainly at the Federal level (although the states can do this too), we ought to stop spending about $100 billion a year of tax money to subsidize conventional fuels and power to make them look cheaper than they really are. That's a very expensive kind of self-deception. In California, the 55 percent state solar tax credit is actually less than the Federal tax subsidies being offered to Alaskan gas. So you start off with solar heat that's cheaper than gas, then you subsidize them both out of your pocket at great expense so that the gas can look cheaper than the solar. That's also nuts, but that's what we're doing.

Third, we ought to move gradually and fairly (as I think we can) toward charging ourselves for depletable fuels and what it will cost us to replace them in the long run. Not doing that is just a sophisticated way of stealing from our children. (There is also a way in which we can get around that problem by not moving to those prices and yet acting as if we had.)

Now it won't be easy to do any of these three things. But I think it is easier than *not* doing them. And if they are done right, they can have a great political appeal, because unlike the hard path, the soft path has advantages for almost every constituency. It offers, for example, jobs for the unemployed, capital for business-people (otherwise their capital goes to energy and they never see it again), savings for consumers, chances for small business to innovate and for big business to recycle itself, better national security for the military, environmental protection for conservationists, exciting technologies for the secular, a rebirth of spiritual values for the religious, world order and equity for globalists, energy independence for isolationists, traditional values for the old, radical reforms for the young, civil rights for liberals, and states' rights for conservatives. It doesn't quite make Westinghouse happy, because Westinghouse might wrongly see it as a threat rather than an opportunity, but it does cut across the kinds of traditional ideological disputes that have been stalling energy policy.

We've just spent two years in the Senate saying that before we could even start on an energy policy we have to agree on price versus regulation, capitalism versus socialism, Jefferson versus Hamilton, the future of the oil companies, the whole shape of our society. We never agreed about any of those things. We never will. Life would be very dull if we did. But if we make them a prerequisite for energy policy, hell will freeze over first—maybe literally. Whereas in a soft path those kinds of disputes don't much matter, because if you're an economic traditionalist and you just want to do what's cheapest for you, that's okay: you can go ahead and build your solar collector because it's cheaper than not doing it. If you're a worker, you might want to build it because it gives you more and better jobs than building power stations or synfuel plants. If you're an environmentalist, you might want to build it because it's benign, or if you're a social transformationalist you might want to build it because it's autonomous. So what? It's still the same collector. You don't have to agree, before or after, about why you built it.

We have in this country an overwhelming consensus that energy husbandry and benign renewable sources are a good way to go. We've got no consensus on anything else in energy, and I doubt we ever will. So maybe what we ought to be doing is starting with the consensus we have and designing an energy policy around it. We've never tried that. But it seems long past time we started.

Yet I think the time left us to do that is short, because although each of these paths is illustrative and embraces infinite variations on a theme, there is a sense in which they are mutually exclusive. I don't mean by that, as some people have supposed, that hard and soft technologies are technically incompatible, because they aren't. There is nothing technical to stop you from putting solar panels on top of Fort St. Vrain; it might even help it work better. Indeed, in a soft path you would start off with a bunch of hard technologies, end up 50 years later with soft technologies, and in between they would be coexisting side by side for those 50 years as the mix gradually shifted. But that shift takes place within a social and political context, and it is there, I think, that three kinds of exclusivity arise.

The first one you might call cultural. The existence of each of these worlds makes the other kinds of world harder to imagine. Where we are now is a great example: there are a lot of people around who cannot imagine any approach to the energy problem except what they have been doing for the past 30 years, just because of this cultural conditioning. Secondly, each of these paths builds up around itself thick layers of laws, institutions, habits, and institutional barriers that inhibit change—just as today we are surrounded by old rules and habits left over from the cheap oil era that are locking us into more of the same rather than something else. The third, and most obvious is that the two paths compete for resources. Every bit of work and skill, every dollar, every barrel of oil (most precious), and every year we put into these very demanding hard technologies is a resource we cannot also use to perform the tasks of the soft path urgently enough so they hang together. I think in this sense, programs like that to develop synthetic fuels are not only unnecessary—they are a positive encumbrance. Committing our resources to them can push the soft technologies so far off into the future that before we can get to them our fossil fuel bridge has literally been burned.

So we ought, with due deliberate speed, to choose one of these broad patterns or the other before one has foreclosed the other (or before proliferation has forclosed both). We ought to ask where we could get to in 50 years or so and then work backwards to see how to get there smoothly, rather than just continuing by incremental ad-hocracy—one plant at a time—not asking where we're going. We ought to be using these relatively cheap fossil fuels thriftily to capitalize a transition as nearly as possible straight to our ultimate energy-income sources, because we won't have another chance to get there. ✻

Why, Where, and How to Conserve Energy

Denis Hayes

We Americans waste about as much energy as we use. Simply increasing the efficiency with which we draw on existing supplies could buy us a new lease on life while we explore and develop alternatives to conventional fuels. This conserved energy would be safer, cheaper, more reliable, better for business, and easier on the environment than would energy from any other source. And conservation need not hurt nor make killjoys of us.

The only carryover from the age of energy abundance is the opportunity to conserve. It is everywhere. The U.S. economy matured on cheap energy, and energy-consumption levels have been maneuvered upward by every tactic known to mass marketers. To encourage growth, fuel prices have been kept artificially low and utility rate structures have rewarded extravagance while environmental and health costs have been ignored. Waste has become second nature for us.

Yet "waste" means one thing to a physicist, and another to an economist or an engineer. Even neighbors cannot agree upon a meaning. This is important because the new and eclectic language of energy policy must become a common tongue if conservation is to become widely understood, which it must if it is to be practiced with results. Energy should be considered to be "wasted" whenever work is performed that could have been completed with less or lower quality energy and without incurring higher total social and economic costs. With that concept of waste as a touchstone, we can assess the potential for energy savings in transportation, heating and cooling systems for buildings, water heating, the food system, electrical generation, industrial efficiency, waste recovery, recycling, and lighting.

The second concept that needs to be clarified as a prologue to any discussion of energy conservation is that of cost. The "costs" of energy are not limited to the capital and the environmental damages of energy-processing facilities. Biologist Paul Ehrlich argues that "one of the best measures of the assault humanity is mounting against the all-important natural systems that support it is the level of society's energy consumption . . . With cheap, abundant energy, the attempt clearly would be made to pave, develop, industrialize, and exploit every last bit of the planet." Making the same point, energy analyst Amory Lovins claims that "even if we had an unlimited energy source, we would lack the discipline to use it wisely."

More and more people oppose unlimited energy growth rates on environmental grounds, and more still are becoming advocates of limited growth because economic necessity leaves them no choice. But how to set the limits remains open to debate. The question of who should do the setting is even more politically controversial. Some believe we have already passed the optimal location; others contend that, if we slow down, we might manage to grow carefully for another half century. But conservation should be begun in earnest in any case.

What Conservation Will Do For You

Energy conservation does not mean deprivation any more than efficiency does. It means making less do more. Increasingly, the question "How much fuel do we have?" must be asked in conjunction with another, "How well are we using it?" Because we never thought to ask *both* questions before, the United States has drifted and shifted into nearly complete dependence upon nonrenewable energy sources over the last century. One hundred years ago 90 percent of our energy came from sustainable sources. Today, petroleum, natural gas, and coal supply more than 90 percent.

Since producing energy requires energy, investing a dollar in wise energy conservation makes more net energy available than does investing a dollar in developing new energy resources. For example, ceiling insulation in a typical home costs about $300 installed and will save about seven barrels of oil each year for the lifetime of the house. Using very conservative discount rates, the present value of the energy to be saved by the insulation in future years is 60 barrels. Thus we are "producing" heating oil at about $5 per barrel when we install ceiling insulation. If heating oil costs only $3 per barrel, the insulation will not be economically attractive. But today heating oil costs over $20 per barrel, so home insulation is a bargain. It may, in fact, provide a higher rate-of-return than any other investment available to the average citizen, earning 20 to 40 percent in saved fuel costs at no risk while boosting to the average citizen, earning 20 to 40 percent in saved fuel costs at no risk while boosting property values.

At the other end of the investment spectrum from home insulation is the nuclear power plant. Electricity from a large nuclear power plant costs upwards of $3000 per delivered kilowatt. (This sum conservatively reflects the cost of the power plant and the distribution system, federal research, federal development and subsidization of the fuel cycle, interest charges, fuel, radioactive waste management, and regulation, etc.) By comparison, replacing electrical resistance heating with an efficient heat pump costs between $50 and $120 per thermal kilowatt, and recapturing waste heat from the chimneys of industrial furnaces costs about $70 per thermal kilowatt. Generating electricity as a by-product of industrial steam production costs $190 to $280 per thermal kilowatt. Clearly, the smart money is on conservation.

Energy conservation by Americans today will allow the earth's limited resource base of high-quality fuels to be "stretched" further. It will enable our children and those in other lands (chief among them those living in underdeveloped countries, where the marginal return per unit of fuel is far greater than in highly developed countries) to share in the earth's finite stock of fossil fuels.

Energy conservation will enable us to set aside a portion of the fossil fuel base for non-energy purposes: drugs, lubricants, and other materials. Without such a reserve system, we will have to bear the astronomical energy cost of manufacturing such substances from carbon and hydrogen when our feedstocks have been exhausted.

Energy conservation will allow us to minimize the environmental degradation associated with all current energy production technologies. Economics aside, reducing pollution from heavy metal particulates, carcinogenic aromatic hydrocarbons, various radioactive materials and other death-dealing agents associated with the production or use of conventional energy sources is itself ample reason to cut back needless energy use. Equally worth avoiding are the poorly understood but potentially grave dangers linked to crossing climatological thresholds. In a sense, recognizing the limits of an ecosystem to absorb injury is admitting our need to limit energy use.

Energy conservation will be one of the best things that ever happened to preventive medicine. The excessive fat in our energy diet contributes to obesity, heart disease, and possibly even to some cancers. By combining exercise with transportation and by eating unprocessed foods, we save energy while following doctor's orders and do our part to reduce pollution to boot.

Energy conservation will substantially bolster employment levels. According to an employment analysis performed by economist Meg Schachter in 1979, conservation measures such as insulation and weather stripping create new energy-related jobs at less than one-third the cost per job nuclear power production does. Other recent studies indicate that conservation holds special promise as a source of jobs for the young and the semi-skilled, many of whom could become involved in recycling efforts. The good news for skilled industrial labor is that the manufacture of energy-efficient appliances requires more labor than does the production of inferior goods. In general, the replacement of human skill, intelligence, or craftsmanship by automation has become increasingly difficult to justify when both unemployment and energy prices are primary national concerns.

Where Conservation Opportunities Lie

Save for that of the Texas Railroad Commissioner, who in 1979 captured press attention in Washington by announcing that "America didn't conserve its way to greatness," opposition to energy conservation in the U.S. is difficult to find. But that is not to say that conservation has yet won the commitment and following it deserves. Apparently, the opportunities are not yet widely appreciated.

In intracity travel, substantial energy savings can be made if commuters switch to buses and fixed-rail transport systems. How much can be saved will depend on the extent of substitution and the load factors of the competing modes. The same principle applies to intercity travel. If passengers would switch from planes and automobiles to buses and trains, substantial sums of energy can be saved. But that is a big "if," since the opposite has been occurring.

Vast amounts of transportation energy can be saved by improving engineering, improving the load factors of all types of transport, switching to more efficient modes, and by reorganizing our society in ways that reduce our transportation requirements. Granted, people would have to switch gears psychologically and adjust their routines—ideas lampooned of late by those whose emotional attachments to their automobiles have gotten the better of their good sense—but some of the changes would pay double dividends. Living near work and patronizing neighborhood stores, for example, would contribute to urban (or suburban) revitalization as well as cut energy needs. In any event, considering that over 40 percent of the nation's energy budget is dedicated to transportation and that the conservation opportunity is commensurately great, the concessions seem minor.

With respect to buildings, the most reliable guide to energy conservation is simple common sense. Windows that can be opened are the most efficient ventilation system, and replacing furnace pilot lights with electric igniters can cut fuel use by 10 percent. Redesigning furnaces and insulating all heating system ducts would save enormous amounts of fuel. More important, though, is tailoring all new buildings to take advantage of their environment. Houses and commercial buildings should be oriented to make maximum use of the sun and prevailing breezes. All new heating, cooling, and hot water systems should be designed for eventual conversion to solar power, and a steadily increasing percentage should use solar energy at the outset. Constructing energy-efficient and passive solar buildings at the start makes more sense than upgrading inefficient structures later. Nevertheless, retrofitting and weatherproofing existing buildings are still wise investments.

Groceries provide a veritable object lesson in conservation. Today we use several times as much energy as fuel to produce, process, retail, and prepare food as the food itself contains. None of the energy in the fuel is actually transferred to the food—food energy comes solely from sunshine. Instead, it substitutes for labor, land, capital, rain, and so forth. In an era when food and fuel jointly account for almost half of our runaway inflation, the increasing fuel-intensity of the food system warrants a closer look.

Cooking, refrigeration, home freezers, and food shopping by car account for close to a third of the total energy expenditures on food—two and one-half times as much as farming uses. More than half the total electricity spent on food is spent at home. Recent years have also seen wildfire growth in the sales of food-related electrical appliances, many of which are functionally redundant. While some domestic energy use has been transferred to the food-processing industry, preparations for many frozen foods now require more energy use at home than their unfrozen predecessors did.

Garbage, sewage, crop residues, and industrial waste also provide conservation opportunities. The organic material that constitutes the bulk of our urban garbage and all of our residential sewage is a rich potential source of energy. Feedlot wastes, agricultural residues, and the by-products of forest industries are other richer energy sources. Energy can be made available from these resources through direct combustion, pyrolysis, hydrogasification, and methane generation.

Standing in the way of a growing national commitment to extracting energy from waste, some fear, is the chance we may develop a vested interest in unnecessary waste. That fear is legitimate. Avoiding an unneeded wrapper is clearly preferable to throwing it away and recovering its energy potential through incineration. The benefits of using cans—even if the metal from the cans is recycled—stack up poorly compared to those of using reusable bottles. The best approach is to save energy directly by eliminating some of the bulk in our solid waste. Archaeology students in Tucson, Arizona, who excavated fresh municipal garbage discovered that between 10 and 15 percent of all food was thrown away. We would obviously do better to consume the food (or cut production) than to recover its energy in a utility boiler.

In industry, the most significant opportunities for savings require a more sophisticated approach than do most other conservation measures. Industrial fuel use falls into four principal categories: 45 percent is used to generate process steam; 29 percent is used for direct combustion heating; 25 percent is used for motors, lighting, and electrolysis; and 1 percent is used for electrical heating. Manufacturers produce vast quantities of steam in-house while purchasing almost all their electricity from utilities. If waste heat in the form of industrial steam is first used to generate electricity and then used as steam, the dividend can be a marketable *surplus* of electricity. The sun can also be used to stretch the 44 percent of industrial energy invested in producing steam. Pre-heating water with elementary solar technologies can triple the output of steam per unit of fuel consumed. Other energy gains could be made by product substitution, modifying manufacturing processes, and paying more careful attention to "housekeeping" matters in production facilities.

Economic production need not suffer as a result of reducing industrial energy use, a fact its recent concern with conservation shows that industry respects. While future efforts to improve energy productivity may eventually run up against technical and systemic barriers, industry has led the way in making conservation gains for fifty years. A strong downward trend in the amount of energy required per dollar of economic product has prevailed, even in the face of declining energy prices. Even the potential obstacles to the continued improvement of the efficiency with which energy can be used in industry pale in the light of certain rises in near-term energy prices. And the need to focus on industry's use of energy speaks to one fact: 40 percent of our energy budget is now consumed by the industrial sector.

Purchases of indirect energy pose a more difficult (but nonetheless solvable) problem for the consumer. The trick is to buy fewer energy-intensive products and services and relatively more whose creation instead requires extra labor. For example, if a commuter switches from a bus to a bicycle and spends savings on restaurant meals, each dollar spent has less than half the amount of energy associated with it than if it had been spent on bus fares. Sports equipment, education, and theater-going also exemplify goods and pleasures that don't require much energy to supply.

In general, a truly well-designed energy conservation program can create a "Snowball Effect" that spells money and convenience to the consumer. If the dollars saved by conserving energy are invested in ways that save even more energy, directly or indirectly, the conservation effect becomes self-multiplying. The bus-to-bicycle savings can be used to plant a home garden; the savings from the home garden can be used to insulate the house, etc. Carried far enough, this kind of thinking would enable the conserver to save enough on energy to purchase a solar collector and, in effect, become an energy producer!

Not all opportunities for conservation lend themselves to direct action by citizens. The average person can do little to transfer a growing percentage of freight from trucks to railroads or to increase the energy efficiency of a high-rise office building. But some do. And a few rules of thumb can help make the most of them. One is to make gasoline mileage the paramount concern when purchasing a new car. Oversized cars, over-powered engines, automatic transmissions, and unnecessary power options should be avoided. Another is to take the most energy-efficient transport to work. Bicycle, walk, use public transportation, or join a car or van pool. For long or short trips, always use the most energy-efficient mode and route of travel that time permits. Another key is to insulate your home amply. At the same time, purchase only the most energy-efficient appliances and reduce the lighting within your control by using smaller light-bulbs and fluorescent bulbs, avoiding "show room" lighting, and turning off all unnecessary lights. Last, if at all possible, plant a home garden. A carefully tended 20' by 20' plot can produce hundreds of dollars worth of fresh produce, saving both fuel and money. If you don't live in a house, urge your management or city government to set aside some outdoor space for resident gardens.

Individual actions alone will not turn the tide toward national energy self-sufficiency. But they will make a critical difference: a strong national conservation program will not develop until an informed constituency demands it. In this light, one of the most conservation-minded acts citizens can perform is to press their political representatives to eliminate tax incentives that encourage the consumption of fuel and other virgin resources, transport rates that discriminate against recycled goods, and utility rate structures that reward energy gluttony. The personal rewards of getting involved in the politics of conservation may or may not be greater than those of cutting energy bills. It scarcely matters since the choice is not either/or. 🌴

VI.   COMING TO TERMS

The Coming
of the Solar Age

Hazel Henderson

The Six Historic Transitions

Mature Western industrial societies are undergoing a profound transition—actually, a confluence of at least six historic transitions.

1. The transition from the Petroleum Age to the now emerging Solar Age, a very rapid cycle most of which is confined to this century.

2. The transition from the Fossil Fuel Age (coal, gas and oil) that began in the early 1700s in England will peak sometime around 2100 and exhaust itself around 2300, according to geologist M. King Hubbert's no longer controversial estimates.

This transition from human societies living on the earth's stored fossil fuel "capital" to its daily "income" (solar energy either collected directly for thermal use, or converted by solar cells into electricity or by the photosynthesis of plants into stored carbohydrate and hydrocarbon energy in biomass; or that stored in falling water, ocean waves, thermal currents and tidal movements, or in the world's climate machine, as wind power) will mean an economic transition for all societies. This transition is already under way in economies that have *maximized* material production, mass consumption, and planned obsolescence based on nonrenewable resources and energy sources, and in economies that *minimize* waste by recycling, re-using and maintaining renewable resources and relying on renewable energy for sustained-yield long-term productivity.

3. Before us also is the transition of industrialism itself, as it matures and makes this painful resource-base shift, whether in Britain

(where it began), West Europe, North America, Japan (where the process was vastly accelerated), or in the Soviet Union, whose younger industrial economy also shows the same inexorable energy crunch and the same sort of social bottlenecks in managing the complexity that characterizes industrialism—be it that of planned or capitalist economies.

I call this transition stage of mature industrialism as it exhausts its potential as a socio-technical system the "Entropy State" (in contradistinction to Daniel Bell's linear extrapolation of a Post-Industrial State, seen as flowering out of the increasing labor productivity of the agricultural and manufacturing sectors). This Entropy State is the stage reached when these societies' complexity and interdependence, their scale and degree of centralization, and the unanticipated 'side-effects' of their technology finally become "unmodelable," and therefore unmanageable. All of these efforts to coordinate anarchistic economic activities and conflicting technological applications; to clean up the mess left by mass production and consumption; to ameliorate the social problems and care for the drop-outs, the addicts, the disabled workers, and other social casualties; to mediate the conflicts, sustain even larger security forces against theft and crime, keep the air breathable and the water drinkable—all lead to a burgeoning of social and transaction costs that finally exceed the actual production costs.

Economists still add these social costs (including, for example, the $2.6 billion in claims and the $22 million in clean-up costs for the Love Canal chemical dump in Niagara Falls, NY, and the $60 billion of public costs of smoking and alcohol addition) to the Gross National Product (GNP) rather than subtract them. In fact, they are probably the only fraction of the GNP that is still growing! Thus, these mature industrial societies wind down of their own weight, as does a physical system, into a state of maximum "social entropy." Thus they face the basic biological problem of evolution: growth creates structure, then structure inhibits further growth. As the dinosaurs' extinction demonstrated, "nothing fails like success."

Mature industrial societies can today be seen drifting to a soft landing in accidental 'steady states,' with inflation masking their decline. Indeed, the Morgan Guaranty Bank of New York portrayed the absurdity of the GNP-measured growth efforts by pointing out in 1979 that the U.S. economy took 200 years to reach the first trillion and just seven years to reach the second, two-thirds of which was just inflation! We have simply overstated "growth" and "productivity" for decades, and now these accrued social bills have to be paid.

Belgian information theorist Jean Voge verifies that narrowly conceived efficiencies in production scale are now meeting diminishing returns, since production gains are arithmetical but generate information requirements at a geometric rate and thus expand the bureaucracy exponentially. Voge demonstrates that when industrial economies reach a certain limit of centralized, capital-intensive production, they have to shift direction to more decentralized economic activities and political configurations, using more laterally-linked information networks and decision-making, if they are to overcome the serious information bottlenecks in excessively hierarchical, bureaucratized institutions. This change of direction amounts to "spontaneous devolution"—citizens simply began recalling the power they once delegated to politicians, administrators, bureaucrats, and business leaders to make far-reaching technological decisions. In all mature industrial countries, movements for consumer and environmental protection, corporate and government accountability, human rights and social justice, worker self-management, the development of human potential, self-help health care, "small is beautiful" technologies, alternative lifestyles, and the rise of ethnic pride and indigenous peoples, as well as the tax revolt, are all parts of this "spontaneous devolution" of old, unsustainable structures.

4. The socioeconomic transition will be accompanied by a conceptual transition as the 300-year-old logic undergirding industrialism's rise exhausts its creativity. The logic stemming from Galileo, Bacon, Descartes, Newton, Leibniz and the Enlightenment philosophers—reductionism, materialism, technological determinism, and instrumental rationality—will fail us. Even the fierce ideological battles of the nineteenth century between capitalism, socialism, and communism become less relevant. They will realign since it is no longer only a matter of who owns the means of production, but also the need to address the ecological, social, and spiritual dilemmas posed by the means of production themselves.

5. We are also undergoing a cultural transition. The great sociologist Pitirim A. Sorokin forty years ago saw this late 20th Century cultural crisis as the decline of Sensate Culture, which has been on the rise since the 16th Century. Sorokin theorizes (and marshalls voluminous evidence to validate the concept) that human cultures express themselves in three major styles: the Sensate, in which truth is that which is empirically validated by human senses; the Ideational, in which truth is revelatory, values are absolute and concerns are otherworldly; and the Idealistic, in which both material and otherworldly concerns and systems of truth or knowledge are balanced and integrated, producing the periods of highest human cultural achievement. Sorokin plotted these three cultural styles in art, music, literature, jurisprudence, technology, systems of knowledge, patterns of war and internal conflict. His charts covered milennia from Before Christ to the 20th Century, and his description of the Decline of Sensate Culture in _Social and Cultural Dynamics (1937–41)_ is uncannily predictive of what we see today. Sorokin saw that "Western culture is entering the transitional period from its Sensate super-system into either a new Ideational or an Idealistic phase. Since such epoch-making transitions have hitherto been tragic periods, the greatest task of our time (since we cannot avert tragedy) is to make the transition as painless as possible."

6. Yet another framework for viewing today's transition is that it also marks the decline of the patriarchal systems that have predominated in most of the world's nation-states for some 3,000 years as the earlier matri-lineal societies were superseded. The nation-state, like all patriarchal systems, is hierarchically structured. It is based on rigid division of labor, manipulative technology, instrumentalist and reductionist philosophies, the control of information, and on competition. Unlike the earlier, small city-states and feifdoms, these nation-states have proved, as Toynbee showed, to be highly unstable, somewhat like large unstable marco-molecules. Quintessentially patiarchal, they are characterized by extreme polarizations of conceptual, bureaucratic, academic, intellectual work in centralized, urbanized, metropolitanized complexes. They are rendered operational by the large statistical aggregates of the formal, monetized GNP economy. They ignore manual tasks, rural and agricultural life, and the unpaid work of the "informal economy." Household production, gardening, canning, repairs, home fix-ups, nurturing and parenting, volunteer community service and all the co-operative activities that permit the over-rewarded competitive activities to be "successful" count for nothing.

Today, patriarchal modes are also reaching logical limits: hierarchies become bottlenecks; excessively conceptual governance becomes divorced from reality. In Washington, Brussels, or Moscow, the bureaucrats try to govern by manipulating statistical illusions using highly aggregated, averaged data that do not fit one single real world case or situation. Similarly, corporate executives make momentous technological and economic decisions using highly selective marketing studies, isolating "effective demand" from real world need as well as from social and ecological impacts. In the same vein, patriarchal academic hierarchies in science and technology have systematically excluded women — denying them patents, admission to professional societies, and access to journals (as Elise Boulding documented in *The Underside of History* in 1977).

Are we not at a very significant turning point in human affairs? We see both elements of cyclical-type crises, such as the cultural one Sorokin describes, but also that these have converged with others that are real and based in the resource transition we must now make and in the catastrophic effects that our psychotic technology is now producing: mental illness, environmental cancer, and stress. Only a drastic reconceptualization of our entire situation will adequately address our need. (It is to this emerging politics of reconceptualization that I have committed myself. At such cultural crisis points, reference points become lost, and the personal search for new meaning and individuality is thus thrust upon us.)

Many cannot bear the burden of living during a period of cultural collapse. As individuals in mass consumption cultures, we are used to simple yardsticks of money-measured "progress" and personal "success." The chief taboo of our industrial culture has been the fundamental exploration of human purpose, meaning, and identity, even our own death. It is painful for all of us, since we can no longer externalize responsibility for the resource-allocation patterns and justness of our society by deferring to what we now know as major rationalization systems of our Enlightenment and Industrial eras: Lockean individualism, private property, technological determinism, and "free market" economics. In other words, we can no longer continue legislating markets and rationing by prices, and then blaming God (the Invisible Hand that Adam Smith found so convenient) for the outcome.

Today, greed has been institutionalized: the economic system is greedy on our behalf. As Bayard Rustin put it, "We have socialism for the rich and rugged individualism for the poor." In fact, we now have an economic system that operates on many of the Seven Deadly Sins—greed, pride, sloth (i.e., labor-saving technology), lust, and selfishness—and whose major logic is based on competition. Our economic system (and, increasingly, our mass media system) does not even recognize that humans are also cooperative, nurturing, and capable of transcending self in the millions of routine volunteer activities and daily acts of altruism.

Right Livelihood and Right Action

Helping to change the worldview and knowledge paradigms of industrial societies necessitates taking a very long view of such a project. One must not expect the personal validation of success, nor demand to see results in the short run, or within our lifetime, since these are historic and evolutionary processes on much larger time scales. Adopting such an outlandish goal, however, does involve imperatives with shorter term consequences. First comes a personal self-help project to deprogram ourselves of many of the goals and values our culture promotes: income maximization, institutional careerist goals, material consumption as an end in itself or for display, conventional ego-rewards, and competitive individualism. Of course, some of these are deeply instinctive motivating forces that need to be sublimated in more useful, appropriate ways than those portrayed in the incessant media bombardment of advertising.

Besides constructing a personal lifestyle that allows us to pursue our concerns, we must also in an interdependent society find relevant means for political expression and action. What do people do after getting right with themselves, after achieving a "right livelihood," except extend concern to community and country and begin to act politically as well? Too many now see virtue in heading for the hills, building a passive solar house, and relinquishing all interest in the evils of politics. But we cannot evade the responsibility for the power we allowed to drift up to the national level.

While the dangers are enormous, the long-term opportunities for the human species to evolve on this planet in accordance with its operating principles—co-operation, honesty, peacefulness, sharing and love—are still waiting for us. However, the next ten years may be a very crucial period, as we have now moved rapidly from the Soaring Sixties to the Stagflation Seventies and into the Economizing Eighties. Since the shift is not yet widely understood as a basic shift of our resource-base and our entire productive systems to renewable-resource sustained-yield systems, confusion abounds. Leaders still talk of "consuming our way back to prosperity" and cutting taxes to stimulate demand, while exhorting us to believe that there is an energy crisis. The new edict of "fighting inflation" is an economic mystification, since what we call "inflation" is just all the social, psychological and ecological variables economists leave out of their models, coming back to haunt us. Ultimately, is there any such thing as a profit that is not either won at the expense of an equal but unrecorded debit entry in some social or environmental ledger or passed on to future generations (for example, the huge uncounted costs of decommissioning nuclear reactors, which our children will pay in some twenty years)?

Shift In Production Systems

Obviously, the necessary huge shift in production systems will cause painful grinding of gears and readjustment. However, renewable resource economies can provide useful, satisfying work for all citizens, as we move to more personal-scale economics and combine our precious capital and resources, involving people in flatter-structured enterprises (cooperative and localized economies of scale that higher transportation costs will mandate). But such new societies of the Solar Age cannot provide windfall profits, large pay differentials, huge permanent war machines, and costly space ventures; nor can they supply us with all the frivolous, unnecessary, and downright harmful goods we have come to expect as our birthright.

Choices between hundreds of brands of headache and sleeping pills, cigarettes, protein hair shampoos for pets, expensively advertised and packaged junk foods, sweetened cereals and candy are also political choices. We choose them at the expense of decent schools, health care, and maintenance of essential urban services. When we begin to account accurately for all of the social costs of these frivolous "goods," we will soon realize that not only can we not afford them, but that we don't want them. As long as advertisers are allowed to bring us only the "good news" about these products and do not have to tell truthfully of the "bad news" of the social and environmental effects that harm us, individuals will not be able to make informed choices, either politically or in the marketplace. If corporations are allowed to continue manipulating media information by portraying our choices narrowly (as between going along with their priorities or being thrown out of work and freezing in the dark) or forcing workers to choose between their jobs and their health, then our debate will remain cloudy and intergroup conflicts will be fomented.

The new challenges to our material expectations in all industrial countries will leave many people frustrated and disoriented. Human services for the poor in cities are already the target for budget-cutting. In the U.S., we see unconscionable proposals to break faith over Social Security entitlements earned long ago. Cutting government spending is an empty shibboleth unless it focusses on special-interest boondoggling and some of the vast tax subsidies to corporations, military contractors, and conventional energy industries (which taxpayers have subsidized over the years), as well as on investment tax credits, which are just as often used to further automate and destroy jobs as they are to create them. We can expect increased inter-group conflict, individual violence and political outbursts, such as Proposition 13 in California, as well as the simplistic demands to cut individual taxes and stimulate investment irrespective of what is to be produced. Our politicians will need to be realistic and help us accommodate and face the fact that incomes for most workers, even in the U.S., have remained flat for the past seven years. If the GNP-pie cannot grow, we will have to face the fact that it is now full of inflationary air and additives unfit for human consumption anyway. We will redefine it more realistically (if economists will let us), and then share the newly-baked, wholesome pie more fairly.

But we might as well prepare for the economists' last-ditch effort to define our problems in their terms as "declining productivity," "loss of innovation," "inflation," and thus to cannibalize the body politic by "deregulating" and "reducing government interference" in the "free marketplace," etc. The rationale is used to lower smog standards, reduce worker job safety, cut children's school lunch programs, and slash funds for summer jobs for idle young people because the costs in social disorder, public health, and safety are borne by the public, not by producers, who wish to continue to "externalize" them from company budgets. Meanwhile, corporate executives continue to make their speeches about private enterprise while lobbying for huge government subsidies and contracts, and military budgets soar.

Decentralists working on pragmatic alternatives in their own lives cannot ignore politics. Instead, they must work to reduce real hardship and speak out against the sick economists' game of trying to wring inflation out of the system by throwing the economy into recession every three years or so. Even some honest economists, such as Arthur Okun, now admit that today "you get so little deflation out of a recession that it's like burning down your house to bake a loaf of bread." Yet Western democracies still seem bent on proving Karl Marx's prediction that late-stage capitalism would need an "industrial reserve army" of hard-core unemployed, as our own poor, minorities, and females must serve as the last hired and first fired in order to stabilize inflation. We also know that the "old time religion" favored by conservatives and Monetarists fails to address the basic new sources of inflation. These new sources are better understood in thermodynamic terms (as they relate to the declining productivity of capital invested in resource extraction) and in general systems and information-theory terms (as regards the burgeoning transaction costs of excessive centralization and complexity).

We must now debate openly our values and our public policy goals, rather than continue the game of throwing specious data and studies at each other, with the pork-barrel prize going to the interest group with the greatest computer fire-power and the largest army of intellectual mercenaries. I hope that we all will boo off the platform politicians who refuse to be honest about what part of the budget they intend to cut: whether nuclear aircraft carriers or children's school lunches.

David and Elizabeth Dodson-Gray see the coming period of social adjustment and accommodation to new realities as analogous to the processes described by Elizabeth Kubler Ross in individuals dealing with death: first denial, then anger, followed by bargaining, depression and, finally, acceptance. But we must remember that in all biological systems decline and death is the precondition for rebirth, and we must propagate the many scenarios of cultural rebirth and point to what are already visible growing edges of the emerging counter-economy and renewable resource technologies as glimpses of the more humane communal, co-operative civilizations of the coming Solar Age. Polls are now showing that Americans are adjusting their earlier expectations, and the now famous Voluntary Simplicity report of the Stanford Research Institute estimates that 4 to 5 million Americans have already dropped out of the "rat-race," leading lives of voluntary frugality and searching for inner growth and psychic riches.

Protection Racket

We can also see how such value shifts are translating themselves into public policy—in, for example, the massive outpouring of interest in solar energy in the international celebration of millions of citizens on Sun Day (May 3rd, 1978). From such public pressure, we see the evolution of official government energy-demand forecasts: since 1972 the forecasts of energy demand by U.S. officials have fallen under public pressure from 160 quadrillion BTUs, to 140 quads in 1974; to 124 in 1976; to approximately 95 quadrillion BTUs in the recent Domestic Policy Review of the Department of Energy's forecasts in 1978. Thus, we slowly move from the technological fix, instrumental "supply side" economists' approach to our problems, to a more subtle, self-aware view of the "demand side" (our own behavior, attitudes, and values).

Similarly, top-down hierarchies are losing their grip. Patriarchal remedies—more centralization, more control, manipulation, technical fixes—become less effective and less credible. We now see the absurdity, as E.F. Schumacher pointed out, of societies that require a breakthrough a day to keep the crisis at bay! Charismatic, patriarchal leadership styles are also becoming hollow. Competitive, patriarchal, nation-states, and all organized systems of distrust and inequality have exhausted their logic. Patriarchal leadership seems to have little left to offer except competition, violence, confrontation, institutionalized paranoia, and ever greater efforts to manipulate nature for short-term goals.

Thus, the value shifts will entail more than redesigning our technologies, reconceptualizing our politics and repatterning our knowledge; we must reinfuse our culture and re-balance our male-dominated industrial culture with those values to which highest lip-service is always paid, but which are most burdensome and challenging to operationalize. These are the values that have always been thrust upon women and sub-ordinated groups in all cultures: co-operation, humility, nurturing, maintenance, openness, spontaneity, peacefulness and love, and which have been most often designated as "female." Not that it is possible to return to the ancient matriarchal systems of our past; nor is it desirable. But a new synthesis that allows individuals to express a healthier balance of these so-called male and female tendencies is now necessary. The Chinese YIN/YANG symbolism is a less painful polarization of the debate and may help us avoid yet another battle of the sexes. Our culture simply suffers from an overdose of YANG.

Indeed, decentralist, communitarian, simple communities embody those values YANG cultures have despised as "feminine"! Yet these "sissy" YIN principles imbue religious doctrines, however patriarchal the formal, administrative church hierarchies. We need to re-examine these deepest roots of our belief if we are to deal adequately with the confluence of crises we face. For today, our shattered cultures need creative nurturing. They need "mothering."

Ethic of Enough

Our decency and goodwill as citizens in the face of all this obfuscation and confusion will be taxed as never before. We must all involve ourselves in the task of behavioral adaption to more shared, communal lifestyles and the ethic of enough, since these will be the new survival-oriented values of adapting to inevitable new realities: holism, ecological awareness, empathy, co-operation to leaven the excessive competition, justice and fair shares for the less fortunate, and what Erich Fromm calls the shift from *having* to *being*. Keeping up with the Jones will need to be replaced by the Shakertown Pledge, and by setting examples to reinforce its points: today we see that ancient faiths are confirmed by empirical events.

All our greatest spiritual leaders throughout history have been the real futurists—but we did not always understand their time frame. Cyclic value changes are the history of human societies. Wholesale value-shifts in human behavior will continue to occur, since we are now receiving direct feedback and reinforcement from the planet itself. Ancient religious concepts become understandable as scientific formulae: the Indian concept in Hinduism of "karma" is merely a general systems theory statement of the behavior of a non-linear system where the vectors of human behavior may be unknown, but what is known is that all such motions initiated will boomerang and create complex effects in delayed and displaced patterns. Similarly, the Christian and Judaic concept of Judgment Day, in general systems theory terms, is simply a complex non-linear system whose information feedback loops are speeding up to real time, where cause and effect are simultaneous, and there is no temporal or spatial dimension in which to hide the consequences of our actions. Even "miracles" are simply general statements of nonlinearity and new mutual-casual paradigms now emerging in information theory and post-Newtonian quantum physics. Indeed, we are still communicating in many disciplinary and sectarian tongues. The Tower of Babel haunts us yet. But the core knowledge and understanding is the same. Morality has at last become pragmatic. ❦

International Environmental Law — Potential and Paradox

Richard Falk

With America's discovery of the domestic environmental challenge early in the 1970s came the recognition that the challenge is global. Many other nations have come to the same conclusion. Officially, the birth of international concern occurred at the 1972 Stockholm Conference on the Human Environment, a gathering that can be viewed either as a momentous success because it staked out the contours of an international policy or as a depressing failure because it confirmed governments' willingness to talk big while doing nothing.

For their part, international lawyers have discovered the environmental challenge and responded to it. But so dizzying is the array of problems that a new framework for classifying and thinking about the environmental agenda is needed. The first step in this clarification process is to eliminate some of the confusion that arises from the present tendency to treat the environmental agenda as if it were a single problem. That entails sorting out the distinct problems often lumped in discussion under catch-all rubrics.

The Challenge

Clarifying our concerns about environmental subjects has been compared to swimming through a sea of tapioca. Should we worry about exotic species? If we worry at all, is it for the sake of wildlife or because its afflictions indicate the precarious condition of the human species? Should we instead worry because in some sense the quality of human life depends on sustaining the diversity of nature? Does the survival of animals have a more vital place than we generally acknowledge? Is agonizing over environmental quality distorting priorities when people are starving?

These questions could be posed with almost equal force for other environmental issues. We have more questions than answers because we have not agreed as to whether it is good citizenship to raise environmental questions at all. Few centers of power, wealth, and influence have more than voiced concern with the environment, and action is not nearly keeping pace with rhetoric. But rephrasing the questions might make answering them easier. Perhaps the pressing questions are to what extent (and on the basis of what evidence) are we concerned with human survival and the planet's habitability as ends in themselves? To what extent are we maintaining environmental quality simply so we can exploit the environment as long as possible? And to what extent are we concerned with abandoning centuries-old homocentric priorities and assumptions—moving at last to challenge assumptions about what constitutes progress and trying to re-establish the harmony between man and nature?

Responses to these questions vary widely. On the one hand, many blacks, radicals, labor leaders, and business executives argue that the poor bear the costs of environmental protection inequitably and disproportionately, and that satisfaction of basic needs should not be deferred or subordinated for the sake of environmental quality. Some among them also assert that the extent of environmental pressure is greatly exaggerated, largely reflecting middle-class aesthetics and nature worship. On the international level, many Third World governments take a similar view, arguing that the rich industrial states are alleging concern to divert attention and resources from the development process, that global environmental problems are caused almost totally by the advanced industrial countries, and that environmental issues should not be featured prominently on international agendas.

In stark contrast to these views are many compelling reports about "the death of the oceans," the imminence of eco-catastrophe or eco-suicide, and the brevity of the interval available within which to end war and redistribute the world's wealth. But even those who argue that the planet is in grave danger disagree as to whether the fundamental issue is population pressure, technologically based growth, or the archaic social and political habits associated with affluence, urbanization, and conflict. Buckminster Fuller stands out among those who contend that the choice for the human race has narrowed to "utopia or oblivion." According to Fuller, utopia is possible if we organize world society to develop and distribute cheap and abundant energy. Fuller's utopia depends upon technological creation of the material basis for a good life for everyone, not just a relative few. He argues that oblivion will result if we allow scarcities and wars to persist. In more restrained terms, advocates of fusion power also maintain a technocratic vision of global liberation based on cheap, clean energy for all a few decades hence, _if_ we can just manage to keep the planetary economy running on diminishing or risky energy sources in the interim. Such optimism collides with alarmism about depleting fossil energy supplies and about the dangers of nuclear power programs.

Whether these competing views can be evaluated, much less reconciled, will depend in part on our ability to see them for what they are— simultaneously matters of evidence, of priority and trade-off, and of action. Here, two complementary approaches to perception and policy can be suggested, both of which need to be assessed in light of the fact that international law can make only gradual or marginal contributions to environmental protection. The first is _World Order Reform_. This approach would entail the evolution of supra-national solutions to environmental issues that do not depend on the sovereign state for implementation.

Can the world order system be reformed? Relevant experience is regretably discouraging. For example, promotion of supra-national solutions for the arms race and the dangers of nuclear warfare have not produced positive results: earlier hopes for disarmament have been quietly shelved and the focus has shifted to a reinforcing process called "arms control." _Intergovernmental solutions,_ the second approach, would require acting within the state system to resolve environmental issues with international dimensions. Practical and realistic for the short term, this approach entails intergovernmental negotiations, rule-making, and institution-building—in short, the traditional tasks of international law and lawyers.

As Leo Marx wrote in _Science_ a decade ago, "we have no choice but to use the nation-states as political instruments for coping with the rapid deterioration of the physical world we inhabit" as long as ecosystems and ecological problems do not stop at national borders and we have no world government. Committed as he is to reform, Marx understands that working within the present structure holds our best chance of minimizing destruction and trauma while we make the transition to a more durable and equitable system. As a practical matter, then, international environmental law must be considered mainly within the context of the world as it is, even though the need for changes grows clearer as interdependence deepens.

The Dimensions

What are the environmental challenge's basic components? The three main types of issues appear to be degradation of the environment in warfare, the variance in the spatial reach of specific environmental problems, and the extension of the environmental challenge to include conservation. Putting the environmental challenge in such broad terms helps us to do several things: identify the actors principally responsible for causing environmental harm (individuals, corporations, etc.) and capable of correcting the abuse, define the relationship between the wrong-doer and the locus of impact, assess the seriousness (rate of deterioration, extent of economic and social consequences, etc.), and determine the type of impact (economic, aesthetic, biological, etc.).

The issue of waste disposal presents an important test of the criteria spelled out here. Solid waste, raw sewage, DDT, PCBs and other persistent pesticides, industrial chemicals and minerals, spilled oil, phosphates, and other toxic substances being released into the environment in quantity are allowed to build up primarily because the numerous localized uses of such substances are generally remote from the places of harmful impact and seemingly inconsequential in relation to the problem posed. Each use seems locally beneficial, serving some socially useful end at minimum cost. The ability to dispose of wastes cheaply obviously enhances market competition, industrial growth, and output. But growth-oriented GNP accounting also encourages the transfer of the economic costs of disposal to the community as a whole, and of the environmental costs to future generations.

International law is of little help in cases such as this one. Yet, a large class of environmental problems involves users who are remote from the harm done and who have no direct incentive to curtail harmful activity.

In contrast to cumulative environmental problems associated with repetitive use are those in which the minimum threshold of natural accommodation is virtually zero (e.g., nuclear radiation, mercury poisoning). To combat these, the regulatory objective would have to be prohibiting use (or disposal) or making precautionary standards as absolute as possible. The user of such ultratoxic substances is likely to be a government or a large corporation, so the mechanics of regulatory prohibition should not, in theory, be difficult to implement. But they are. For example, the official commitment to increase national energy supplies to sustain economic growth by relying on nuclear power creates incentives to understate all hazardous consequences. There is no trustworthy means to ensure the public interest, as the government is itself compromised.

This type of problem also resists international legal response since individual nations remain committed to maximizing GNP without loss of geopolitical maneuverability. Standards and procedures for the storage, transport, and disposal of radionuclides and other dangerous wastes cannot be set as long as energy policy is treated as a domestic matter. No political or legal mechanisms for challenging national policies that endanger the international environment exist, and world energy shortages have intensified the nationalist element in policy-making.

Another class of events involves national threats to global well-being. An example is the accidental release of poisons into air and water systems. As matters now stand, the acceptability of these risks is generally not subject to prior international review. In fact, the offending party is under no clear obligation to compensate for actual harm unless the victim or complainant can demonstrate fault and causation. For example, if a train carrying chlorine is derailed in Canada near the U.S. boundary, relief for injury will depend on being able to show a causal impact. The controversy surrounding the use of the high seas for testing nuclear weapons illustrates the same point. In November of 1971, the United States detonated an underground nuclear explosion on Amchitka Island in the Aleutians that had 250 times the explosive force of the Hiroshima bomb. Before the blast, the Japanese government had voiced concern about tidal waves hitting the Japanese Islands, and Canadian opposition was even more vigorous. The only effective opposition came from within the United States, where a rather small and poorly financed citizen organization, the Committee for Nuclear Responsibility, lost by just one vote in the Supreme Court a last-minute effort to obtain an injunction.

While the citizens' worst fears never materialized, the Cannikan controversy remains of interest. Its lessons? First, the opposition of foreign governments held little weight in the face of alleged national security considerations. Second, there was no coordinated effort to represent an overall global interest. Third, a legal precedent of national discretion was set. Fourth, the most formidable opposition to Cannikan came from domestic quarters, including recourse to the courts and efforts to organize a congressional initiative. Finally, there was no tradition or mechanism with which to mount environmental challenges against government policy.

The outcome of the Cannikan incident also bears looking at with such other crucial environmental issues in mind as the disposal of nerve gas and other chemicals of warfare, the future of supersonic transport, the preservation of the ozone shield, and the discharge of CO_2 into the atmosphere. A jurisdictional problem exists in each case because the locus of activity is not within national territory and no government is therefore legally able to prevent harm or to assess responsibility for harm. Indeed, the government most directly responsible likely has the most to gain by acting irresponsibly.

Disasters pose yet another category of important environmental issues. Who is ultimately accountable for a tanker collision or break-up on the high seas and for the oil spill in the wake? The Torrey Canyon accident in 1967 was the Hiroshima of the ecological age, awakening world consciousness to a new danger arising from large-scale oceanic oil transport. Off-shore oil blow-outs and accidents are generally associated with deep-sea mining operations, which go on within a regulatory vacuum.

Looking beyond the isolated but newsworthy event, we should consider extending the concept of environmental harm to encompass both the wasteful use of resources and conflicts of interest between the world's rich and poor (and between this generation and successive ones). Also at question is the impact of national governmental action on the global ecosystem. What is to keep a nation from failing to enforce reasonable standards of seaworthiness if registration fees represent a major source of foreign exchange?

Less tangible than those other types of threats are those to the preservation of our heritage. Trade-offs are often possible, and yet the discretionary powers of exploiters stand in the way. Egypt's decision to build the Aswan High Dam to obtain electrical power for development at the cost of destroying cultural monuments and natural wonders is one example of this type of problem. Should the United Nations have intervened? Should the world community have had an opportunity to help Egypt pay for maintaining its own (and the world's) cultural heritage? Is there a legal concept of world trust?

The unnatural extinction of species raises problems of the same type. For example, no effective international regulation has resulted even though whale hunting has pushed the population of many whale species way below the level of maximum sustainable yields. With thousands of jobs and a major source of protein on the line, Japan has no incentive to renounce its pro-hunting policy. The "facts" of the case depend upon one's vantage point. At the level of the hunters or factory ships, self-interest tends to be perceived in terms of the size of annual catch, return on investment, and national gains; and self-restraint is viewed merely as a senseless transfer of profits to rivals.

The last category of problems includes the ravages of war. Among the many horrors born of the Viet Nam War was large-scale pre-meditated environmental warfare. Used to deny insurgent forces the natural sanctuary of foliage, brush, and forest, these tactics included the massive spraying of herbicides, the bulldozing of timber areas with Rome plows, carpet bombing, weather modification, fire-storming, and occupying cultural monuments.

Throughout the history of warfare, concepts of military necessity have evolved to justify new instruments and techniques of warfare. Viewed thus, environmental warfare is part of the counter-insurgent response of high-technology societies to the rise of guerrilla warfare. As long as high-technology governments dominate the law-shaping process and high-technology weapons are being shipped to governments in low-technology regions of the world, how can legal prohibitions on environmental warfare succeed?

These many types of environmental issues will be difficult to resolve within the state system since a characteristic feature of each is the *uneven distribution* of harmful impact and regulatory costs. Voluntary self-regulation must certainly fail in the absence of perceived mutual interests, and this unevenness makes it difficult for international lawyers to negotiate appropriate standards and virtually impossible to implement them. After all, international law is now itself a creature of the state system.

Prospects

Ecological demand—the sum of all humankind's demands on the environment—grows along with GNP and all-out efforts to boost GNP.

In _Blueprint for Survival,_ British scientists argued that if current growth rates continue, total ecological demand on a global scale "will increase by a factor of 32 over the next 66 years." In this light, is optimism anything but foolhardiness?

There are some encouraging developments, including the recent upsurge of national and global concern about environmental issues and related issues of food supply, resource adequacy, and population pressures. Some observers also regard the revival of subnational and transnational ethnic, religious, and linguistic bonds and a consequent rise in political militancy as positive signs. Even though such developments may breed violence, this logic goes, they also reflect a broad historical trend toward self-identification that is weakening the state as the main unit of political organization in global affairs. Arguably, the growth and expansion of the multinational corporation as a major instrument of capital development and business also challenges the statist logic of maximizing the territorial well-being of national units. At any rate, all these developments suggest a more _complicated_ pattern that creates some basis for increasing the role of international cooperation.

On the short term, national governments clearly face a choice. To promote environmental quality, they can act as parties to bilateral and universal arrangements that establish common norms, procedures, and institutions. Alternately, they can unilaterally take such steps at the national level to protect their national environment from external intrusion.

The prospects for the international legal order involve the sum of cooperative and unilateral undertakings. Naturally, not every extension of national prerogative contributes to international order. But national governments acting alone are important law-creators in the global realm, and national governments alerted to the environmental danger can help mitigate adverse global impacts. They can, to take just one example, impose off-shore environmental standards on shipping operations.

Many international governments are also in a position to further ecological goals. U.N. agencies such as the World Health Organization, the Food and Agricultural Organization, and the Fund for Population Activities have been wrestling with global environmental problems, while the International Maritime Consultative Organization has facilitated the growth of treaty law bearing on ocean pollution. The proliferation of treaties, even of specialized ones, does not assure compliance with their terms, especially if there is no machinery to detect violations, much less to apprehend and hold violators accountable. But international institutions are becoming important instruments of intergovernmental cooperation. Similarly, _nongovernmental_ groups such as the Sierra Club and transnational actors such as Friends of the Earth or Greenpeace can spur governments' re-examination of unsound environmental policy and practice.

Levels of Defense

What can all these actors hope to accomplish? Where are the opportunities? The gaps? Are some types of environmental problems more easily solved at one level than at another? Or is action at all levels the key?

If international lawyers would inventory achievements, projects, and proposals, they could begin to develop an overview of existing legal initiatives and set an environmental agenda. A simple matrix with types of issues listed on one axis and arenas of action on the other would help the legal community set its priorities and lay its plans. But to construct such a matrix, the action possible at each level must be spelled out.

Global undertakings—the highest level—require the participation of virtually all governments in a world conference or an international institution. Such cooperation probably won't restrain controversial behavior, but it may prompt participants to include broad affirmations of duty in general lawmaking treaties. The Stockholm Conference on the Human Environment (1972) represents the most dramatic effort yet in this direction, although its chief value lay in providing a forum for comment and criticism and in providing some momentum.

A more promising global undertaking is the U.N. Governing Council for Environmental Programs. This Nairobi-based institution, a direct legacy of Stockholm, gathers and exchanges information and monitors critical indicators of fundamental eco-stability bearing on temperature, weather, carbon balance, and oxygen supply. It also measures pollution, develops expert techniques and some capabilities for responding to environmental disasters, trains environmental specialists for national service, alerts the public to environmental dangers and emergencies, and helps create environmental standards for various activities. A much more ambitious effort is needed, however. The current institutional initiative is, at best, part of a holding operation assigned to international law while a new eco-political base forms.

Two examples suggest other "global area" opportunities to arrest ecological damage. A treaty conference to rewrite the laws of war to encompass environmental issues is obviously needed; so is a prohibition on the release of ultratoxic substances into the atmosphere.

Inevitably, the global arena is most significant for framing responses to environmental challenges. The capacity of the state system to strike bargains of global scope and to implement them effectively is critical to interim efforts to meet the environmental challenge on the international level. Sooner or later, supranational procedures and institutions will be needed to express trends toward global integration, and whether such trends can be accommodated peacefully is part of the basic historical drama of our era. Determining whether this will happen in the decades ahead is partly a matter of weighing fact and feasibility (the needs and pragmatics of problem-solving) and partly of expressing preference (ethical priorities and values). Such perspectives are far from self-evident to international lawyers, who tend to work in relation to the *status quo* and to dress up their normative predispositions in the obscure language of legal discourse.

The key to regional or sub-regional cooperation is a simple geo-political fact: in highly industrialized areas composed of groups of countries, the threat of environmental damage tends to be perceived as a common danger, and responsive action—both inward- and outward-looking—is therefore relatively easy to agree upon. Within the region the challenge is to set common standards, agree on ways to implement them, and equitably mete out the benefits and burdens (for example, rights to discharge wastes or to exploit marine resources versus duties to limit such discharges and provide compensation). The key here is to develop procedures for settling disputes and enforcing agreements.

Another kind of regional or sub-regional arrangement is aimed at staking out claims against outsiders, imposing barriers upon access or behavior, and outlining implementation procedures. Perhaps the most spectacular recent instance of such a regional initiative has been Latin America's effort to proclaim and uphold 200-mile exclusive fishing zones off its Western coast. Of course, the primary motivation here is economic nationalism, but scarce resources are also conserved in the process. In this sense, regionalist or sub-regionalist environmental policy can resemble traditional security alliances.

Bi-national or multi-national cooperation, the third level of action, can take many forms. In each, the character of the arrangement reflects the bargaining relationship. A regime designed to sustain the environmental quality of an international river exemplifies this sort of international legal arrangement. So does the allocation of fishing rights among many states.

Traditionally, international law has depended heavily on treaty law of this sort, partly because the number of participants is flexible and the level of obligation can be specific (as with catch quotas) or rather vague (as with the obligation to refrain from dumping noxious substances into international waters). But the development of international law at this level remains disappointing because national governments have failed to consent to environmental standards or procedures that impinge on perceived national advantage, even if the advantage is to a small group or short-lived.

The fourth level, national governmental initiatives, involves individual nations' claims based on alleged environmental standards. Influential countries such as the U.S. can exert considerable pressure by erecting environmental barriers, either by establishing boycotts or by extending territorial claims. This approach holds appeal because it is comparatively easy both to implement and to enforce appropriate policies within one nation's territorial jurisdiction. It can backfire, of course, resulting in such events as the accelerated spread of harmful products like cyclamates to foreign lands. Its other drawbacks relate primarily to the further build-up of state power and the encroachment of national claims upon the resources of the global community. When the state system seems unable to manage intensifying economic or ecological interdependencies or to fulfill the basic human needs of so much of the world's population, relying on unilateral extensions of state power does seem perverse. That, in effect, is the *paradox of world order*—so long as the state system exists, national governments are the most effective agents of global law-creation and enforcement, but the longer the state system persists, the more difficult it becomes to uphold global interests.

The final level, non-governmental initiatives, includes the work of the gamut of non-governmental actors. Just as the International Committee of the Red Cross spurred the development of the law of war, so public interest groups (and individuals) have stirred up interest in environmental issues. In the U.S. and Western Europe they have pressured governments to take the environmental agenda seriously, insisting on the development of rules, procedures, and regimes, and helping to keep governments and their spokesmen relatively honest with each other and with the media.

In the U.S., the action of local communities has been crucial. Grassroots activists have prevented the construction of oil refineries, power-plants, jetports, and pipelines in economic contexts where a decade ago profitability and GNP would have been virtually the only criteria of policy, and construction a virtual certainty. Never-the-less, economic gain still carries most weight with policy makers, and evidence of ecological decay continues to grow.

Probability and Ideals

If international law is to protect the environment, then international lawyers must eventually design central planetary-guidance capabilities that do not require a super-centralized world polity. In the immediate future, we will probably have to content ourselves with a drearier achievement—plugging holes in the ecological dike and hoping that more ambitious reform builds into a world movement. The glamor of environmental reform will be mainly confined to global conferences on population, food, and the oceans, but more genuine progress may occur closer to home. The most impressive steps are likely to be government and local initiatives, but the linchpin of the whole process is a change in human consciousness. It comes down at last to the public's ability to overcome the paradox of world order, to struggle against vested interests and narrow outlooks. In the end, our quest is for a planetary network of institutions and values that is both politically viable and ecologically sensitive.

Corporate Responsibility and Toxic Chemicals: The 'I' of the Storm

Gus Speth

It sometimes takes calamity to teach big lessons. The failure of a dam brings the dam safety issue into painfully clear focus. India's explosion of a nuclear bomb brings home the realization that atoms for peace can become bombs for war. And Kepone contamination in Hopewell, Virginia, helps shape public awareness of the risks associated with toxic chemicals.

Nothing will be the same after Kepone. Americans from all walks of life were horrified by dramatic television interviews of Kepone victims—workers for an Allied Chemical Corporation contractor in Hopewell who, sometimes with slurred voices or shaking hands, told how exposure to kepone had blurred their vision, damaged their coordination, or caused joint and chest pains and loss of memory. Kepone contamination from the Hopewell plant poisoned the James River, forcing a ban on fishing in the James that is still in effect, and then spread to the Chesapeake Bay, where fish contamination has been detected.

In August of 1976, Allied Chemical pleaded *no contest* to 940 criminal charges of illegally discharging Kepone into the James River. The company was fined $13.2 million—one of the largest penalties levied in a pollution trial—but the fine was later reduced to $5 million when Allied donated $8 million to an independent environmental foundation in Virginia. Two executives of the Allied contractor that operated the Hopewell plant were convicted of conspiracy to violate federal anti-pollution laws and were also fined, as was the city of Hopewell for allowing the discharge of kepone-laden wastes into the municipal sewer system.

The Kepone incident is all the evidence we need that a nightmarish possibility of our chemical age can become the morning's grim reality. It justifies strong governmental regulation to ensure that such neglect, destruction and injury is never repeated, in Hopewell or elsewhere.

The Kepone incident no doubt influenced those polled not long ago by Lou Harris. The Harris survey indicated that two of every three Americans are seriously concerned about toxic substances. Yet, the pollsters detected an attitude that runs counter to these healthy fears: since 1976, they found, the percentage of people who think toxics will be less of a problem in the future has grown from 14 to 36 percent.

That show of confidence may indicate the public's relief that, after five years of temporizing, Congress finally passed the Toxic Substances Control Act. It may also suggest that American citizens feel we have finally cracked down on this issue and that it's only a matter of time before we stop introducing troublesome chemicals into our air, water, and food. Perhaps the Harris findings even signal a sense of confidence in the public officials responsible for finding a solution to the hazardous substances problem.

Whatever it suggests, those Americans who feel that toxic substances will be less troublesome in the future than in the past are in for a disappointment. True, recent legislation has for the first time given us broad authority to control dangerous chemicals, but the problem is at least a generation old and we have just begun to address it.

The widespread use of synthetic chemicals started after the second World War, but we are only now learning how extensive—and how persistent—the harmful side effects of that chemical revolution can be. Not long ago, chemicals began seeping from a disposal site beneath a housing subdevelopment in Niagara Falls. The trauma suffered by the residents of the Love Canal area has helped galvanize public sentiment behind a national program to clean up hazardous wastes. Since Love Canal, other problems have cropped up. In Hardeman County, Tennessee, at least 17 chemical contaminants were found in local well water a short distance from a ridge where 350,000 drums of wastes from a pesticide plant are buried. In Lowell, Massachusetts, health officials got an emergency appropriation from the state legislature to remove 17,000 barrels of toxic chemicals that were leaking into the Merrimack River. And in Michigan, state officials sued to recover the $1 million spent to clean out an industrial site in Pontiac.

These incidents could portend even more problems in the future. Approximately 762,000 American facilities generate hazardous wastes, some 20,000 transport them, and 20,000 more process or store them. The Environmental Protection Agency estimates that between 1,200 and 2,000 dumpsites that contain some hazardous wastes could pose significant leakage problems; 500 to 800 of these sites may have been abandoned.

In short, toxic chemicals pose a serious threat. How well are we prepared to address it? Our federal environmental laws, though imperfect, are one of Congress' major achievements in this century. The Toxic Substances Control Act and the Clean Water Act provide strong authority to protect the public from dangerous chemicals. But improvements, adjustments, and new initiatives are badly needed. Of special urgency is new legislation addressing the problem of inactive hazardous waste dumps. In mid-1979, the Carter Administration proposed the so-called "Superfund Bill"—the Oil, Hazardous Substances and Hazardous Waste Response, Liability and Compensation Act—which would create the nation's first comprehensive program to deal with spills of oil and hazardous chemicals and with inactive and abandoned dumpsites. The "Superfund Bill" would fill the gaps in our existing authority to protect the public from these hazards.

Along with securing passage of this essential legislation, other challenges must be addressed. Federal agencies today are making a concerted effort to control toxic chemicals by making regulation more efficient, more effective, and better coordinated. For example, recent efforts have been directed at developing a government-wide cancer policy, coordinating regulatory actions on particular chemicals and industries, and building new systems for acquiring and sharing data on toxicity and exposures. But all this is taking place in the face of a powerful anti-regulation movement spearheaded by the offending industries.

In recent years, as the size and influence of corporations has expanded, the pace of legislation to control them has quickened. Since 1963, Congress has enacted at least 150 major laws to regulate the social impact of business activity. Some businesspeople seem to believe that we now have all the regulatory control any economy can withstand. In fact, some major corporations have launched extensive campaigns to convince Americans that government regulation is out of control.

And yet, year after year, some new piece of corporate neglect or law-breaking either mocks the controls we have or suggests that those controls have failed again. These are not minor infractions, but serious violations—sometimes condoned at the highest corporate levels—of our laws and of the norms of responsible business behavior. PCBs from General Electric Plants, for example, have profoundly damaged the Hudson River, making a ban on commercial fishing necessary. And a new "inside" account of corporate decision-making at General Motors reveals that top management insisted on marketing the accident-prone Corvair despite strong objections by the company's engineers.

In the context of continuous revelations of this type, most corporate protests against environmental and consumer regulation ring hollow—especially when companies and entire industries are quite willing to support other government regulation when it works to their advantage. For instance, despite all the praise lavished upon the concept of competition by business' spokespeople and their copywriters, the trucking industry today is fighting deregulation tooth and nail.

Some corporate complaints about government regulation are understandable. But most pay no respect to the fact that every environmental regulation has its genesis in some problem that threatened the public and finally brought a legitimate public demand for governmental action.

Regulation is not going to go away until the problems do. The way we regulate can and must be improved, but vigilant government regulatory activity is essential to national goals of paramount importance: to controlling cancer and protecting health, to preventing consumer fraud and deception, to cleaning up our air and water, to reducing oil imports and conserving energy, to protecting us from nuclear accidents, and to fulfilling a long list of other national objectives.

The short-sighted attack environmental regulations by charging that they are inflationary. But that claim cannot withstand scrutiny. A comprehensive analysis of the inflationary impact of pollution control regulations, performed by Data Resources, Inc., at the behest of the Council on Environmental Quality, makes that clear. Between 1970 and 1986, federal air- and water-pollution control requirements will add an average of 0.3 of one percentage point to the annual rate of increase in the consumer price index, with the 1980 figure estimated at 0.1 of a percentage point. Even judged by standard economic measures, the inflationary impact of environmental programs is thus quite minor. Moreover, any likely modification of federal environmental regulations would produce no significant reduction in the overall consumer price index. If the inflationary impact of these requirements could be reduced by a fourth—a substantial relaxation—the CPI's increase would be restrained by less than 0.05 of one percentage point. Since the net effect of even Draconian measures could amount to no more than the difference between a 7.00 percent increase and a 7.05 percent increase in the CPI, we must look elsewhere for the sources of inflation and for targets of our anti-inflation efforts.

Another challenge—improving existing regulatory efforts by supplementing them with new and innovative approaches—entails a variety of possibilities. Chief among them is the increased use of economic incentives such as emission charges and noncompliance fees as a complement to direct regulation. We must continue to build increased economic incentives and disincentives into our pollution-control efforts.

A related idea deserving wider attention than it has so far received is victim compensation. Victims of exposure to toxic chemicals, be they workers or members of the general public, should be fully and adequately compensated by the company or companies responsible for the exposure. This compensation, on the "polluter pays" principle, would not only be equitable from the injured party's perspective but would also provide a strong deterrent against harmful releases and exposures by manufacturers and others. Numerous mechanisms—from improving state worker's compensation programs to creating a new federal right of action that victims can pursue in court without having the entire burden of proof on their shoulders—have been suggested for ensuring this type of compensation. They deserve careful examination.

At the heart of the issue of toxic chemicals and their regulation is the question of corporate responsibility and accountability. Two types of nonmarket forces influence the corporation: external government controls and the internal controls exercised by those who directly manage or run the firm. Government and the public alike have tended of late to force good citizenship on corporations from the outside, instead of promoting social responsibility on the inside. Government regulation has been spurred by real problems, but it has prompted business to abandon its own sense of responsibility and to operate under the assumption that everything that is not proscribed by law is permitted. This leads to questionable corporate activities that in turn provoke still greater regulation. The cycle is not only vicious; it is self-perpetuating.

Both business and government stand to gain from following a new approach that combines traditional regulation with a new focus on efforts to improve corporate governance. As former Secretary of Commerce Juanita Kreps pointed out in Congressional testimony, "to the extent business helps (through improved corporate social performance) to deal with issues that might otherwise prompt government regulation, it serves its own economic interests." Secretary Kreps made another point that every business leader agitated by government intrusion should remember: business cannot responsibly call for less government regulation without also addressing those social issues and needs that prompt the calls for more regulation.

Business leaders, government officials, and the public must work together to put the concepts of corporate social responsibility and accountability into routine practice. But this alliance is not likely to form as long as the laws that determine the way corporations conduct their "internal" affairs remain so primitive. As far back as the 1890s, New Jersey and Delaware competed to see which state could water down its laws most to attract corporate charters. (Delaware won; by 1934, one-third of the corporations listed on the New York Stock Exchange were incorporated in Delaware.) Regrettably, this ethic of laxity has endured.

Partly because corporate controls are relaxed to attract business, the legal institutions for U.S. corporate governance—the stockholders and the directors—function as little more than rubber stamps for management decisions. Those that are affected most by the corporation's decisions—labor, consumers, the community at large—have even less to say.

It is time for a healthy dose of democracy in corporate decision-making. Two fundamental elements of democracy are participation by and accountability to the people whose lives the corporation affects. There are at least two steps that can be taken now to bring greater participation and accountability into corporate affairs—neither of which risks the economic benefits that corporations must provide.

First, to insure that the boards of directors of all large corporations are independent and representative, every large corporation should be required to have on its board a strong majority of members—perhaps two-thirds—who come from outside corporate management. In this way, most of the directors of these companies would be unencumbered by significant corporate ties that would limit their ability to provide an independent review of management. Of these independent directors, about half—or a third of total directors—should be directly representative of the public communities affected by the company's activities: consumers, environmentalists, employees, citizens from plant towns, and so on.

Not just anybody should be dragged in off the street to sit on a board simply on the strength of belonging to an environmental group. Such "public directors," besides representing a company's constituencies, would have to wear two hats and share responsibility with other directors for the corporation's profitability. Finding the right people for these positions requires sensitivity, but one possible mechanism is straightforward enough: simply let the shareholders vote for candidates for the potential slots, much as they vote for directors now.

The second step is to require major corporations to prepare a periodic social audit or report that will give the public enough information to determine whether the company is a good citizen. Such an audit would also provide shareholders with the information they need to make socially responsible decisions in buying and voting their shares. Social reports are now required in several European countries. There they are viewed in part as an alternative both to central government control and to the traditional market, which is no longer judged capable of meeting the broad spectrum of social needs.

What type of information could such a social audit contain? With respect to environmental impacts, the public and many investors want corporations to disclose a succinct factual account that shows what the company's activities do to the environment, whether the company follows enlightened environmental practices, and whether it complies with federal and other laws that protect the environment.

Economic incentives, victim compensation, and corporate accountability can all be used to supplement traditional regulatory approaches. If we pursue these newer ideas while continuing our commitment to enforcing the goals of the Toxic Substances Control Act and the Clean Air and Water Acts, the suffering of those caught in the calamities of Hopewell and Love Canal will not have been for naught. ☘

Neighborly Power

David Morris

A longing for neighborhood is sweeping this country. Even in mobile, ad hoc America a new generation yearns for a sense of place. We are, after a long period of amnesia, remembering that, after the family, the neighborhood is the basic building block of society, and we are feeling the breakdown of the blood bonds of neighborhoods and the fracture of life between work and play. As one urban observer has written:

> The structural faults (of our cities), whether social, material, economic, or administrative, can be seen to hinge upon one factor, dispersion and separation—separation of people from people, work from homes, homes from shopping and leisure activity, financial needs from financial resources, patterns of governmental authority from patterns of need for governmental action or aid.

The automobile has played a major role in this process. Leopold Kohr has described the multiplier effects of using the car to move out of the urban village:

> My wife feels we live too far from the market to continue shopping on foot. My children are too far from playgrounds and school. We all are too far from the theater, the recreation facilities, the restaurants, the library, the pubs, in fact from every location that was within pedestrian distance as long as we lived in town. In other words, my move into the outskirts has increased the distance to be negotiated not arithmetically but geometri-

cally. The addition of a single mile has added not only one two-mile journey per day, but a whole cluster of such journeys, and this not only for the family collectively, but for each of its members individually.

Public policy since World War II has reinforced the destruction of geographic community. Federal financing agencies, such as HUD and FHA, have for twenty years pursued a policy that can only be described as a search-and-destroy mission. Those neighborhoods that lacked an economic base were razed, despite the presence of a viable social structure.

These programs supported high-rises and freeways as efficient ways to house and to move large numbers of people. Even after these programs have been proven erroneous, they live on, sapping the energy of neighborhoods that have to spend years fighting against policies whose very designers have since admitted their folly. Thirty years after his support of high rises was translated into national and global policy, architect-planner Constantine Doxiadis recanted, noting:

> Such buildings work against nature by spoiling the scale of the landscape. The most successful cities of the past have been the ones where man and his buildings were in a certain balance with nature, such as Athens or Florence. Furthermore, these buildings work against society because they do not help the units of social importance—the family and the extended family, the neighborhood—to function as naturally and as normally as before.

As individual transportation systems fragmented work and play, and vertical construction destroyed the human scale of society, our neighborhoods have become increasingly single-purpose, residential areas. Even when they retain a business base, it is no longer one that acts to hold the community together. Neighborhood commerce now consists of branch stores and franchises. The manager lives outside the community. The products sold come from outside as well. And this trend has given way to an even more sinister and debilitating one. The local gas station has been replaced by a self-service station. The attendant sits behind bullet-proof windows, taking cash and pushing buttons. Branch banks are being replaced by electronic bank tellers, and supermarkets are introducing automated checkers.

These developments may be efficient when viewed in terms of the corporation's bottom line; but they reinforce the growing image of the neighborhood as an outpost of civilization rather than its center. No longer can we get a flat tire repaired or ask for financial planning assistance. The human interaction of commerce is being eliminated.

Yet, despite this onslaught, human communities survive and persevere. Neighborhoods that have fought against freeways, high rises, local school closings, traffic dangers, and the like are now seeking some way to guarantee their security. The strongest demands usually stem from those neighborhoods located in the ring around downtown, for it is here that the daily pressure of speculators and builders has been most intensive. But the revival of localism has spread beyond inner city neighborhoods to those residential communities on the edge of the city, and beyond to the sprawling housing developments that constitute the new suburban communities. This sense of geographic identity and turf is being reinforced by a growing support for local self-reliance, for a return to a human scale of society, where decision-making can be done through face-to-face contact, and where production takes place within walking distance.

Neighborhoods have learned that struggling against something, be it a high rise, a park closing, or increased traffic, is debilitating. Too often confronted with decisions after the fact, these communities have gained organizational strength and maturity, and begun to demand active participation in planning.

Neighborhood Planning

Planning that strives for community self-reliance will blend the ancient and modern. It will adopt the pre-industrial concept that geographic community should be the locus of society, that the urban village, with its rich human interaction and culture, should be preserved and reinforced. It will integrate the modern advances in technology and science, which can reinforce holistic planning through contemporary ecological concepts.

The goal of this kind of planning is transforming neighborhood residents from consumers to producers, from passive observers of society to active participants in planning its future.

For the neighborhood to once again become productive it must utilize the wealth it generates. This means stopping the leakages of wealth from its borders. There are at least two kinds of leakages that decentralized planners must minimize. The first is the outflow to the public and private sectors of money that could be recirculated within the area for local economic development. The second is the outflow, or just plain waste, of the enormous natural resources the community has access to. The energy that falls on its territory, the soil and rooftop space, the so-called organic and solid "wastes" that should rather be considered raw materials by local planners, the rich human resources— these are the natural resources common to all geographic communities.

By plugging the natural resources "leakages" in our communities, and recycling finance capital into local economic development, we can begin to build a productive base and regain a measure of self-confidence and cohesion that has been lacking in our neighborhoods for some time.

Stopping the Leaks: Capital

Although studies of neighborhood capital flows are in their infancy, neighborhoods are beginning to recognize that vast quantities of public and private money flow through their boundaries very rapidly and with few beneficial effects on the area. As Milton Kotler observed:

The important features of a poor neighborhood are, first, the discrepancy between the aggregate expendable income of the neighborhood and the paltry level of its commerce, and second, the discrepancy between the considerable tax revenue the neighborhood generates and the low level of benefits it receives in public services and welfare. In both cases, the neighborhood exports its income.

For the public sector, one of the earliest studies, done in 1969, examined the Shaw-Cordozo neighborhood in Washington, D.C., with a population of 87,000. Even in this low-income area, $10 million more flowed out of the community in taxes and fees than returned in services and public welfare. These figures in fact understated the impact on the neighborhood because the money that did come back in services went mainly to pay the salaries to teachers and police officers who live outside the neighborhood, coming in only to perform their jobs.

The government is not the only source of leakage. One study examined the neighborhood balance of payments of Bedford Stuyvesant, a large neighborhood of 250,000 residents in New York City. It found a favorable balance of payments, primarily due to the huge impact of public assistance moneys from federal and local governments. However, it also found that the amount of money that flowed out of the community for drugs and gambling equaled the amount that came in as public assistance payments. Organized crime was the source of leakage in Bedford Stuyvesant. It was grossing more money than the federal government was collecting in taxes. Not surprisingly, the gambling operation in the area is the second largest single employer—second only to the government itself.

Private business is, if anything, worse than the public and criminal systems. The money you deposit in the local bank rarely benefits you or your neighbors. The persistence of neighborhood activists led to the uncovering of the redlining practice. Insurance companies and banks have traditionally refused to make loans in areas they decided were declining. When redlining occurs, a neighborhood does deteriorate: there is no money for home improvement and no financing for property transfers.

Even the money that is loaned rarely goes to neighborhood enterprises. In the Adams Morgan neighborhood in Washington, D.C. (population 25,000), chain stores deposited 20 percent of the money in the local bank, while the locally owned and operated independent retailers deposited 80 percent. However, when loans were made, the giants gained 72 percent, the independent businesses 28 percent.

The proliferation of branch stores has aggravated the basic problem. To appreciate just how much, consider the conclusions of a study of the books of one fast-food franchise—McDonalds:

Fully 20 percent of this store's costs immediately leave the community: advertising; rent (paid to a corporate subsidiary); a service fee paid to the corporation; accounting and legal fees;

insurance; depreciation and amortization; and debt service. This restaurant, like all other outlets, purchases its food and paper supplies from other centralized corporate subsidiaries. These costs are 41.81 percent of total expenses. Management costs go toward paying salaries outside of the area . . .

These figures are particularly disheartening since franchised businesses constitute the most rapidly growing part of the retail economy.

Neighborhoods striving for self-reliance will try to keep as much of this money within their borders as possible, recycling money the way they recycle natural resources. This means substituting local services and products for those previously imported. It is a concept that has been used with varying success in developing countries and that is gaining popularity in our capital-starved and hemorrhaging big cities.

Stopping the Leaks: Natural Resources

Just as capital flows out of our communities, so do natural resources. And, as in the case of dollars, neighborhoods interested in self-reliant planning must develop mechanisms for capturing these resources for local use.

F.H. King, writing many decades ago in *Farmers of Forty Centuries,* noted the ironic waste of nutrients in America:

. . . The people of the United States . . . are pouring into the sea, lakes, or rivers, and into the underground waters 6 to 12 million pounds of nitrogen, 2 to 4 million pounds of potassium, and 75,000 to 3 million pounds of phosphorus per million of adult population annually, and this waste we esteem one of the great achievements of our civilization.

In most cities there are millions of square feet of roof space on warehouses, office buildings, and residences that can be used for energy generation, food production, or both. Utilizing intensive agricultural techniques such as hydroponics, a city dweller can raise significant quantities of vegetables. One study done of a densely populated neighborhood in Washington, D.C., found that by using only part of the roof space and soil available, the neighborhood could supply over 40 percent of the vegetables it needed.

Solid waste is also a neighborhood resource. Twenty thousand people generate ten tons of paper a day, an equivalent amount of organic waste, and significant quantities of metal and glass. This material wealth can be processed locally and turned into products.

So too, the energy on our rooftops and streets is wasted. The solar energy that falls on our neighborhood each day could meet all our energy needs. Yet, only recently have the first signs of solar technology entered our communities. The technology is available currently not only to collect low-grade heat for heating our domestic water and the interiors of our buildings, but for higher grade heat for air conditioning.

Solar cells and wind generators are available to convert solar energy to electricity. Increasingly sophisticated technologies are coming on line, including storage systems. Given their availability, it is time we began to view our neighborhoods as energy producers, and solar collectors as means of turning houses into utility companies. As communities begin to assess their energy potential, they cannot help but see how renewable energy can replace imported energy.

Consider the case of the electric car. Electric vehicles can be produced economically by relatively small plants for relatively small market areas. The electricity for these cars could come from solar cells or wind generators. In one study done of Washington, D.C., it was discovered that if all the parking lots were covered with solar cells, enough electricity would be generated to supply 65 percent of all the energy required for work-related trips by electric vehicles, and approximately 100 percent of work-related transportation during the summer months. This case study raises a vital question: why import oil from Saudi Arabia or Texas when we can use wind and sunlight falling on our own turf?

Why Self-Reliance?

At this point, the reader may ask "Why self-reliance?" Why should our neighborhoods seek a degree of autonomy? Might this pursuit not fragment systems and lead to a balkanized inefficiency in both production and delivery?

By striving for self-reliance, a neighborhood will build a sense of cohesion and self-confidence. People will be involved directly in decisions that affect their own lives. The process itself is important. To be self-reliant, neighbors need to rely on each other more, and in that spirit of cooperation they may prove ingenious.

Self-reliant neighborhoods must do more with less, creating new ways of providing high quality goods and services at lower cost with fewer materials and less energy. Their most important resource is people. Yet, ironically, only recently has the value of the voluntary labor that neighborhoods produce in quantity been recognized. Cohesive communities have an important, even critical, barter economy. People watch other parents' children. They swap recipes and share emotional support systems. They barter goods and services. The strength of neighborliness in all its forms should not be underestimated.

Beyond this, there is the broader range of unpaid services, what Scott Burns in *House Incorporated* dubbed the "household economy." Several studies have found that if we gave the minimum wage for such tasks as house-cleaning, child care, and the like, we would find that unpaid services are worth as much as the entire national income.

There are other important aspects of self-reliance. As neighborhoods become more productive, they gain and retain a knowledge about production that makes the residents better citizens. Youth growing up in a community that has light industries and food- and energy-production programs can use the neighborhood as a school. In earlier times, the youth dropped by the blacksmith's forge to learn how to shoe horses. Modern neighborhoods have very few, if any, places of learning outside the schools. Community businesses can provide the knowledge that residents need to evaluate large entities. Just as the Tennessee Valley Authority was a benchmark for the production of electricity for private enterprise, so the neighborhood farms or production facilities will show how much cheaper and better locally made goods are than national brands.

Neighborhood self-reliance can even promote world peace. It is trite by now to note that the rest of the world is neither so affluent nor so fortunate as is our country in terms of natural resources and technologies. Although much of that problem is traceable to a maldistribution of income and to the kinds of political regimes in power, part of the problem results from a lack of natural resources and technology appropriate to local conditions. It may be that as we utilize the creativity of our neighborhoods to develop ecologically sound systems we will both lighten our resource consumption and develop techniques of use beyond our borders.

In the last twenty years of this century we will face an extraordinary need for experimentation, creativity, and invention. This is best done on a small scale. As James Madison once observed, a diversity of experimentation on the local level can only lead to progress. If the experiment fails, no great harm is done. If it succeeds, the experience can be rapidly transferred and adapted to still other localities. It is this need for creativity and diversity that may be the greatest justification for neighborhood self-reliance.

Economies of Scale: Production

Any discussion of decentralization must confront the conventional wisdom that bigness is efficient. How far can one community go in producing the goods and services it requires?

Many discussions of this question stem from the need for a new definition of efficiency, one that stresses human involvement. Is it efficient to use half a glass of oil to produce a glass of milk? Is it efficient to produce thousands of cars a week, while each worker does nothing more than turn one bolt or screw? Is it efficient to centralize production so that hundreds of thousands of employees must travel miles to and from work and spend hours commuting, rather than decentralize plants and lessen the human toil?

However, even if we approach efficiency in traditional terms, we soon discover that most production systems are small. The myth of the efficiency of bigness stems mainly from a confusion between plant size and company size. Companies *have* grown large. Multi-national corporations are colossal. But the typical plant has not changed very much. Even most manufacturing plants are small: more than 95 percent of the 275,000 companies in the United States own only one plant.

Several studies of the consumer goods manufacturing sector have estimated the minimum efficient production unit. These studies are remarkably consistent. They indicate that for the production of many consumer goods, plants can be very small. One study found that for almost 70 percent of all the industries for which a minimum efficient scale could be identified, fewer than 250 employees were needed; 44 percent required fewer than 100 employees. And 70 percent of the industries required capital assets of under one million dollars to enter the industry. These figures may seem high for a neighborhood of between 10,000 and 30,000 people, but even the sacrifice of optimum efficiency may be no great loss. Studies show that we may be able to scale plants down to a size at which they produce for very localized markets goods that cost only slightly more than those of outside competitors. The cost difference would be slight indeed if the loyalty of the neighborhood could be won and the high costs of advertising, distribution, and overhead cut radically.

This is the picture we get from examining the current state of production. The future may be even brighter, for new technologies and materials advances are decentralizing even those industries such as steel-making and automobile-producing. At the same time there is a rapidly developing movement around the world that presumes that in many cases we can scale down our technology without sophisticated scientific advances. This movement has many names: intermediate, community, or appropriate technology. It began in developing countries, where small markets, scarce capital, and an abundance of labor, make imported capital-intensive machinery that requires large market areas seem wasteful and often even injurious to use.

Take the use of construction materials: the late E.F. Schumacher (author of *Small is Beautiful*) states that for us building material has come to mean Portland cement. "Why Portland cement:" he asks.

Go around Europe, to Asia, and you will find the most magnificent, wonderful buildings. The Taj Mahal or the cathedrals of Europe were not made with Portland cement, and they are still standing. Why have we fixed ourselves on Portland cement? Maybe you need Portland cement to build skyscrapers, but that is a minority phenomenon. Most buildings are not skyscrapers. What about other cementitious materials? It turns out that there are many other materials that can be made into cement at half the temperature of Portland cement. And for most normal human requirements, they are totally adequate and can be made on a small scale.

We can expect, with the growing awareness of appropriate technology and the federal and local government's interest, that neighborhoods may soon call on technical expertise much as the developing countries have done. These engineers and scientists will be asked to redesign production facilities so that local materials can be utilized, smaller markets can be reached, and more labor can be used in creative capacities. As this occurs, neighborhood planning will become largely a matter of deciding what kinds of trade-offs the neighborhood will accept.

The question of trade-offs is an important one, for there is no right decision. Planning, like politics, is the process of choosing that option among many that is most advantageous. For instance, the Intermediate Technology Development Group in England examined the manufacture of glass to assess the potential for one developing country's capacity for producing its own. It found that soda ash, which is used as a flux, can be obtained from wood ash or from seaweed. If only seaweed is added to the melt, the glass is slightly green. If arsenic—an extremely expensive trade ingredient—is eliminated, the final product has tiny bubbles. By eliminating these two basic materials, we make the process simpler and cheaper. The price we pay is slightly green glass with tiny bubbles. (Ironically, these bottles are of the very type that bring the highest prices at roadside auctions in rural areas.) Although such material substitutions have not been made in most industries, these trade-offs must be explored by neighborhoods seeking a high degree of self-reliance.

Economies of Scale: Service Delivery

The service area of the economy has become as concentrated, capital-intensive, and remote from neighborhood participation as the goods-production sector. The problem? We have too rarely noted the different dynamics between prevention and treatment. The more we prevent, the smaller the system, the less the capital expense, the greater the role for para-professionals, and the greater citizen involvement. Prevention systems, whether they be in health, criminal justice, or the like, tend to be decentralized. Self-reliance clearly involves prevention rather than treatment for most of our economic, social, and bodily ills.

Getting from here to there, though, will not be easy. Still, what may appear like so much fantasy has a basis in experience. Neighborhoods can and have started with nothing more than a zip code, and have begun to build an identity as a turf on which people cooperate to build self-reliance. Such cooperation has usually been catalyzed by a defensive struggle against external forces. Increasingly, though, the fight is for something—a struggle to create a viable economic base in the community. One neighborhood in the Bronx is converting 70 tons of vegetable waste a week to rich compost that is being used to rebuild the soil for massive urban farming projects. This project has economic development implications as well. After the neighborhood's soil has been rebuilt, the production plant will export the compost to Long Island potato farmers, thereby helping to reverse the fiscal drain that is traditional in low-income neighborhoods. Another neighborhood on the western edge of Newark, New Jersey, has formed a cooperative housing authority; the group now manages 54 buildings with a thousand tenant-owners and operates a day-care center and health facility. Its maintenance crew is now installing solar energy systems for domestic hot water on the neighborhood buildings.

In San Francisco, a food system that is neighborhood-based and worker self-managed now grosses $10 million a year. It has retail outlets, wholesaling and trucking networks, and even some production facilities. It has become a significant force in the food sector in that city.

Thus, by engaging in everything from cooperative housing to solar energy, to small enterprise developments, to composting and food retailing, to banking, neighborhoods are beginning to regain a sense of autonomy and destiny. Will federal efforts soon catch up with the reality of localism? Possibly. The Department of Housing and Urban Development has recently changed its policy focus from urban renewal to neighborhood preservation. Community Development Block Grants are increasingly being tied in with other neighborhood-oriented funds to develop comprehensive planning. Using those Block Grants, communities around the country have established energy-conservation and neighborhood development programs. The Department of Energy has an office of small-scale technology. The Commerce Department has an office of special projects that works directly with community organizations on economic development efforts.

But while "neighborhoods as planning and production mechanisms" is part of the national dialogue, many barriers remain to be overcome. No city willingly relinquishes power to its sub-units. No bureaucracy wants to think of itself as useless. No large utility company will encourage its own obsolescence by supporting the spread of decentralized solar technologies. No major corporation can accept widespread small-scale production units. And, most importantly, few cities consider themselves federations of neighborhoods. The reform movement of the early twentieth century wiped out most ward-based politics, leaving power with at-large delegates and city managers. Yet, returning to neighborhood autonomy and representation and moving toward neighborhood self-reliance is not the same as eliminating the city. City, neighborhood, and individual residents can and should work together. The city is our society's basic political and economic unit at the moment. Under our political system it holds immense power to encourage or discourage local self-reliance. Cities retain taxing power, bonding authority, financing power, and legislative ability. Their bureaucracies can make or break local initiatives.

Imaginative cities can utilize their powers to promote decentralization, moving toward municipal self-reliance. Already Detroit and cities in New Jersey require certain municipal employees to reside inside the borders. Some cities are using their purchasing power to encourage local economic development. Santa Clara, California, is leasing solar systems to its residents. Washington, D.C., bans commuter parking in local neighborhoods. Hartford, Connecticut, helped establish a neighborhood-based corporation that owns a solar energy company and a fire-place-heater manufacturing plant.

Although we are only beginning on the road to local self-reliance, we already have an extraordinary pool of experience to share and build upon. Neighborhoods and cities must take into account new technologies, new concepts, and new modes of cooperation as they plan for the future. Planning for self-reliance is an enormous task. But the benefits are also very great: an informed citizenry, reduced resources use, more cohesive communities. Local self-reliance can mean local democracy, an extension of our definition of citizenship from that of pulling down a lever in a voting booth once every few years to that of actively deciding on the future of our communities. ❦

Easing or
Plunging into Frugality

Warren Johnson

The goal of most people is to minimize change. This is not surprising, given the disturbing nature of so many changes today. But what may be surprising is that such an orientation is not necessarily in conflict with the process of moving toward frugality. It is possible to ease toward frugality slowly, and with a minimum of change. The trick, as far as the individual is concerned, is to be in a good position to take advantage of opportunities as they evolve and to avoid the traps. The most dangerous thing to do is to rigidly resist all change. As for society, "business as usual" is the surest way to bring on a dangerous pace of change later.

Easing

To try to go "back to the land" and to be economically self-sufficient is not a realistic alternative for many people today. In many ways it is not appropriate. We are still at the peak of the urban, industrial economy, just the opposite end of the economic spectrum from a self-sufficient, agricultural economy. To try to abandon all that when the modern system still has so much power and momentum left in it is premature. Besides, when we reach equilibrium sometime in the distant future, it is unlikely that we will have nearly as large a percentage of our population in agriculture as did earlier traditional societies. With the scientific and technical understanding we have, agriculture will inevitably be more productive than in the past, even if we become totally dependent on renewable resources. This increased productivity will leave broad opportunities in cities and towns. A great movement back to the land is not only unnecessary but could even be undesirable if it contributes to instability. The charge against the doom-sayers is well taken—they tend to cause people either to overreact or else to fear change so much that they rigidly resist it. Both are undesirable responses.

Indeed, easing into frugality today, even while we still live in cities, can leave us with plenty of time to enjoy the authentic pleasures available in our society. Some are unique to the affluent society—the education, the books, the good communications, the opportunity to travel, and the extraordinary experiences possible in our fluid, individualistic society. Others are more universal—family, friends, eating, drinking, working, playing in the park, or walking down the avenue. Whatever one's tastes, there are pleasures to be enjoyed and cultivated. There is no reason to abandon them.

This is not to suggest that we should behave as if there were no tomorrow. Some sensible, modest steps should also be taken to protect one's future prospects, to avoid getting too far into a corner. The greatest concern will be for one's livelihood. If it looks as if higher prices for energy and raw materials will seriously weaken one's job, it would be a good idea to keep an eye out for a stronger industry to work in. Even this, however, is not absolutely essential; those who intensely enjoy their work are probably doing a good job and would be in a good position to survive a retrenchment. The auto industry will keep on producing cars under the worst of circumstances, even when cars become glorified bicycles on four wheels run by lawn-mower motors. Others, who do not feel strongly about what they are doing, will be more apt to remain open to other opportunities. But the most foolish thing to do is to fight to hold on to an uninspiring job in a declining industry; this is simply defending one's place in the trap.

Another prudent step is to learn simple but useful skills around the house, the garage, and the garden. Learning how to work with your hands can be enjoyable. It can also be valuable when a personal financial squeeze develops (which for some people has already occurred). But the basic advantage of knowing how to do many things is that having a range of skills may be enormously valuable if one is laid off or if the economy moves in a more labor-intensive direction. It is, of course, hard to know what skills will make the difference; whatever is most pleasurable is as logical a choice as any. But the feeling of being a little bit better prepared to cope with economic reversals can be a good feeling. And one's self-confidence in the face of uncertainty is as effective a tool as any.

There are a number of other practical steps that will not only improve one's ability to weather economic set-backs, but will also contribute to the easing of scarcity as well. A number of these steps are obvious and are already being taken by some: buying a smaller car, insulating the home, and generally reducing material consumption. A significant step in this respect would be to move closer to work and shopping areas and reduce dependence on the private car. From a conservation point of view—which will more and more be analogous to a dollars-and-cents point of view as energy gets more expensive—the best place to live will be in an area with high population density. High density has a number of practical advantages: town houses and apartments insulate each other and tend to reduce energy demands; they consume less land; they can be served efficiently by public transportation; shops and services are usually nearby, often within walking distance; and the cost of maintaining streets and utilities is substantially less because distances are shorter. On top of these material advantages, there are social ones as well. With a higher population density, there are more things to do, more chances to run into friends in shops or on sidewalks, and more opportunities for all the truly urban experiences that Jane Jacobs describes well in *The Death and Life of Great American Cities*.

It is sad that there has been so much opposition to high density. This opposition has contributed to the rapid sprawl that is now so characteristic of modern cities. True, sprawl would have occurred anyway, without the opposition; the suburban house has been the preferred type of dwelling for a long time now, as evidenced by the high prices we are willing to pay for them. (Builders naturally respond by building suburban houses since they are profitable.) As resources get scarce, however, suburban areas will become more and more expensive to live in, and if discretionary use of the private car is restricted, they will become traps as well. The prudent thing is to anticipate this possibility and to relearn the urban pleasures we have largely forgotten during our sojourn in the suburbs. The hard part of all this is, of course, that the city centers are often old and run down. Yet, in many cities, restoration is going on, particularly by young people who cannot afford new homes in the suburbs. This is the economics of resource scarcity working as it should.

Several surveys have shown that many Americans would prefer to live in small towns or rural areas if they could. A 1972 Gallup survey found that only 13 percent of Americans prefer to live in cities, down from 22 percent in 1966, while 55 percent prefer small towns or rural areas. I must admit to some skepticism about these figures; I cannot help feeling that we are more addicted to urban diversions than we realize. The real ideal, most likely, is to live in a rural area within driving distance of urban amenities. But this is the ideal that created suburbia; the only trouble was that there was no way for the first suburbanites to keep others from following them into the countryside around cities. Soon, rural values were destroyed by more and more subdivisions, while the abandonment of the city centers deteriorated urban values as well.

Still, from a resource point of view, the tendency to move away from the largest urban areas is a sound one (providing it is not just a longer commute). Already, unemployment is highest in the largest urban areas, particularly the industrial ones, and the cost of living is going up rapidly. As resource scarcity takes its course, we are likely to see a new urban scene evolve, one in which regional cities and towns are more prominent than the largest urban areas that dominate the pattern of population distribution today. The tendency to move to a smaller city is a good one, for the individual as well as for the process of adapting to scarcity.

A consequence of frugal behavior today should be the accumulation of savings in one form or another, at least for those of us with decent jobs. But frugality is not parsimony; there is no point in denying everything to prepare for a future we cannot know, just as it is foolhardy to live only for today and let the future take care of itself. Many of the surest pleasures are inexpensive. It is primarily ostentatious consumption, the trying to keep ahead of the Joneses, that is so expensive. A movement that tended to ignore what the Joneses had and replaced it with the cultivation of simple pleasures would undermine the economic pressures of our society. With the niche of industrial society filling up, this can be expected to happen; there will be fewer opportunities to make a fortune, just as the opportunities to secure what is currently considered a middle-class standard of living are being constricted. To carefully consider what is personally important and satisfying, in effect to "know thyself," would be a reasonable and deliberate step toward living successfully with scarcity.

Plunging

It is sometimes suggested that if economic growth ended, it would mean the end of change; life would become repetitious and monotonous without the challenges and opportunities we have had in the past. This, of course, is virtually an impossibility. The challenges will be different, but we will not get away from change that easily—not for a long time, anyway. When a degree of stability is finally reached sometime in the obscure future, our descendants will probably be ready for it.

The word *adapt* comes directly from the Latin word *adaptare*, meaning to fit. To be well-adapted is to fit. To be well-adapted is to fit well into one's situation, to be at ease and relaxed, instead of restless and dissatisfied. We have all known well-adapted people at one time or another who are perfect for the time and place they are in—a great teacher or salesman, a grizzled old fisherman, or a tramp. It is an envious position to be in, to fit so well, but it can also be a hazardous position with the world changing as much as it is today. The great teacher may be forced to use new teaching techniques or textbooks; the salesman may be forced by a merger from a small personal operation to a large bureaucratic one; expensive modern fishing boats may destroy the livelihood of the old fisherman; and prosperity may reduce the fellowship of the open road.

It is the "maladapted" who have created the modern world. They were the ones eager to capitalize on the changes that were undermining the well-adapted. Certainly, our society seems to reflect the restlessness and the dissatisfaction of those who shaped it. The steady stream of efforts to improve things, both from the personal point of view and for society as a whole, must say something about our assessment of ourselves and our society.

In our fluid society it is a normal thing for individuals to maintain a running comparison of their situation with alternatives that come to their attention. Everyone has some dissatisfactions that cause one's mind to wander down different roads to see where they go—to look around with the kind of eyes that put oneself into the picture seen, and to compare it with one's own situation. If the prospect pleases and seems possible, it generates excitement and anticipation. In this comparison between the existing situation and an alternative, the pros and cons of the existing situation are normally well known—how secure the job is, how happy the family is, what friends one has, what pleasures can be enjoyed, and what torments and hostilities are to be endured. The alternatives are more questionable; this is where the risk comes in. Even if the present situation is barely tolerable, it is usually necessary to have a fairly well-defined alternative before an individual, and especially a family, can make a major change.

Most people investigating alternatives will run into barriers of one sort or another—inadequate capital, lack of economic potential, and awkward transition—or the alternatives may just not appear so attractive on close examination. But even if nothing comes of such investigations, just the consideration of an alternative will make it a little harder to go back to the old job, and the excitement and anticipation will remain.

Sometimes fortuitous circumstances make a change possible. Some "half-way house" may be found in which the alternative can be tried without cutting off the security of the old job completely, or friends may offer a cooperative arrangement that makes it easier for both parties, as well as provides a degree of mutual support. Perhaps the risks will be reduced when the children's education is completed and they are off on their own. Or an inheritance may provide some capital. Even a setback can force a change—the loss of a job, a particularly disturbing crime nearby, or not getting admitted to graduate school. Or perhaps the impetus will just be the long-term trends—income falling behind prices, higher taxes, rising crime rates, or declining mobility. Whatever the trends may be, as the current situation declines, the choice will shift toward a major break with things as they are.

The most important obstacle to small-scale alternatives is the difficulty of finding a way to obtain a living. There will be only a limited number of new economic opportunities until prices for energy and raw materials go up substantially over present levels. In the meantime, the uncertainties are great. How much easier it would be if we knew for sure how fast the price of energy will go up, how the rising cost of transportation will affect population distribution, or how land prices will change. For example, it could be very advantageous to buy a small farm if the price of food went up in the future along with present increases in the prices of farm equipment, energy, and chemicals; such a combination would make a small, labor-intensive farm economically viable. But if a recession were to come along or agricultural surpluses reappeared, the same small farm might not produce enough income to make mortgage payments.

In a sense, there is no point in struggling with these economic imponderables. The current market values for businesses and land are a broad composite assessment of their economic potential as judged by buyers and sellers, and it is pretty hard for anyone to claim better knowledge. Every investment has its risks, and whether the risks are worth undertaking depends primarily on the individual's assessment of how desirable life will be as a result. People willingly accept a low income if they love the work and the way of life that goes with it.

Whether the alternatives are viable does not depend entirely on how much money can be made. More and more, the key to economic survival will be to learn how to get by with less income. There are many opportunities to make a modest income; they will become economically viable opportunities to the first people that are able to get by on the small income generated. It is frugality that has allowed the Briarpatch network, a group of small independent entrepreneurs doing what they want to do on reduced incomes, to flourish in the San Francisco Bay Area. It is also what has allowed the Amish to thrive and expand on small farms all during the period when most small farms were going out of existence. A low income is the heart of frugality.

It takes a highly motivated and creative person or family to undertake the risk of developing his own work while getting by with less and learning how to become more self-sufficient. For the first pioneers, it can be lonely and difficult work in unfamiliar territory. The frequently heard criticism that says these people are "dropouts," and that they do not contribute their skills and energies to solving society's problems, is totally wrong. They are doing a task that is essential for our future, developing new skills and ways of living that will provide models for others as necessity pushes more of us in that direction. Nothing could be more important. The pioneers are opening up new economic territory where subsequent settlers can join them.

Families are also more likely to pull together for many of the same reasons mentioned earlier. Arrangements between family members do not entail such involved legal arrangements as between unrelated parties, and the traditional separation of labor in a family, where the older members help around the home so that the younger generation can devote more of their energy and attention to an economic enterprise, may again be of real assistance.

What is now being called the household economy, in fact, may emerge as a key adaptive strategy between easing into frugality and plunging in all the way. The logic of the household economy has its basis today in the affluence of parents, who often have secure, well-paying jobs and mortgage-free homes, at a time when their sons or daughters cannot find work. These young people could give up the discouraging task of searching for a regular job if they could find some way to earn money on their own. If they are living at home anyway, any work is better than none, and parents might be expected to help financially to get them started. There are many possibilities: taking care of lawns; repairing neighborhood cars, bicycles, or appliances; refinishing furniture; taking care of children for working parents; washing store windows; installing insulation or solar heaters; or restoring old houses—anything to make some money. This kind of work could enable the young person to gain valuable experience and, in time, to become fully independent. It would also reduce the feeling of being trapped by unemployment. And it involves the labor-intensive kind of activities appropriate for the future. It could lead, in time, to profitable businesses.

If unemployment rates continue to rise or incomes to fall, the family will undoubtedly become more significant as an economic unit than it is now. Especially if unemployment hits the breadwinner, everyone in the family will have to pitch in and help. Or, an extended family could sell their assets in a region with declining economic prospects, pool their capital, and use it to get started somewhere else where the prospects look better. This could be an excellent way of adapting to scarcity and would benefit the family at the same time.

Individual and family economic alternatives will develop as circumstances and individual ingenuity make them possible. That could take time. We could use more large-scale community alternatives right now, if for no other reason than to absorb unneeded labor. The commune movement was a discouraging one, on the whole. The best that can be said for it is that it demonstrated a good deal about what was practical and what was not. It showed, most significantly, that it is not possible to have the best of all possible worlds—combining togetherness, sharing, and simplicity with complete freedom in personal relationships and sexual matters, and asking for no sense of duty to stick out the hard times or to be on good terms with one's neighbors. That vision of the good life, in which there were to be huge benefits at practically no cost, has, at least for the time being, been put to rest.

The communes that survived, greatly reduced in number, have much more structure and usually have a religious basis. A notable one is The Farm, which was organized by Stephen Gaskin after he and a group of followers had left San Francisco in 1971 in a small fleet of old buses. They finally settled in Tennessee and purchased land in a thinly populated county, and now 1,000 people of all ages (though mostly young) support themselves quite well on 1,700 acres of land. A dozen other Farms have been spawned elsewhere and together support another six hundred members. Besides farming, The Farm operates its own banks, construction company, private utilities, schools, and medical clinic, where the group delivers their own babies. They also ask pregnant women to come and have their babies there instead of having abortions

and, if they wish, to leave the babies with The Farm as long as necessary. Membership in The Farm is only granted after a trial period, and
it requires a vow of poverty and the turning of personal wealth over to
the cooperative, so membership is not taken lightly. The Farm has
enough surplus, after being in existence for only three years, to form an
international aid service called Plenty, which provided substantial
assistance to Guatemala after the earthquake of 1976.

The main weaknesses of these "technicolor Amish," as they describe
themselves, seems to be their dependence on the charismatic religious
leadership of Stephen Gaskin and the traditional difficulties of sustaining a communal way of life. Although aspects of many societies are run
communally, complete communal societies are a very rare phenomenon
in history, which suggests that they are difficult to sustain. The loss of a
strong leader often leads to an organization's break-up, unless a sound
operating structure has been built. A better basis than communes for
decentralized groups would seem to be communities—for example, a
community organized under the auspices of an established organization.
A community based on a known organization, philosophy, or religious
faith would be more apt to receive financial support and local acceptance. Bureaucracy has its usefulness too. Established organizations
could better assure the continuity of the community and would be
more likely to attract members from all parts of society than just the
affluent young, the main group involved with the communes. The Black
Muslims and the Congress of Racial Equality have both developed cooperative economic activities in the South, since they concluded a long
time ago that northern cities would never provide a good life for poor
blacks. Cooperatives are also an attractive alternative to what is often
experienced as the lonely and threatening world of commercial competition. Individuals with land or economic enterprises could work them
cooperatively, if they felt strongly enough about the particular philosophical basis on which the cooperatives were organized.

Any alternatives that might evolve, whatever their form or function,
will make a major contribution to the economy and to the choices
available to people. If their numbers were to increase substantially, it
is possible that the shortfall in jobs could be reduced, greatly easing the
adjustment to scarcity. But whatever their numbers, successful communities will be valuable additions to the range of models available to
others in the future. New communities may have to struggle for a long
time before getting firmly established, but this should not be held
against them. Such tasks are not easy and straightforward.

The Politics of Decentralization

American society has always honored independence and the pioneer
spirit. In general, it was not hostile to the utopian and socialistic experiments of the nineteenth century. Even the commune movement of the
1960s received quite a bit of approval from American idealists in the
beginning. There is no reason to assume this general attitude will

change, especially since the decentralized alternatives offer the promise of removing some of the overload from the economy and will enable the rest of society to go on with less unemployment and less scarcity. From now on, anybody who leaves a regular job for one that effectively removes him or her from the labor market will be doing society a favor. The kindest thing I could do for my unemployed colleagues with advanced degrees would be to quit my teaching job so one of them could have it. For this simple but basic reason, there is not likely to be any general opposition to decentralization, although there may be opposition to some of the specific consequences in areas receiving an influx of outsiders.

Because of these benefits, the government is not likely to hinder the movement to frugality. But could it do very much to encourage it? Not too much, probably. Decentralization will occur primarily because of slowly intensifying scarcity and the government is not likely to speed this up. One traditional function of government is to facilitate the flow of information and research, but this is already being done by the growing number of books and magazines that report the grassroots economic experiments going on in many parts of the country. If the government plays a role in the process of adjusting to scarcity, it will probably be by reducing the financial risks of change.

The risk of failure will always inhibit change. It is a pretty gutsy thing to do what a lot of people would like to do—quit an unrewarding job, sell the house, and start out independently somewhere else. It is hard to give up security, even a rather unpleasant security, for something that is uncertain. The government could help here by putting a floor under the risk, so that bankruptcy and trying to get the old job back are not the specters that hang over every hopeful scheme. If our present welfare system were replaced by a single guaranteed income, it would act as such a floor. Then, if the first economic venture failed, or took longer to get started than expected, the guaranteed income would help one to weather the lean period.

A guaranteed income would have a number of advantages compared to present forms of unemployment and welfare programs. A federal guaranteed income would provide uniform benefits nationwide, encouraging people to move to places where the cost of living is less, such as small towns and rural areas. Existing programs pay higher amounts in urban areas because the cost of living is higher there, but this encourages the poor to stay in the cities. Once drawn away from economically stressed urban areas by uniform benefits everywhere, people would be better situated to find day-labor jobs, to learn new skills, to have a garden or cut firewood, and to take advantage of decentralized economic opportunities as they evolve.

One of the most disturbing visions of the future is that of a vast number of destitute people stuck in cities that increasingly assume the appearance of ghettos. Any program that tended to reduce that situation would be very valuable. Welfare cannot be eliminated since it sustains life in many parts of the inner city, but welfare could be modified in order to encourage a personal response that is more consistent with the long-run interests of the poor as well as the overall needs of society.

There is one more thing the government could do that would almost surely facilitate the response to scarcity, and that would be to loosen up the regulations that currently make unorthodox economic activity and housing so difficult. Zoning, labor restrictions, and building codes all had their logic at one time, usually to control rapacious factory owners, developers, and retailers who were trying to exploit their workers or the public—activities characteristic of the heyday of capitalism. These regulations will be less appropriate for the needs of a decentralizing economy. A number of these regulations could be dropped without difficulty, as time passes, while others could be modified. This process is sure to be slow and messy. Those who benefit from the regulations will try to maintain their advantage as long as they can. But an alliance between conservatives and liberals can already be seen forming in current deregulation cases. The conservatives, who are opposed to government regulation on principle, align themselves with liberals who are opposed to subsidizing powerful industries. This alliance seems certain to gain strength as the disadvantages of various regulations become more obvious. As these regulations are eroded, the process of decentralization should quicken. ✼

The Monastic Paradigm and an Economics of Permanence

Theodore Roszak

If there is any hope of saving the rights of the person and planet in the years ahead, we—by which I mean the ordinary, chronically power-less people who live in the belly of the urban-industrial leviathan—we are going to have to find our way back to a comparable sense of mutual aid, a comparable capacity to live self-reliantly within more local and domestic economies, a comparable appreciation of the wealth that lies in modest means and simplicity of need. We are going to have to re-think some of our most firmly held assumptions about property and privacy, security and success, recognizing that there is simply no livable future for the competitive, self-regarding, high-consumption, middle-class way of life which we have been taught to regard as the culmina-tion of industrial progress. And we are going to have to undertake that reappraisal from the bottom up, expecting no encouragement from leaders and experts who are the chief products and principal benefi-ciaries of our high industrial compulsions. It will be up to us to begin coming together, talking together, working together. We are going to have to stop keeping our cares and material goods, our troubles and our talents, our wealth and our psychic wounds to ourselves and begin sharing our lives like mature, convivial animals.

But how are we to get together? In what spirit, in pursuit of what guiding vision? The modern world is littered with unhappy experiments in collectivism, large and small—failed Utopian communities, authori-tarian cults, soul-destroying mass movements. Brook Farm in nine-teenth-century New England was a way of getting together; it lasted five years and then the philosophers and writers who were its too-fastidious residents tired of the hard work. The totalitarian people's republics of Asia and Eastern Europe are ways of getting together; but how long would they last in the absence of nationalist propaganda and state censorship? The Manson Family, B.F. Skinner's Walden II, Huxley's Brave New World, Orwell's nightmare of 1984 . . . they are all ways of getting together. Where do we look for a model of common life and work that is competent, humane, and liberating?

I think it is a kind of new monasticism we will need to carry us through the coming generation of social uncertainty and economic dis-location; I suspect that is the general style of life to which more and more people will find themselves turning spontaneously at the grass-roots level where we meet one another as friends, family, and neigh-bors. What does such an admittedly odd conjecture call to mind, I wonder. Medieval chapels, robes and bells, hair shirts and incense? No, I will make no case for the mortification of the flesh or the celibate life; less still is it my intention to encourage any form of sectarian retrench-ment or doctrinal exclusiveness. I take it for granted that the planetary culture which it is our task to build will have to be universal and eclectic—_panclusive,_ even in its professions of faith. It can learn from the past, but it must be open to the present moment and to our species-wide experience.

The word "monastic" is hard to work with, precisely because it belongs to an ancient, well-defined tradition that has endured long enough to leave its distinctive mark on history. Let me make it clear, then, that my interest is in monasticism as a model—a tested, historical paradigm of creative social disintegration. I turn to it because it illumi-nates the way in which the top-heavy and toxic institutions of an ex-hausted empire were sifted down into civilized, durable communities where a vital, new sense of human identity and destiny could take root. The spirit in which I approach monasticism is somewhat that in which E.F. Schumacher wrote of "Buddhist economics"—with the intention of evaluating the hidden ethical assumptions that guide our lives, and perhaps with an eye to extrapolating a viable, contemporary alternative from an old and exotic idea. But in this case, the exercise is not merely hypothetical. There _was_ a monastic economics, as well as a monastic politics and sociology; the tradition is still with us, lingering at the fringes of the modern world. The achievement is a real one, there to be examined as a significant social institution which, as a matter of histori-cal fact, managed to embody many of the values Schumacher credited theoretically to Buddhism.

I suppose it is an historian's habit, when confronted with a problem, to go rummaging about in the past for precedent and tradition. Perhaps that is the peculiar contribution I can draw from my work and train-ing—to salvage a few of the human possibilities that existed before history-making became the monopoly of industrial cities. Certainly, I take heart in knowing that a social form containing so much that our time cries out for—an economy of simple yet ingenious means, a communitarian culture of nonviolence and spiritual growth—has been tried in the past during times of extreme disorder and has worked, not as a marginal oddity, but as a cultural force that in time became so deeply implicated by its success in the political, economic, and intellectual mainstream of its society that it was constantly in danger of being co-opted and corrupted, constantly in need of being reformed.

The achievement that I would hope the monastic tradition might especially model for us is its remarkable capacity to synthesize qualities of life that have become fiercely polarized in our world. I have in mind the tragic way industrial society has pitted the personal against the convivial, the practical against the spiritual. As we live today, these values make war upon one another like deadly enemies. Yet, the task of saving the person and the planet demands that we make peace among them. And here we have a tradition reaching back more than a thousand and a half years in Western history, which gives us reason to hope that such a harmony of opposites can be made to exist. Specifically, it presents us with two significant facts.

First, the tradition began in the seclusion of the private cell, in the depths of the lonely soul struggling toward personal salvation. Yet, soon enough, these solitary cells were surrounded by supportive communities that still hold their place in history as a standard for convivial sharing and principled egalitarianism.

Secondly, the tradition began as a desperate search for spiritual purity on the part of men and women who had abandoned the world and all concern for success, wealth, power, even bare physical survival. Yet soon enough, these unworldly exiles had created a network of independent domestic economies that were the most stable, orderly, and productive in their society, with more than enough surplus to provide charitable care for the needy, the aged, the indigent.

In these two facts there is much to be pondered by those who assume that the need for personal solitude and spiritual growth must necessarily lead to a narcissistic dead end devoid of social conscience and historical influence. For what are we to make of the seeming paradox that people who did not put social obligation "first" or make it the monopolistic concern of their lives, nevertheless achieved one of the most culturally vital forms of egalitarian fellowship? And further: that people who did not allow practicality to dominate their lives nevertheless developed an economic style of astonishing inventiveness and productivity? I suggest that the key to the paradox lies in recognizing how much can be achieved if we once allow the social and economic necessities to become "secondary" considerations, trusting that they will draw their best motivations from a psychology of wise indirection. Then we allow other energies to rise within us—energies that are born of personal need, but which unfold naturally into the surrounding world. It is perhaps somewhat like the paradox involved in recognizing that feats of great physical exertion are often best achieved by relaxing into them; the muscles give up their distracting strain, the breath regains its even rhythm, and we achieve a smooth flow of easy effort. Similarly, we may become more authentically convivial, more resourcefully practical by relaxing the bullying anxieties that insist we _must_ be socially engaged, and so discovering that we _need_ to be, we _want_ to be. Of course, we are social animals who must fulfill a social responsibility; of course, we must feed, clothe, and shelter ourselves in order to survive. But is it not possible that these things fall most gracefully into place in our lives if we do not let them become our constant obsession, but instead trust that they will emerge with just the right urgency and ingenuity from the process of self-discovery?

In the case of monastic communitarianism, we have a way of life in which, both historically and psychologically, the claims of the person have always been given an unquestioned priority. At the very outset, as people come forward to announce their vocation, each is granted a place of personal sanctuary and much time for solitary withdrawal. From the beginning and as a matter of unconditional right, there is the guarantee of absolute privacy and inviolable solitude; the disciplines of contemplation are taken up in a spirit of principled detachment from the pressures of material necessity. Yet, inevitably, both sociability and practicality come to surround the inner quest, because their sources have been tapped within the person; they grow out of, instead of being imposed upon. If the socialist and communist ideologies of our time had not opted to become so fanatically antireligious in orientation, they might have learned a great truth from the communitarian experience of the monasteries. They might have come to see conviviality, not as a difficult social duty that must be strenuously inculcated upon us as a matter of class consciousness (an approach that only produces mass movements), but as a culminating relationship between free and unique persons. They might have come to respect the existence of a personal reference that supports, but also delimits, the claims of the collective will.

At first sight, it may seem an unlikely comparison to make, but in many respects Maoist communism may be the nearest, large-scale equivalent we have in the modern world to the monastic tradition—the nearest, and yet how far off. So much that Mao wished to achieve—the social ethic of self-sacrificial service, the tight agrarian communalism, the integration of manual work and intellect, even the economic development he hoped to see spring from collectivized labor and folk technology—all this is part of monastic history. The monks also committed themselves to "going among the people," voluntarily assuming the social role of serfs and peasants; they preached and taught in their localities; they became the best farmers and craftsmen of their age, the inventors and disseminators of many new technologies. From their contemplative commitment, they reached out to share knowledge and resources with the surrounding society. They traded goods, kept school, distributed alms, and transmitted the culture. Often, at their Christian finest, they sought to bring "the peace of God" to their neighbors, or at least to offer shelter from the endemic violence of the times. With the world around them, they practiced an economics of charitable sharing and hospitality that might almost be seen as the earliest antici- pation of the modern welfare state. But what did this impressive range of social interaction and neighborly responsibility finally rest upon? Again, we come back to the private cell, the soul in search of personal salvation. *That* first of all . . . *then* the rest.

But with Mao's communism, every effort is made to subtract the personal and spiritual elements of the monastic tradition; the ideal is totally secularized. And then what motivation is there left to tap? We fall back upon the familiar repertory of modern political propaganda: the belligerence of patriotic pride, the appetite for vicarious collective power, competitive material standards of national production, constant agitational appeals to comradely duty that draw their force from people's guilt and fear. Finally, everything is subordinated to the col- lective project of building still another "Great Power" in the world, still another urban-industrial colossus, where—as now seems likely in the People's Republic—policy-making after Mao will rapidly gravitate toward technocratic methods and conventional industrial values.

Admittedly, the conviviality that grows from personalist sources will never serve to build societies on such a giant scale. Its natural focus is the small community, or, at largest, an anarchist network of com- munities—the form that most monastic orders finally assumed as each house, having reached an optimum size, sent out its members to find new land and to make a new, small beginning. For those whose measure of "society" is pegged at the level of nation-states, social classes, mass political movements, multi-national corporations, megalopolitan cities, this is bound to seem a negligible scale of human association that falls shamefully below the horizon of politically realistic discussion. But, then, my interest here is precisely in those social forms that disintegrate such bigness, seeking to replace it with socially durable, economically viable alternatives. The question I address myself to is "Where do the little people of the world turn when the big structures crumble or grow humanly intolerable?" At that point, it becomes important for us to know what a political and intellectual leadership devoted to the big sys- tem orthodoxies will never tell us: that there are small alternatives that have managed to bring person and society, spiritual need and practical work together in a supportive and symbiotic relationship.

There is one more feature of the monastic paradigm that deserves to be mentioned—another instructive synthesis that follows from the per- sonalist approach to the social and economic necessities. This has to do with the highly sensitive way in which the monastic economy has gen- erally managed to balance technical innovation and ecological intelli- gence.

A strong argument could be made (as has been done by Lewis Mumford) that the monks played an indispensable role in laying the agricultural and technological foundations for later European industrial development. Their contribution in this respect might almost be seen as medieval Europe's "great leap forward." Many of the most hostile wilderness areas of Europe were pioneered by the monks; many of the Western world's most basic techniques and machines were either invented and perfected in the monasteries: the water mill and windmill, the animal-powered treadmill, the clock, rational accounting, new methods of farming and grazing, fulling and tanning, brewing and wine making, stockbreeding and metallurgy. These were indeed crafty and assiduous communities of work. Yet, their relations with the land remained frugal and gentle, their technology was always kept to a moderate scale. This was because the monasteries never regarded economic activity as an end in itself, never idolized productivity, never measured their success by profit or by any criterion of competitive national power. Instead, their economics sprang from a work ethic that regarded manual labor as a spiritual discipline. _Ora et labora_—and one worked as one prayed, in the pursuit of personal sanctification. In this respect, Mumford credits the monks with having found the secret of true leisure—"not as freedom _from work_ . . . but as freedom _within work_; and along with that, time to converse, to ruminate, to contemplate the meaning of life."

The economic style of the monastic communities assumes that, with sufficient ingenuity and hard work, one can reach a point of balance with the land and the life upon it that will, dependably, yield enough. The challenge is to zero in upon that point of ecological "climax," to adjust and revise and reassess, to make one's way forward, not by force, but by finesse, until one arrives at what E.F. Schumacher has called "an economics of permanence." There, the community finds itself firmly centered amid a grand series of natural rhythms and cosmic reciprocities that can support it indefinitely at a moderate, but substantially secure standard of life. It is this finely tuned steady state of existence the monks were after, where each day is much like the last—another welcome chance to stand in the presence of the ordinary and eternal splendor. Such idyllic images have doubtless always been represented in the human cultural repertory as part of an age-old Utopian yearning. What the monastic tradition contributes to that dream is the disciplined conviviality and the work ethic that can alone make Utopian gardens flourish. It offers us a philosophy of work that dignifies and democratizes labor, instead of making it a dehumanizing tyranny we would prefer to give over to machines or impose upon a subordinate class. And it adds one more vital ingredient: the inner spiritual dimension of the dream. For this is no way of life that can be evaluated by purely external criteria or achieved by purely economic means. There is an _inside_ to this economics which teaches us that we cannot set our sights on material plenitude or permanence without a proper culture of the person.

One might say that the monasteries created a healthy economic style because they simply had no economics—not as a body of abstract theory that stood apart from the daily round of work and worship. Rather, their economics was left to take shape from the prerequisites of personal growth. This clearly did not preclude the possibility of prodigious technical innovation; a machine or a more efficient technique might still be valued as a way of relieving drudgery. But the economics of the monasteries was kept "labor-intensive" because it was clearly understood that work is a necessary attribute of the personality, while limitless affluence is not.

Out of their commitment to the sanctity of the person, monastic communities have tended to find their way to an economic order that respects the rights of the planet. As a matter of spontaneous experience, if not of doctrine, they achieve a wise and harmonious rapport with the Earth. This is most marked in the Taoist, Tantric, and Zen communities of the East, where the traditions have blended into a mature nature mysticism. But even in the West, where Christian dogma forbids the adulation of nature, the monks have generally been drawn into comradely, if not reverent, relations with the natural setting in which they make their home. ✲

List of Contributors

A. KARIM AHMED is a scientist with the Natural Resources Defense Council in New York. He is the co-author with Frederica Perera of *Respirable Particles: The Impact of Airborne Fine Particles on Health and the Environment.*

KENNETH BOULDING is with the Institute for Behavioral Sciences at the University of Colorado at Boulder. His books include *The Meaning of the Twentieth Century, Macroeconomics,* and *Eco-Dynamics.*

ROBERT BOYLE is a journalist. He is author of *The Hudson River, A Natural and Unnatural History* and one of the authors of *Malignant Neglect.*

LESTER BROWN is President of Worldwatch Institute in Washington, D.C. His books include *World Without Borders, The Twenty-Ninth Day: Accommodating Human Needs and Numbers to the Earth's Resources,* and *Running on Empty,* which he wrote with Christopher Flavin and Colin Norman.

MICHAEL BROWN is a free-lance writer. He is author of the forthcoming *Laying Waste: The Love Canal and the Poisoning of America.*

BARRY COMMONER directs the Center for the Biology of Natural Systems, part of Washington University in St. Louis. His books include *The Closing Circle, The Poverty of Power,* and *The Politics of Energy.*

KATHLEEN COURRIER is Publications Director of the Solar Lobby and the Center for Renewable Resources. Formerly she was editor of *Development Communication Report.*

JACQUES COUSTEAU is head and founder of The Cousteau Society and captain of the *Calypso,* an oceanographic research vessel.

HERMAN DALY teaches economics at Louisiana State University. Formerly a Research Associate at Yale, he wrote *Steady-State Economics.*

ERIK ECKHOLM is a member of the Policy Planning staff of the U.S. State Department. A Senior Researcher at Worldwatch Institute until 1979, he wrote *Losing Ground: Environmental Stress and World Food Prospects* and *The Picture of Health: Environmental Sources of Disease.*

DAVID EHRENFELD teaches biology at Rutgers University. He wrote *Conserving Life on Earth* and *The Arrogance of Humanism.*

ANNE EHRLICH is a Senior Research Associate in Stanford University's Department of Biological Sciences. She is a co-author of *Ecoscience: Population, Resources, Environment.*

PAUL EHRLICH is Bing Professor of Population Studies at Stanford University, where he also teaches biology. He is author of *The Population Bomb* and co-author of *Ecoscience: Population, Resources, Environment.*

RICHARD FALK is Milbank Professor of International Law at Princeton University.

MARCIA FINE is a Science Associate with the Toxic Chemicals Program of the Environmental Defense Fund. She is one of the authors of *Malignant Neglect.*

DENIS HAYES is Executive Director of the Solar Energy Research Institute in Golden, Colorado. Formerly a Senior Researcher at Worldwatch Institute and chairman of the Solar Lobby's board of directors, he wrote *Rays of Hope: The Transition to a Post-Petroleum World.*

HAZEL HENDERSON is author of *Alternative Futures* and the forthcoming *The Politics of Reconceptualization.* She was until 1979 a co-director of the Princeton Center for Alternative Futures, Inc.

JOSEPH HIGHLAND is chairman of the Toxic Chemicals Program of the Environmental Defense Fund. He is one of the authors of *Malignant Neglect.*

WARREN JOHNSON is chairman of the Geography Department at San Diego State University. He is the co-editor of *Economic Growth vs. The Environment* and author of *Muddling Toward Frugality: A Blueprint for Survival in the 1980s.*

HELENE KENDLER is a poet and copyrighter. Formerly she was editor of the Natural Resources Defense Council's quarterly newsletter.

THOMAS LOVEJOY is a scientist and wildlife conservationist. He is a Program Director with the World Wildlife Fund in Washington, D.C.

AMORY LOVINS is the British representative of the Friends of the Earth. His books include *Soft Energy Paths: Toward a Durable Peace* and *World Energy Strategies—Facts, Issues, Options.*

WESLEY MARX lectures on marine affairs in the Program in Social Ecology at the University of California at Irvine. He wrote *The Frail Ocean* and *Acts of God, Acts of Man.*

IAN McHARG is Chairman of the Department of Landscape Architecture and Regional Planning at the University of Pennsylvania. He wrote _Design With Nature._

DAVID MORRIS is co-founder and co-director of the Institute for Local Self-Reliance in Washington, D.C. He is author of _The Kilowatt Counter_ and co-author with Karl Hess of _Neighborhood Power._

RICHARD MUNSON is Coordinator of the Solar Lobby and the Center for Renewable Resources in Washington, D.C. Formerly, he was Director of Environmental Action and co-coordinator of Sun Day.

NORMAN MYERS is a conservation scientist based in Nairobi, Kenya. Affiliated with the Natural Resources Defense Council and the World Wildlife Fund, he wrote _The Sinking Ark: A New Look at the Problem of Disappearing Species._

FREDERICA PERERA is a resource specialist with the Natural Resources Defense Council in New York. She is co-author with A. Karim Ahmed of _Respirable Particles: The Impact of Airborne Fine Particles on Health and the Environment._

MARC REISNER holds an Alicia Patterson Journalism Fellowship, which he is using to write a book on water policy and development in the western United States. Formerly, he was editor of the Natural Resources Defense Council's quarterly newsletter.

THEODORE ROSZAK is chairman of General Studies at California State University at Hayward. His books include _The Making of a Counter Culture, Where the Wasteland Ends,_ and _Person/Planet: The Creative Disintegration of Industrial Society._

STEPHEN SCHNEIDER is a scientist with the National Center for Atmospheric Research. He wrote _The Genesis Strategy._

GUS SPETH is chairman of the Council on Environmental Quality. Formerly with the Natural Resources Defense Council, he has written widely on numerous environmental issues.

ROBERT STOBAUGH teaches at the Harvard Graduate School of Business Administration. Director of the Energy Project there, he is co-editor of _Energy Future: Report of the Energy Project at the Harvard Business School._

ARTHUR WESTING is Dean of the School of Natural Science at Hampshire College in Amherst, Massachusetts. He is author of the forthcoming _Warfare in a Fragile World: Military Impact on the Human Environment._

LANGDON WINNER has taught at MIT, the University of California, and the College of the Atlantic in Bar Harbor, Maine. He wrote _Autonomous Technology: Technics-out-of-Control as a Theme in Political Thought._

DANIEL YERGIN lectures at the Kennedy School at Harvard. Author of *Shattered Peace*, he is also a co-editor of *Energy Future: Report of the Energy Project at the Harvard Business School.*

DAVID ZWICK is co-founder and director of the Clean Water Action Project in Washington, D.C. He is the author of *Water Wasteland*, and the co-author with Mark Green and James Fallows of *Who Runs Congress?*

NOTES

NOTES